Football, Power, and Politics in Argentina

This book examines the interplay between football, politics, violence, passion, and morality in Argentina. Drawing on original ethnographic research, it considers the role of fans, club officials, politicians, and others in the spread and perpetuation of corruption and violence within football and in wider Argentinian society.

Argentina's triumph in the 2022 World Cup brought millions onto the streets of Buenos Aires in celebration, but this book argues that beneath the veneer of sporting success lie networks of power and practices that have naturalized corruption and violence within Argentinian football and, by extension, in Argentinian society as a whole. It shows how the actions of club officials, politicians, barras (groups of organized, violent fans), and the police, which together represent a system of clientelism, exemplify in the world of football the system of organized chaos that habitually defines Argentinian politics. With the barras given licence to engage in violent behaviours linked not only to sporting passion but also to economic and political interests, this book argues that football, politics, and violence have become entangled in a web of social relations that illustrate Argentina's struggle to break the vicious cycle of corruption and impunity.

Shining new light on the significance of sport in wider society and the centrality of football in one of the world's greatest footballing nations, this book is essential reading for anybody with an interest in the anthropology, sociology, politics, or history of sport, or in political science, corruption, or Latin American studies.

Eugenio Paradiso works for North York Community House, an organization that assists newcomers to Toronto during their settlement process by providing information, resources, referrals, and education in matters related to immigration. He completed his PhD in Social Anthropology on the social, cultural, and political dimensions of violence in Argentinian football at Simon Fraser University, British Columbia, Canada.

Critical Research in Football
Series Editors:
Pete Millward, Liverpool John Moores University, UK
Jamie Cleland, University of Southern Australia
Dan Parnell, University of Liverpool, UK
Stacey Pope, Durham University, UK
Paul Widdop, Manchester Metropolitan University, UK

The *Critical Research* in Football book series was launched in 2017 to showcase the inter- and multi-disciplinary breadth of debate relating to 'football'. The series defines 'football' as broader than association football, with research on rugby, Gaelic and gridiron codes also featured. Including monographs, edited collections, short books and textbooks, books in the series are written and/or edited by leading experts in the field whilst consciously also affording space to emerging voices in the area, and are designed to appeal to students, postgraduate students and scholars who are interested in the range of disciplines in which critical research in football connects. The series is published in association with the *Football Collective*, @FB_Collective.

Available in this series:

The Politics of Football
Christos Kassimeris

The Safe Standing Movement in Football
Fan Networks, Tactics and Mobilisations
Mark Turner

LGBT Football Fans
Authenticity, Belonging and Visibility
Rory Magrath

Football and Diaspora
Connecting Dispersed Communities through the Global Game
Edited by Jeffrey W. Kassing and Sangmi Lee

Football, Power, and Politics in Argentina
Eugenio Paradiso

For more information about this series, please visit: https://www.routledge.com/Critical-Research-in-Football/book-series/CFSFC

Football, Power, and Politics in Argentina

Eugenio Paradiso

LONDON AND NEW YORK

First published 2024
by Routledge
4 Park Square, Milton Park, Abingdon, Oxon OX14 4RN

and by Routledge
605 Third Avenue, New York, NY 10158

Routledge is an imprint of the Taylor & Francis Group, an informa business

© 2024 Eugenio Paradiso

The right of Eugenio Paradiso to be identified as author of this work has been asserted in accordance with sections 77 and 78 of the Copyright, Designs and Patents Act 1988.

All rights reserved. No part of this book may be reprinted or reproduced or utilised in any form or by any electronic, mechanical, or other means, now known or hereafter invented, including photocopying and recording, or in any information storage or retrieval system, without permission in writing from the publishers.

Trademark notice: Product or corporate names may be trademarks or registered trademarks, and are used only for identification and explanation without intent to infringe.

British Library Cataloguing-in-Publication Data
A catalogue record for this book is available from the British Library

ISBN: 978-1-032-60399-5 (hbk)
ISBN: 978-1-032-60400-8 (pbk)
ISBN: 978-1-003-45893-7 (ebk)

DOI: 10.4324/9781003458937

Typeset in Goudy
by codeMantra

Contents

List of figures	*vii*
Glossary	*ix*

1 Introduction   **1**
Football for All 6
Methodological approaches and considerations 7
Access to participants 11
A note on what this book is not about 14
Research questions and chapter outlines 15
Notes 17

2 Violence in Argentinian football   **19**
The "River Experience" 19
Obtaining the tickets 21
Outside the stadium 22
A night at the Monumental 25
Violence and aggression 26
Definitions 27
Civilization and barbarism: On race and class 28
Chants 32
*A grounded and emic approach to interpreting fan behaviour at
    football stadiums 37*
Cognitive dissonance and role play 39
Words can kill: The case of Emanuel Balbo 49
Spectators 51
Supporters 52
Fans 53
Barras bravas 55
Aguante 62
Notes 65

vi Contents

3 Corruption in Argentina   69
Definitions and approaches 69
Corruption and violence in Argentina: A brief background 77
A culture of impunity 82
Corruption in football 84
Notes 90

4 Anthropological perspectives on clientelism and politics in Argentina and beyond   92
Definitions 92
Clientelism in Argentina: A brief background 93
Clientelism in ancient Rome 96
Clientelism in anthropological studies 98
Clientelism in football 107
Notes 112

5 Morality in Argentinian football   113
Moral relativism 113
Moral issues and dilemmas 114
Hinchadas Unidas Argentinas: The "stigmatization" of barras 123
Moral inconsistencies 126
The rival is the enemy: Passion and morality 130
Notes 132

6 Conclusion   134
Foreign solutions 134
On change: Social and cultural impediments 138
A new paradigm 147
Notes 151

Appendix A: A note on methods   *153*
Appendix B: On subjectivities and the validity of research findings   *154*
References   *160*
Index   *169*

Figures

1.1	Life-size statues of three Argentinian football stars in the tourist neighbourhood of Recoleta, in Buenos Aires. From left to right: Gabriel Batistuta, Diego Maradona, Lionel Messi 2
2.1	Map of the Autonomous City of Buenos Aires showing the location of Núñez, Belgrano, and River's stadium 23
2.2	A poster depicting an expression of *aguante* 63
5.1	An advertisement promoting the candidacy of Mariano Cúneo Libarona for president of Racing Club 124

Glossary

Aguante Endurance. In football, this term refers to the physical, emotional, psychological, and financial endurance displayed by fans during adverse conditions.

Barra brava Literally "brave gang." Name given to a group of organized and violent Argentinian football fans. Also called *barra*.

Barrabrava Member of a *barra brava*. Also called *barra*.

Blat Russian term used to define a set of informal relationships based on close personal contacts that allow people to gain access to goods and services by bypassing official rules.

Bostero Nickname given to fans of Club Atlético Boca Juniors. It comes from the word *bosta*, meaning dung.

Caudillismo Social system structured upon the interdependence between the head of a political faction, called *caudillo* (often a military leader), and his followers.

Compadrito Henchman hired by a local political *caudillo*.

Comadre Godmother.

Denarius An ancient Roman unit of currency.

Guanxi Chinese term that means social relationships or social connections. More specifically, the term refers to the practice of gift giving.

Hincha (de fútbol) (Football) fan.

Salutatio Ancient Roman social ritual at which clients would receive favours or cash from their rich patrons in exchange for votes.

Superclásico This term refers to the games between Argentina's two biggest football clubs: Club Atlético River Plate and Club Atlético Boca Juniors.

Tablinum In ancient Roman architecture, name given to the relatively large room used as an office, often found between the atrium and the peristyle.

Torcida Group of organized and violent Brazilian football fans.

Trapito This term, which literally means small piece of cloth, is used to refer to individuals who extort people who drive to concerts or sporting events into paying protection money for their cars when they park on the street. *Trapitos* often work for *barras bravas*.

Ultrà Group of organized and sometimes violent Italian football fans.

Unidades Básicas Buildings that act as local "headquarters" where clients meet with their brokers to receive goods, services, and favours.

Chapter 1

Introduction

Coming back from a friend's house after watching the *superclásico*[1] on TV (Boca 1 – River 2, played at Boca's stadium, where River had not won in ten years), I got off the bus and overheard a man in his sixties talking on his cell phone. He was sitting outside a café in the Buenos Aires neighbourhood of Palermo. In an annoyed tone of voice, he told his interlocutor: "I missed the entire River game, do you understand? Beyond the final score, which I don't give a crap about, I missed the game. All because I had to go see an apartment!" Considering that, in Argentina, football is often referred to as a religion, the man's reaction was understandable. As a fellow River fan, I empathized with him, as his obligations had denied him the opportunity to witness an exciting *superclásico*. This might seem like a trivial matter, but according to the *Encyclopedia of Anthropology*, "Argentines are religiously devoted to their favourite sport, *fútbol*" (Dyer 2006:274). Additionally, the encyclopaedia *Countries and Their Cultures* (Ferradás 2001) describes football as Argentina's strongest symbol of national identity.

Indeed, even though outsiders might think of tango music and dance as defining characteristics of Argentinian culture, it is football that acts as one of the very few nationwide markers of identity. This is particularly important considering that football in Argentina "does not simply reflect society or culture but is part of a general process of the way society models some of its central existential, moral and political issues" (Archetti & Romero 1994:46). Unlike tango, which is predominantly popular in the city of Buenos Aires, the passion for football transcends social classes, economic disparities, ethnic and geographical origins, and religious affiliations. In the words of Gaffney,

> Attending a soccer game in one of Greater Buenos Aires' 69 stadiums is one of the most spectacular and vibrant urban experiences in the world. The exuberance and passion of the fans is matched on the field by intense physical, and highly skilled, competition. Even lower division games are highly charged affairs with thousands of spectators waving flags, burning flares, chanting, singing and threatening rival groups.
>
> (2009:160)

DOI: 10.4324/9781003458937-1

2 Introduction

Figure 1.1 Life-size statues of three Argentinian football stars in the tourist neighbourhood of Recoleta, in Buenos Aires. From left to right: Gabriel Batistuta, Diego Maradona, Lionel Messi. Photo by author.

Behind the veneer of passionate crowds engaging in carnivalesque and picturesque expressions of support for their teams, the world of Argentinian football is characterized by violence and political and economic interests. In response to a continuing concern within political anthropology with the social and personal roles of the face-to-face, dyadic, instrumental, and emotional relationships that characterize patronage politics (Eisenstadt & Lemarchand 1981; Eisenstadt & Roniger 1984; Fox 1994; Gledhill 2000; Hopkin 2006; Kettering 1988; Szwarcberg 2013), my research looks at the mechanisms through which clientelist relationships in Argentinian football are established and maintained. In simple terms, clientelism refers to a "relationship between individuals with unequal economic and social status ('the boss' and his 'clients') that entails the reciprocal exchange of goods and services based on a personal link that is generally perceived in terms of moral obligation" (Briquet n.d.). The presence of clientelist networks and widespread corruption in football is particularly relevant to an analysis of political corruption and impunity in Argentinian society as a whole (Goldstein 2012; Haller & Shore 2005; Hopkin 1997; Saba & Manzetti 1997), especially considering the strong ties that exist between football and politics. Argentinian football clubs are non-profit civil associations (i.e. they are not privately owned); this creates opportunities for politicians at the municipal, provincial, and national levels to double as club officials, often with the intention of recruiting followers from a club's group of organized fans by exchanging favours for votes through patronage politics . Similarly, club officials with no prior experience in politics often use football clubs as political platforms from which to launch their careers. As Duke and Crolley explain,

> Argentine *fútbol* operates a hierarchical structure that is common to many other institutions. The AFA[2] is responsible for the running of *fútbol* and is answerable only to the state. The clubs, whose chairmen and directors double as politicians, are governed by the AFA's structures and rules. Most of the club *presidentes* and *dirigentes*[3] are associated with a political party. A well-known example.... is that of Pedro Bidegain at San Lorenzo de Almagro,[4] who was also a leading figure in Unión Cívica Radical.[5] In many countries, the fans traditionally have little power in the formal structures of football; they are merely the masses that constitute the crowd and provide the gate money. However, in Argentina, because of the unique ties between politics and *fútbol*, the role of the fan is of utmost importance in the running of a club and to a politician's career (to this day rival political lists appear in club elections).
>
> (2001:99–100)

In this context, groups of organized fans known as *barras bravas*[6] enter into mutually beneficial agreements with club officials and politicians. These agreements allow the *barras* to profit from football's businesses, while club officials and politicians benefit from the *barras*' political support within and beyond the clubs. Duke and Crolley go on to explain that "what is distinctive about Argentina is that sport and politics are inextricably linked. *Fútbol* is an extension of politics; it is part of the political system and anything that begins as a sports issue rapidly becomes politicised" (2001:93). Taking into account the status of football as a national passion, its politicization has consequences at the national level. The interactions observed in Argentinian football clubs provide a useful barometer of the issues that affect society as a whole, such as the lack of transparency and accountability in public institutions as well as the widespread corruption that characterizes Argentinian politics.

In line with Duke and Crolley's assessment of Argentinian football as an extension of politics, my research considers the sport's political ramifications at all levels of government. Thus, far from being confined to what can be observed at football matches, an analysis of Argentinian football elucidates ways of experiencing and thinking about corruption, impunity, morality, passion, discrimination, and violence in Argentinian society.

As I will later discuss, the links between football and politics have repercussions beyond the stadiums. Relationships between politicians, club officials, and

4 Introduction

barras receive extensive media coverage. News of political projects and alliances as well as of cases of corruption involving these actors often make headlines in national and local newspapers. Throughout this book, I shed light on the political connotations of football at a macroscopic level by presenting examples that emphasize its influence in everyday politics. Conversations with research participants regarding the ties between football, politics, corruption, impunity, and violence further highlight the role of football in Argentinian society and politics.

Given the sport's public prominence, an analysis of clientelism in football brings to the fore one of Argentina's most pressing problems: the inability (or unwillingness, depending on the actors being considered) to break the cycle of impunity and corruption that has affected the country for centuries. Through the actions of club officials, politicians, *barras*, and the police, the world of football exemplifies the system of organized chaos that informs Argentinian politics. Understood as an inversion of Radcliffe-Brown's (1952) structural functionalism, with its emphasis on harmony and stability, the system of organized chaos, although certainly stable, revolves around the political and/or economic interests of particular groups of social actors. Many of these actors have a personal interest in maintaining a system that allows them to exploit the opportunities provided by exorbitant levels of impunity at the expense of the country's general welfare. In short, the world of Argentinian football provides a particularly compelling opportunity to dive into the issues that hinder the country's socioeconomic development.

Although in some cases direct connections between the topics I explore might not seem immediately apparent, corruption, clientelism, impunity, passion, violence, and morality are interrelated and intertwined. My argument is that corruption and clientelism in football enable violent behaviour in and around football stadiums[7] by granting *barras* special status within the clubs. As a result, stadiums become stages where *barras* express their passion for their clubs by engaging in acts of violence and verbal aggression. The political and economic ties that characterize the relationships between politicians, club officials, the police, and *barras* perpetuate the conditions that grant *barras* the freedom to engage in violent behaviour, which may be tied to passion, performances that reinforce group identities and create a sense of belonging, economic interests, or any combination of these factors, depending on the occasion. Hence, football, politics, and violence become entangled in a web of social relations that illustrates Argentina's struggle to break the cycle of corruption and impunity.

Before discussing corruption and clientelism in football and beyond, I analyze the varying manifestations of violence and verbal aggression at football stadiums among spectators and *barras*. *Barras* often employ intimidation and/or violence to achieve their goals. As noted above, however, the violence of the *barras* does not have a single cause. Although it is increasingly common for *barrabravas* to engage in internal confrontations (i.e. confrontations between members of the same *barra*) over the control of the *barra's* businesses, acts of violence inside and outside the stadiums are often unrelated to economic interests, being instead the result of a form of passion that is manifested through displays of physical and psychological dominance over the rivals, who are perceived as enemies to be overpowered and humiliated. According to Archetti and Romero, *barras bravas*

> are evolving into kinds of elite military regiments dominated by the formation of small well-trained commando groups with a material infrastructure which includes weapons and cars. Operations are planned. It seems a task for professionals. The main leaders are well known and some of them are public figures with good relations in the world of football and politics.
>
> (1994:66)

Although it is common for the media to blame most of the violence in football on *barras*, I examine the role of club officials and spectators in the creation of hostile environments that perpetuate antagonizing practices. These practices, in turn, promote a culture of *aguante*[8] that exalts displays of physical violence and verbal aggression.

In light of the specificities that characterize Argentinian football and society, I argue that legal measures aimed at reducing violence and corruption in football will prove ineffective unless they are accompanied by cultural change. The current "everyone for themselves" mentality (MacLachlan 2006), combined with high levels of corruption and a culture of impunity that enables politicians, club officials, and *barras* to pursue their personal interests without fear of legal punishment, perpetuate social and political environments where those who do things "under the table" get rewarded. Furthermore, the club officials' emphasis on preserving the traditions that characterize Argentinian football matches (traditions that are partly responsible for perpetuating particular types of violence and verbal aggression) is at odds with attempts at reducing levels of violence and discrimination. Plaza Schaefer and Cabrera ask, "what is a professional football club willing to 'lose' to adopt a comprehensive program against violence?" (2021:98; my translation). Although it would be unwise to suggest that importing solutions that have been successful in countries with vastly different sociocultural and political contexts would provide a quick fix for the issues that plague Argentinian football, the need to develop local solutions should not overlook the analytical contributions made by foreigners who might be better able to maintain a critical distance when examining particular behaviours and interactions. In short, locally developed measures would benefit from a combination of emic and etic perspectives. As I will show, the system of organized chaos maintained by a variety of actors who have access to political and economic resources precludes the development of solutions aimed at reducing corruption and violence.

The prominent place that access to football as a source of psychological well-being occupies in the minds of millions of Argentinians was highlighted during a nine-year period in which the national government funded televised matches. Based on a conversation I had with Sergio, founder of Hecho Club Social,[9] this government programme serves to illustrate the emotional bonds that Argentina's ruling political party sought to establish with the general population. These bonds could then be turned into votes during presidential elections. The following section, which describes this programme in detail, emphasizes the political relevance and reach of football in Argentinian society.

Football for All

From 2009 to 2017, the national government implemented a programme, called Fútbol Para Todos ("Football for All"), that enabled people to watch any and all games of the Argentinian First Division in high definition on public television or online for free. Needless to say, people were divided – mostly along party lines – over the ethical implications of a programme that used public money to fund the broadcast of football matches. My conversation with Sergio revealed that he thought about access to football (whether televised or in person) as an inalienable right. Considering that Football for All was well received by millions of people, the social and political role of football in Argentina and the importance that people attach to it became apparent.

> Sergio: Football for All is a public policy, and that's fine, why shouldn't it be? If it (*access to televised football*) is something that, that used to be a great example of a privatization policy that curtailed the possibility of a lot of people to access football and forced you to humiliate yourself to watch a game through the window of a bar, and it felt as if they told you "if you do not come inside to have a coffee or a beer, you are useless." It seems to me that in Argentina it is a good investment so that people do not feel unprotected and do not feel worthless because they cannot watch a football game on television. I hate that ideology of saying "well, those who don't have money, can't do things." And I felt humiliated when I couldn't watch a football game, or had to go to a relative's house to watch it.

Far from being a mere source of entertainment, Sergio elevates football and its relevance to society to the level of institutions such as healthcare and education. The argument is that football is a right and a basic necessity rather than a privilege. Still, it is unclear how providing free access to televised football might contribute to people feeling "protected" in the way that they might feel protected by having access to free healthcare. To describe football as a basic necessity is problematic. If one person claims that access to football is absolutely necessary, who is to stop another person from demanding free access to ballet, rock concerts, theatres, or tennis matches, and on what grounds? What is it that grants football special status (other than its popularity) among other forms of entertainment?

Sergio also emphasized the psychological benefits of Football for All, which he saw as a programme that dignified people by making them feel valued. It should be noted, however, that far from being a programme that focused exclusively on the psychological well-being of the population, Football for All served as a vehicle for political propaganda. From 2009 to 2014, the government invested 6.12 billion pesos (approximately 852 million Canadian dollars by 2014 rates) (Vázquez & Cayón 2014) in Football for All. In 2014, the programme cost roughly 4 million pesos (556,000 Canadian dollars) per day (idem). This was public money that could have been invested in social housing, infrastructure, education, public works, and other projects. What is more problematic is the view that the government was doing society a favour, as promoting the programme as "free" diverted attention away from the fact that people were paying for it, at least partially, with tax money. At one point, the government considered covering part of the programme's costs through private advertisement. In the end, however, televised football matches became animated political pamphlets. The 15-minute halftimes afforded the government ample opportunities to praise its own investments in projects such as power plants, roads, housing, and others. Thus, instead of partially offsetting the costs of Football for All by receiving money from private advertisers, the government invested *more* public money on publicity.

The fact that the national government made access to televised football a matter of public policy through its Football for All programme sheds light on the emotional attachments that people form to the sport as a source of well-being. Similar to the emotional ties (Wolf 2001) that characterize the relationships between brokers and clients in patronage politics, Football for All appealed to the prominent place that football has in the lives of millions of people to project an image of a caring, protective state that looks after the "needs" of its citizens. The federal government's use of the programme for propaganda purposes highlights the powerful influence that football has on Argentinian politics. Consider the fact that Sergio, for example, a staunch opponent of a type of welfare system that, in his view, generates dependency and perpetuates poverty, eagerly sang the praises of Football for All for restoring the dignity of those who could not access televised football matches. The programme was scrapped in 2017 after the party that created it (Front for Victory) was defeated in the 2015 presidential election.

As the Football for All programme demonstrates, it is important to keep in mind while reading this book that in Argentina, football and politics are inseparable and feed off of each other.

Methodological approaches and considerations

This book is informed by a methodological approach that is simultaneously ethnographic, interpretive, inductive, and based on grounded theory. Creswell defines ethnography as "a strategy of inquiry in which the researcher studies an intact cultural group in a natural setting over a prolonged period of time by collecting, primarily, observational and interview data" (2009:13). Interpretivist strategies of inquiry are often, though not necessarily, an integral part of ethnographic studies. According to Mason, "what is distinctive about interpretive approaches.... is that they see people, and their interpretations, perceptions, meanings and understandings, as the primary data sources" (2002:56). In a similar vein, Beuving and de Vries explain that interpretivism or naturalistic inquiry "adopts the view that social order follows from how humans understand their situation and act upon that" (2015:28). Furthermore, they emphasize that "understanding is a prerequisite to explaining. In order to explain human actions, we first have to understand what those actions mean to those who perform them" (2015:29). Grounded theory, understood as "a strategy of inquiry in which the researcher derives a general, abstract theory of a process, action, or interaction grounded in the views of participants" (Creswell 2009:13), is therefore strongly linked to interpretivism. Put differently, grounded theory is often the result of an interpretivist analysis of fieldwork data.

I argue that ethnographic methodologies based on grounded theory are better equipped than quantitative and grand theory approaches to produce well-informed accounts of social life through an examination of a wide variety of interactions that take place under locally specific circumstances. As Mills explains, the level of abstraction that characterizes grand theory approaches is ill-equipped to develop analyses that are rooted in people's interactions, beliefs, desires, and agency:

> The basic cause of grand theory is the initial choice of a level of thinking so general that its practitioners cannot logically get down to observation. They never, as grand theorists, get down from the higher generalities to problems in their historical and structural contexts. This absence of a firm sense of genuine problems, in turn, makes for the unreality so noticeable in their pages.
> (Mills 1959:33)

By contrast, the collection of fieldwork data using a variety of ethnographic methods such as observation, participant observation, and semi-structured interviews, enables researchers to analyze and interpret their findings in culturally competent and contextually sensitive ways. Furthermore, the degree of familiarity and cultural competence acquired through the long-term involvement in the life and activities of the research participants facilitates the development of well-grounded understandings of social and cultural processes in ways that more "mechanistic" and impersonal approaches such as statistical, quantitative, and survey-based ones cannot match.

Although it is quite common for ethnographers to adopt an emic (i.e. insider) approach to the study of social and cultural groups and institutions, I argue that it is impossible, given the researchers' habitus and life histories, to collect and interpret data *only* from an emic perspective. For example, no matter how hard I may try to understand and analyze the practices of the dowayo people of northern Cameroon by putting myself in their place, my findings will inevitably contain an etic component that is at least partly based on my upbringing and social conditioning. Thus, although ethnographers should strive for an emic understanding of the people and contexts they study, they should nevertheless openly acknowledge the impossibility of going "full native."[10] Kottak describes the emic approach as follows:

> an emic approach investigates how local people think. How do they perceive and categorize the world? What are their rules for behavior? What has

meaning for them? How do they imagine and explain things? Operating emically, the ethnographer seeks the 'native viewpoint,' relying on local people to explain things and to say whether something is significant or not.

(2009:53)

Needless to say, what is significant for the research participants might not coincide with what the researcher considers significant. Furthermore, an excessive emphasis on the native viewpoint can at times be counterproductive. Given the fact that I was born and raised in Argentina but moved to Canada before the start of my post-secondary education, I consider myself a hybrid anthropologist. Put differently, I am familiar enough with the social and cultural context of my research project to be categorized as a native; on the other hand, having received my post-secondary education in Canada has afforded me the opportunity to examine the specificities that define Argentina's context with the critical distance that often characterizes outsiders. A researcher's willingness to adopt the locals' viewpoint is often celebrated by anthropologists. This approach, however, might be somewhat romantic when adopted on its own. To be able to see, understand, and interpret a particular context from the participants' point of view is certainly important, but going "full native" arguably makes it difficult for researchers to identify certain considerations that escape the participants' experiences and locally acquired knowledge. This will become apparent during my discussion of the possibility of producing cultural change in Argentina.

When describing the etic approach, Kottak states:

The etic (scientist-oriented) approach shifts the focus from local observations, categories, explanations, and interpretations to those of the anthropologist. The etic approach realizes that members of a culture often are too involved in what they are doing to interpret their cultures impartially. Operating etically, the ethnographer emphasizes what he or she (the observer) notices and considers important. As a trained scientist, the ethnographer should try to bring an objective and comprehensive viewpoint to the study of other cultures. Of course, the ethnographer, like any other scientist, is also a human being with cultural blinders that prevent complete objectivity.

(idem)

As I have discussed, an etic perspective is not only inevitable but also desirable to some degree. In other words, neither the emic nor the etic approach should be given absolute priority. As Agar explains, researchers need not choose between one or the other:

because of acrimonious debates between "materialist" or etic and "symbolic" or emic approaches to anthropology...."etic" and "emic" turned into labels for competing kinds of ethnographic descriptions. This was a fundamental error, since neither the original linguistic concepts nor their development in cognitive anthropology had defined an "either/or" use of the terms.

(2007:1372)

I have mentioned above that the system of organized chaos that characterizes Argentinian politics represents a sort of inversion of structural functionalism, to the extent that the focus is on the perpetuation of practices that maintain chaos rather than harmony. In any case, it should be noted that I do not equate society with a living organism in the way that Radcliffe-Brown (1952) described it. A better alternative to the analysis of the ways in which a variety of actors challenge or replicate social structures is Ortner's (2006) version of practice theory. As she explains, structural functionalism is a theory of constraint since, in the minds of functionalists, "human behavior was shaped, molded, ordered, and defined by external social and cultural forces and formations" (Ortner 2006:1). As a constraint-based theory, functionalism failed to properly consider the role of agency in relation to the actors' desires, motivations, and interactions beyond and, in some cases, in spite of a society's perceived "necessary conditions of existence" (Radcliffe-Brown 1952:178). To be sure, Ortner's understanding of practice theory does not negate the existence of structural constraints. Rather, practice theory "restored the actor to the social process without losing sight of the larger structures that constrain (but also enable) social action" (Ortner 2006:3). In Argentinian football and politics, club officials, *barras*, and politicians act as social subjects who shape the world through their practices (i.e. through agency) while simultaneously being shaped to varying degrees by the social world around them. According to Ortner, practice theory provides "a dialectical synthesis of the opposition between 'structure' (or the social world as constituted) and 'agency' (or the interested practices of real people)" (2006:16). An important point in relation to a consideration of the possibility of producing cultural change in Argentina is that practice theory incorporates the concept of culture in its analyses of social practices, interactions, and agency. As I will later argue, Argentinian society is in need of a sweeping cultural transformation, rather than institutional reform. In the words of Ortner,

> what social transformation in a deep sense means is not only the rearrangement of institutions. It involves the transformation of 'culture,' in both its new-old and its newer senses. Taking culture in the new-old sense, as the (politically inflected) schemas through which people see and act upon the world and the (politically inflected) subjectivities through which people feel – emotionally, viscerally, sometimes violently – about themselves and the world, social transformation involves the rupturing of those schemas and subjectivities. And taking culture in the newer – public, mobile, traveling – sense, social transformation works in part through the constant production, contestation, and transformation of public culture, of media and other representations of all kinds, embodying and seeking to shape old and new thoughts, feelings, and ideologies. In both senses, then, to adapt an old adage, social transformation must also be cultural transformation or it will be nothing.
>
> (2006:18)

Access to participants

I conducted my research in the Autonomous City of Buenos Aires,[11] Argentina's national capital, from January to December 2014. With a population of approximately 3 million, it is the country's largest city. More than 13 million inhabitants live in the Greater Buenos Aires area, a number that represents almost 30% of the country's total population. According to the Spanish newspaper *El País*, the Greater Buenos Aires urban agglomeration has the most football stadiums in the world, with 36 of them having a capacity of 10,000 or more (Rebossio 2015). Three of Argentina's so-called "big five" football clubs are located in the Autonomous City of Buenos Aires, while the other two are in the Greater Buenos Aires area, just over one kilometre south of the border with the city proper. Buenos Aires has by far the largest concentration of football clubs in the country, which allowed me to interview people from different clubs.

Taking into account that some research participants were well-known public figures who worked in places (such as office buildings) that did not lend themselves to the sort of fieldwork that would have allowed me to hang out with them and observe their activities, I relied on semi-structured interviews as the main source of firsthand accounts of violence, corruption, and politics in Argentinian football.

Although I recruited the participants through personal contacts, the fact that some of them were used to talking about violence in football in media outlets such as newspapers, radio, and television, meant that the prospect of discussing the subject with an unknown researcher who lived abroad, with no tangible reward for their participation, was – understandably – far from exciting and appealing. Thus, finding participants who would be willing to share their experiences was not without difficulties.

Considering football's public prominence, media appearances allow a variety of actors – some of whom might have political aspirations beyond football – to insert themselves into discussions on violence and corruption in football and to present their ideas and/or proposals. When it comes to public figures , social science research on the subject is not generally afforded the same value as the opportunity to make public appearances on TV, newspapers, radio, magazines, etc. To be clear, this is not a criticism of the ways in which high profile actors engage with debates on the issues that affect Argentinian football. Having said that, the difficulties I encountered when trying to arrange face-to-face meetings with potential participants were disheartening at times.

Unlike many anthropologists who live in Argentina and study football, I did not have the privilege of being able to become acquainted with participants prior to departing for fieldwork. This means that I was not able to establish personal, face-to-face relationships with potential participants during the course of my studies. The inability to establish these types of relationships beforehand would not have been much of a problem had I conducted research on a different topic, such as tourism in, say, Purmamarca, a small tourist town of approximately 900 people in northwestern Argentina where store clerks and street vendors selling regional handcrafted products are easy to find and approach. Put differently, participant observation in small and relatively isolated communities, where one can observe the research participants going about their daily business as well as certain aspects of the communities almost in their totality, is quite different from fieldwork in highly and densely populated urban settings where ethnographers do not have the privilege of "being there" (i.e. where the research participants are) *all the time* and interacting with them. Conducting research in Buenos Aires, where the mere act of "showing up" in the field does little to guarantee access to participants who have the knowledge required for a particular project, is quite a departure from the types of projects that anthropologists such as Malinowski, Boas, and Evans-Pritchard tackled decades ago. Having said that, the fact that I do not live in Argentina is not without its advantages. Beyond the methodological advantages of being a hybrid anthropologist, living in Canada affords me the opportunity to talk openly about topics such as corruption and clientelism among club officials and *barras* that could be potentially problematic in terms of personal safety for someone living in Argentina. To name one example, during my stay I met with Marcelo, a member of a third division club's fan subcommittee. He was active in opposing a politician's takeover of the club. In his role as a union organizer, this politician had a large number of followers within the union he represented, many of whom doubled as *barras*. Marcelo explained to me that, after having received a death threat, he was being watched by these *barras* and, as a result, was living on the run, meaning that he had moved out of his house and was staying at his friends', changing residence regularly. This is the sort of scenario that I was able to avoid mainly by making a point of not hanging out with a *barra brava* in the context of a study on corruption, clientelism, and violence in football. Still, the added "benefit" of living in another country contributed to a sense of long-term personal safety.

While in Buenos Aires, I arranged 20 semi-structured interviews with a variety of actors. O'Neill explains that

> it is not always possible or even necessary to obtain a representative sample of informants. The purpose will 'often be to target those people who have the knowledge desired and who may be willing to divulge it to the ethnographer'.
> (2005:11)

Traditionally, studies on football violence have tended to favour the voices of fans such as hooligans and *barras*. While their contributions are extremely important, my goal was to include other actors whose voices are not often heard. Thus, instead of focusing primarily on the fans' perspectives, I have incorporated the experiences of other actors who had firsthand knowledge of and were directly involved in the workings of Argentinian football. In line with O'Neill's statement, my approach targeted people who were deeply familiar with the connections between football, violence, and politics.

With the exception of a former leader of a *barra*, whom I was able to locate and interview through a personal contact, I chose not to approach *barrabravas*. It is extremely difficult for someone who has never been around *barras* to earn their trust. Seemingly minor details regarding their activities that would have likely emerged during interviews or informal interactions could have been perceived as a threat and created suspicion regarding my intentions. More importantly, my safety might have been compromised as a result of my involvement with *barras*. In the words of Gaffney,

> the world of the *barrabravas* is closed and extremely dangerous to outsiders.... Relationships between club leaders and their *barrabravas* are very guarded, primarily because they involve national political figures and institutionalized violence. Because of this it is unlikely that the details of the relationships between them will ever be fully brought to light.
>
> (2009:170–171)

The anthropologist Silvio Aragón (2007) described instances of his fieldwork experience where he had to endure beatings by the police and spend time in jail due to his association with San Lorenzo's *barras*. Gaining entry to the Butteler, as the club's *barra brava* is known, was not without its limitations.

> Access to my informants, mainly to the Butteler environment, was not easy, since I did not know anyone well enough to open the way for me without generating distrust. I only had the experience of attending stadiums for years, which somehow made me a familiar face. This allowed me not to arouse any suspicions while participating as a fan, although I had to be careful about what I did and especially what I asked when I approached the core of the Butteler. I took the decision to participate as a fan after a conversation with Eduardo Archetti,[12] who told me that his attempts to contact members of this same *barra brava* had been unsuccessful, since they frequently asked him for money, tickets or invitations to eat out, without being able to obtain relevant information.
>
> (2007:20–21; my translation)

Although his research benefitted from the interactions he had with *barras*, my official role during the course of my fieldwork was confined to that of an anthropologist. Put differently, I stayed away from the exciting yet sometimes painful heroics of the anthropologist/adventurer. Thus, instead of hanging out at a club hoping to have conversations with random fans about impunity, clientelism, and violence, I approached my research in a way that allowed me to identify participants who were knowledgeable *and* willing to talk about these issues openly. I chose not to become a member of a club because it would have been difficult for me to know exactly who I was talking to when "hanging out." Taking into consideration that *barras* spend quite some time at the clubs, I would not have had the freedom to bring up certain topics without compromising my safety.

14   Introduction

To recap, I chose to focus my attention on participants who had firsthand experience with violence, clientelism, and politics in football and who were willing to share their experiences and perspectives, as I did not want to be constantly on alert or worried about the comments I made and the questions I asked.

A note on what this book is *not* about

Media coverage of corruption, violence, and politics in Argentinian football is widespread. Bearing in mind the social status of football as well as its political ramifications at all levels of government, it comes as no surprise that newspapers pay considerable attention to the ties between football and politics. Needless to say, it is impossible for an anthropologist to witness firsthand most (if any) of the major cases of violence and corruption in football. This is mostly due to the fact that there are too many games and stadiums throughout the country where violence could potentially erupt. When it comes to corruption, on the other hand, the level of secrecy surrounding deals and transactions means that these are not amenable to observation. When discussing the difficulties in conducting qualitative research on corruption, Pardo states:

> in this field it is particularly difficult to meet the disciplinary commitment to the in-depth investigation of the micro-level – not only are official statistics notoriously unreliable and 'closed' questionnaires useless (when not counterproductive); but the traditional methods of participant observation, interviews and case-studies of relevant people and situations are not easily applied.
> (2004:3)

I was fortunate enough to interview people who had witnessed corruption in football. Still, I have relied on newspaper articles for specific examples of prominent cases of violence and politics in football. It should be noted, however, that I have *not* approached the material as a journalist. Rather, newspaper articles serve to support my analysis of the fieldwork data I have generated. Contrary to what many investigative journalists do, it is not my objective to openly denounce particular actors or institutions. My approach seeks to understand a social and cultural context in which a variety of actors engage in questionable practices for different reasons. In other words, the focus is on the practices, behaviours, motivations, and interactions, *not* on individuals. From a disciplinary perspective, this means that I had to adhere to a code of ethics that protected the identity of the research participants.

It is also important to keep in mind that this book was not written in the style of an autoethnography understood as autobiographical reflexivity (Meneley & Young 2005). Although I personally related to and was affected by fieldwork experiences, the research I conducted was, as obvious as it may sound, not about me. I was in the field for a limited time. Much of what happened in the field had no long-term implications in my life; it is the people whom I studied that were left to experience the realities of their social and cultural

Introduction 15

context on a daily basis. It would, therefore, be pretentious and misplaced to put the limelight on myself, which is not to say that relevant personal fieldwork experiences have been put aside. Rather, my approach places the focus on the research participants while incorporating personal experiences where appropriate. In cases where my own upbringing and experiences were pertinent, these were included in ways that elucidate the larger arguments I present.

Research questions and chapter outlines

Taking into account the methodological considerations discussed above, my study explores the following questions:

- What does corruption look like in Argentina and what are the mechanisms that perpetuate a culture of impunity?
- How are clientelist networks of exchange established and maintained?
- How does patronage politics work in contemporary Argentinian football?
- How are instances of physical violence and verbal aggression manifested at football matches and who participates?
- What changes need to take place within the Argentinian context in order to effectively reduce the levels of violence in football?

Given the amount of overlap between some of the topics discussed in my study, it is not always possible to neatly compartmentalize them, as they often inform and influence each other. Having said that, I have organized the chapters thematically in a way that allows the main arguments to flow from one chapter to the next.

Chapter 2 focuses on physical violence and verbal aggression at football matches. Through my experience at a match between River and Libertad, I introduce the concepts of cognitive dissonance and role play in the context of football crowds. Although cases of violence are often attributed almost exclusively to *barras*, who in the eyes of spectators represent a minority made up of "social misfits and savages," I argue that spectators contribute – both wittingly and unwittingly – to the creation of hostile environments at football stadiums by joining the *barras* in their provoking and discriminatory chanting. I also introduce the definitions of violence and aggression that inform my analysis before turning to an overview of the historical context that gave rise to particular interpretations of the concepts of civilization and barbarism in Argentina, which characterize race relations and discriminatory chants at football stadiums to this day. My focus then shifts to the importance of an emic approach to the study of fan mentality and behaviour when seeking to understand a variety of match day practices and performances. With this in mind, I present the case of Emanuel Balbo as an example of the tangible consequences that verbal aggression can have. In addition, I describe the differences between spectators, fans, supporters, and *barrabravas* before explaining the concept of *aguante* and its relevance to the study of football-related violence and aggression.

In Chapter 3, I compare different definitions of corruption and highlight the need to interpret it in relation to particular social and cultural contexts. From this relativist perspective, I point to the near impossibility of defining corruption in objective terms. Rather, I employ a grounded theory approach informed by an emic perspective that places the emphasis on examining practices that are considered corrupt by those who are directly or indirectly involved and/or affected. In order to understand the conditions that gave rise to widespread corruption in Argentina, I provide a brief historical sketch of events that contributed to its proliferation since colonial times. Furthermore, I describe the features that define and perpetuate a culture of impunity, which is closely related to what MacLachlan (2006) refers to as an "everyone for themselves" mentality, supporting my argument with interview material. In the final section of this chapter, I analyze corruption in football by focusing on the intersection of football and politics, with particular attention to interview material generated through semi-structured interviews conducted with a variety of actors from different social and professional backgrounds who have or had strong, personal ties to the world of football.

In Chapter 4, I define clientelism before providing a general overview of the historical context of clientelism in Argentina. I then present an example of patronage politics in ancient Rome as evidence of clientelism's resiliency, pointing to its enduring relevance as a mechanism that relies on dyadic and mutually beneficial relationships – both emotional and instrumental – to solve people's problems. The following section focuses on the importance of ethnographic approaches to the study of clientelism by looking at different understandings and evaluations of gift-giving and patronage politics that emerge from a variety of cultural contexts in different geographical locations. Relying on a cross-cultural analysis of differences and similarities, the comparative perspective adopted here, which includes a discussion of instrumental and emotional friendships, helps to identify the contextually situated ways in which people think about and experience clientelism in Argentina. Turning my attention to the Argentinian case, I then look at the mechanisms through which patron-client relationships in football are established and maintained. As my conversations with research participants reveal, these relationships contribute to the role of football clubs as environments where *quid pro quo* agreements between club officials, *barras*, politicians, and the police take root.

Chapter 5 situates my analysis of violence, corruption, and politics in football within the field of moral relativism. Here, I focus on the ways in which different actors negotiate their actions through the lens of morality, with particular attention to moral inconsistencies and the effects that certain choices have on the perpetuation of violence and corruption within football clubs. Crucially, I explore the actors' moral inconsistencies in relation to particular actions, events, and circumstances, showing the varying degrees to which they negotiate their personally held moral values and adjust their statements when describing potentially compromising situations. In addition, I discuss the role of patronage politics in the creation of Hinchadas Unidas Argentinas ("United Argentinian Fandoms"), a non-governmental organization that sought to establish inter-*barra* ties of cooperation in support of Argentina's national team. The plan, according to one of the organization's co-founder, was to use the *barras* for votes and political mobilization by turning them into "social leaders" (i.e. neighbourhood brokers). I end the chapter with an examination of different interpretations and moral evaluations of the social role of team sports. Here, I argue that moral assumptions regarding the role of team sports must be examined in relation to the social and cultural specificities that define particular contexts and circumstances. In Argentina, it is not unusual for fans to conceptualize rivalries as enmities, a factor that contributes to cases of violence within and beyond football stadiums.

In Chapter 6, I discuss the suitability of adopting foreign measures aimed at reducing football violence and implementing them in the Argentinian context. Contrary to the grand theory model proposed by some social scientists, I argue that violence, corruption, and politics in football need to be properly contextualized. Universal explanations are ill-equipped to account for the multiplicity of social, cultural, and historical factors that characterize the ties between football, violence, and politics in different countries. The interview material presented in this chapter suggests that foreign interventions often lack an in-depth understanding of the social circumstances and cultural features that impede the development of effective measures aimed at reducing violence in Argentinian football. On the other hand, solutions proposed by club officials and politicians often revolve around legal and punitive measures, which do little to discourage and disrupt the practices that promote violence, whether it is motivated by passion, economic interests, political interests, or a shared sense of belonging to a *barra*. Social scientists tend to distance themselves from solutions that involve punitive measures by proposing alternatives such as educational campaigns. The goal of these campaigns is to raise awareness of the ways that people think about violence in football. I suggest that a cultural transformation, including a change in mentality, needs to take place in Argentina if the solutions that are currently being proposed are to succeed in the long term. Taking this into consideration, I conclude by assessing the feasibility of producing cultural change under the current social, cultural, and political conditions.

Notes

1 The name *superclásico* refers to the games between Argentina's two biggest football clubs: Club Atlético River Plate and Club Atlético Boca Juniors, popularly known as River and Boca, respectively.
2 Argentinian Football Association.
3 Officials.
4 San Lorenzo de Almagro is one of Argentina's most important first division clubs.
5 The Unión Cívica Radical (Radical Civic Union or UCR for short) is a centre-left political party.
6 *Barra brava* means brave gang. The term *barra brava* (plural: *barras bravas*) refers to a group, while somewhat confusingly, the term *barrabrava* (plural: *barrabravas*) refers to a member of a *barra brava*. The word *barra* (plural: *barras*) can be used to refer to either a group (*barra brava*) or an individual (*barrabrava*), depending on the context.

7 The *barras'* violent behaviour is not always motivated by football. Economic interests, which *barras* often (but not exclusively) pursue through clientelist ties with politicians and club officials, play a prominent role in cases of violence. Consider, for example, the role of *barras* as "goons" at political rallies, hired by politicians to intimidate or harm political rivals.

8 *Aguante* means endurance. In football, the term refers to the physical, emotional, and psychological endurance displayed by fans during adverse conditions, and is often used to provoke rivals. The term's significance will be discussed in more detail in Chapter 5.

9 Hecho Club Social is an NGO dedicated to the promotion of football as a tool for social inclusion and individual empowerment among homeless people. The NGO's members compete in the Homeless World Cup.

10 Although the term "full native" is often considered racist, my inclusion makes reference to the ways in which anthropologists have historically talked about conducting fieldwork from an emic perspective.

11 The city of Buenos Aires is an autonomous district. Although it is surrounded by the province of Buenos Aires to the north, west, and south (the Río de la Plata lies to the east), it is not politically a part of it. Thus, the governor of the province of Buenos Aires has no direct influence over the city's politics. Autonomous City of Buenos Aires is the city's official name.

12 Argentinian anthropologist who pioneered the study of the social and cultural aspects of football in Argentina.

Chapter 2

Violence in Argentinian football

The "River Experience"

While doing fieldwork, I met Malik at Hecho Club Social. Malik was a young Californian who had made his way to Buenos Aires to participate in a two-month internship programme with the hope of conducting basketball training sessions at the NGO. Mix Up Exchange, the company that organized his stay in the city and put him in touch with Hecho Club Social, offered a variety of activities for foreigners who wanted to "go native" and experience the "real" Buenos Aires from the locals' perspective. Among their activities, they offered a "Boca Experience" and a "River Experience." While it is not uncommon for tourists to attend football matches accompanied by *barras*,[1] Mix Up Exchange offered little in terms of a package. Indeed, its role as an intermediary between the clubs and the foreign visitors they served consisted simply in reselling tickets for approximately three times the original price. Initially, I thought that it was dishonest and misleading to refer to the company's ticket scalping practices as a Boca or River "experience," but on second thought, it occurred to me that perhaps Mix Up Exchange's approach to ticket marketing – which, needless to say, omitted any mention of the fact that ticket scalping is illegal in Buenos Aires – was what made this a true Argentinian experience.

Lured by the prospect of attending a football match in Argentina, where crowds are reputedly passionate in their ways of expressing support for their teams, Malik contacted me to ask me if I was interested in going to a South American Cup game between River and Libertad, a Paraguayan team from the capital city of Asunción. He explained that Mix Up Exchange had tickets available. Being a River fan, and considering how difficult it was to obtain tickets from the club,[2] I eagerly agreed to go to the game with him. The fact that we were going to buy tickets for the so-called "River Experience" (which, as I mentioned, consisted only in buying tickets for more money than they were worth) is not a minor detail. Opting for the "Boca Experience" would have been problematic on a personal level for various reasons. Admittedly, my reluctance to spend 105 minutes – 90 minutes of regulation time plus a 15-minute break – surrounded by Boca supporters has its roots on my background as a River fan, although it would be simplistic to assume

DOI: 10.4324/9781003458937-2

20 Violence in Argentinian football

that the sheer mental effort and willpower required to watch River's main rival play at their stadium and among their supporters is merely a matter of allegiances. As a hybrid anthropologist, my outsider perspective is informed by a healthy dose of critical distance from the fieldwork experiences. Thus, taking this approach into consideration, I should have been able to attend Boca's matches by putting aside personal feelings and toxic rivalries. My Argentinian upbringing, on the other hand, makes me cautious about the idea of being a lonely River fan in a sea of Boca supporters. This fact would make for a very uncomfortable experience, as I would be constantly worried about being found out. Celebrating Boca's goals by screaming at the top of my lungs in an attempt to blend in (a fake reaction) would be out of the question, as would be celebrating the opponents' goals (an honest reaction). Undoubtedly, these safety concerns are closely tied to my personal history, and it would be naïve to believe that they can be simply brushed aside by adopting the "scientifically detached ethnographer's persona." In dealing with human affairs, anthropologists should not be expected to artificially compartmentalize their fieldwork by creating relational boundaries that may not exist in particular social situations. As Amit (2000) notes, the pressure to separate the personal from the professional when conducting fieldwork is predicated on the notion that scientific validity requires distance and detachment if the results and conclusions are to be objective. Ironically, however, ethnographic research revolves around the idea of immersion. While some degree of consideration should be given to the ways in which the ethnographer's background and interactions inform their analytical focus, it should also be taken into account that these interactions occur in the real world – be it in the context of fieldwork or beyond – and are not, by definition, artificially fabricated and "inserted" into an alternate fieldwork reality. To pretend that personal life and fieldwork are (or *should be*) separate domains is therefore problematic. In the words of Callaway, "ethnographic research involves prolonged interaction with others, yet anthropological discourse conveys the understanding gained in terms of distance, both spatial and temporal" (1992:30).

The main point for the purposes of this section is that I cannot pretend that I am not a River fan or that in my role as an ethnographer I am able to suppress aspects of my identity in the name of research. Given the tensions and personal safety concerns that would have arisen from attending a Boca match, opting for the "River Experience" was, both personally and ethnographically speaking, the logical and sensible choice. Needless to say, not all aspects of the researcher's identity play an equal role in their interactions, nor are they equally significant to the research project. Thus, while the fact that I am a River fan may be of little significance to a project that focuses on, say, the commodification of Indigenous arts and crafts in northwestern Argentina, it is hard to ignore its repercussions on a project that examines the social and political aspects of football. This is especially true if one considers that identities are both chosen and enforced (Eriksen 2004), meaning that people are not always free to choose how others see them. In my case, telling the research participants that I was a River fan may have led them to develop an idea of the kind of person that I am based on the club's history and values as well as on the fans' social, political, economic, and cultural backgrounds.

Obtaining the tickets

Malik informed me that he was going to buy our tickets from Mix Up Exchange. In my naivety, I asked him if the company had an agreement or partnership with the club, thinking that perhaps the club had given Mix Up Exchange a limited number of tickets to sell legally to the exchange programme's participants. My reason for considering this possibility was that I had trouble believing that an exchange company that dealt with foreigners would risk ruining its legitimacy and reputation over the illegal sale of football tickets. Surely, I thought, Mix Up Exchange would refrain from selling tickets illegally to foreigners under the guise of a Boca or a River Experience. In short, my own naivety stemmed from the fact that I did not suspect that the company's owners would be naïve enough to try to scalp tickets, especially considering how easy it would have been to prove that they were engaging in an illegal activity. The company's practices serve as an example of impunity by pointing to the ease with which it was able to profit from the illegal sale of tickets without the need to conduct operations discreetly, as its "packages" were openly advertised on the internet.

The tickets, which are made of plastic and are the size of a credit card, come with the full name and identification number of the buyer printed on the front. This made it extremely easy to identify the original buyer who chose to scalp the tickets, but was not enough to deter scalpers from selling tickets illegally, as it is usually the buyer who runs the bigger risk. Before meeting with Malik to obtain my ticket and give him the money, I explained to him during a telephone conversation that, at the discretion of the security personnel, people are sometimes required to show the DNI (Documento Nacional de Identidad or "National Identity Card") before being granted access to the stadium. I wondered if the tickets Malik had bought would circumvent this requirement by being specially designated for tourists, but he told me that the person who sold him the tickets had not given him any special instructions.

When Malik and I met a few days before the game, my doubts were finally put to rest. He handed me my ticket, which included the buyer's details. According to the ticket, and for the purposes of attending the game, my name was now Martín, and the National Identity Card number listed on it indicated that I was slightly older than I really was.[3] As it turns out, I had been sold a ticket illegally without my knowledge. It would have been immediately obvious for a local that getting access to the stadium with those tickets might prove difficult, but Malik was unaware of the implications. As a foreigner, he had no reason to mistrust the company that had facilitated his stay in Buenos Aires. The marketing approach, which relied on a fancy name (i.e. the "River Experience") to attract foreigners eager to witness the excitement of a live football match in a country where the sport features prominently in public life, added an air of legitimacy. Although I worried about not being granted access to the stadium, the manner in which we had secured the tickets created an opportunity for ethnographic research. Having tickets with details that did not match our identification cards allowed me to observe the degree to which the security personnel controlled access to the stadium. This was particularly important considering that many fans complain about *barras* being given preferential treatment by the police. It is not uncommon for *barras* to be granted access without being searched. Furthermore, they often pass through the turnstiles that lead them into the stadium without having to wait for other fans to go through security. The fact that the *barras* are "pampered" by the police while other fans are treated as potential troublemakers is problematic to say the least. The irony does not go unnoticed. Understandably, this expedited process angers many fans – be it club members or single ticket holders – who have their National Identity Cards checked, are searched multiple times, and have to wait much longer to be able to get into the stadium. The argument is not that all fans should be able to enter the stadium without having to go through a screening process. Rather, common sense dictates that *barras* should be subjected to the same level of scrutiny as the rest of the fans.

Outside the stadium

Although in the minds of the general public the club is usually associated with the middle class neighbourhood of Núñez, which boasts a strong River fan base, it is officially located in the neighbourhood of Belgrano. The confusion stems partly from the fact that the stadium is right on the border with Núñez, and given the predominant presence of River fans in Núñez, the media also refer to River as Núñez's club. Both neighbourhoods are located in the northern area of the city of Buenos Aires, with Núñez being the city's northernmost neighbourhood, bordered by the Greater Buenos Aires district of Vicente López to the north, the Río de la Plata (sometimes called River Plate in English; it is the river from which the club takes its name) to the northeast, and Belgrano to the south. Belgrano is also bordered by the Río de la Plata to the northeast. In general terms, the northern half of the city of Buenos Aires, with its imaginary border drawn along Rivadavia Avenue, is considered wealthier and more prosperous than its southern counterpart. Boca Juniors, River's main rival, is located in the southeastern neighbourhood of La Boca, bordered by the Greater Buenos Aires district of Avellaneda to the south.

Although I attended a South American Cup game between River and Libertad, Boca's geographical location in a humbler area of Buenos Aires is important to an analysis of verbal aggression, as many of the chants uttered by River fans during the match were directed at Boca rather than at Libertad. This will become apparent in the following section.

On the day of the highly anticipated game, I met with Malik and Carol, a Californian woman from Mix Up Exchange who had decided to join us. Since they were both staying in a building that was relatively close to mine, we went to the stadium together by bus. Bus rides to River's stadium on game days are never comfortable, and our ride was no exception. The bus was packed with River fans chanting and jumping, creating an entertaining spectacle that resembled a virtual travelling circus. When we got off five blocks from the stadium equipped with tickets that, legally speaking, belonged to other people, we began our journey to the gates with some anxiety.

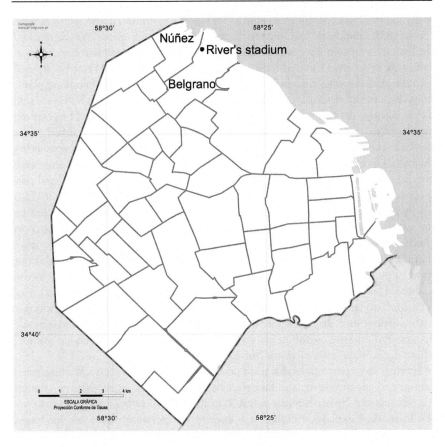

Figure 2.1 Map of the Autonomous City of Buenos Aires showing the location of Núñez, Belgrano, and River's stadium.
Source: mapoteca.educ.ar.

We were now at the mercy of the security officers, who could, at their discretion, choose to let us pass without giving too much attention to the information on the tickets, or demand that we show them some form of identification. I was particularly anxious about Carol and Malik. Unlike me, both of them stood out in the crowd. Malik's Middle Eastern and Carol's African-American features, combined with the fact that neither of them spoke Spanish, made them more vulnerable to identification checks by security officers. To complicate matters further, we had to go through *three* security checks before we could enter the stadium. Two of these checks were located along the five blocks that we had to walk from the bus stop, while the remaining one was located at our designated access gate that led to the stands. Although being searched three times – a testament to the expectation of violence at football matches in Buenos Aires – seemed excessive, the identification checks proved to be the real hurdles on our way to the stands. Having made it

24   Violence in Argentinian football

past the first check, Malik and I waited for Carol to join us. As the searches were conducted by hand, she had to go through the women-only queue. As she reached the female security officer, we noticed that she was trying to explain her situation to her. A male officer joined them, telling Carol that she would not be allowed into the stadium with that ticket. I tried to intervene on Carol's behalf, explaining to him from a distance that she was a tourist and that her ticket had been sold to her without her full knowledge of the ticketing system. He replied by pointing out the fact that her ticket said "Jorge" (George in Spanish). He then asked, "does she look like Jorge to you?" As unfair as the situation was, especially considering that Mix Up Exchange had taken advantage of foreigners who believed they were getting valid tickets, the officer was right. I knew that from a strictly legal perspective, Carol – and Malik and I, for that matter – had no valid argument. This is why I explained her situation to the officer *from a distance*. Needless to say, by intervening on Carol's behalf I was exposing myself to yet another identification check. It would have been easy for the officer to suspect that I also had a ticket that did not legally belong to me. As much as I wanted to help Carol, I did not want to press the issue to the point where I would also be denied access to the stadium. Fortunately for me, the officer was not interested in knowing who I was. For Carol, on the other hand, that first hurdle was the end of the line. It was not without frustration and guilt for the fallen comrade that we had to watch as she disappeared into the crowd on her way back to the neighbourhood's main avenue, where she would take a cab back home.

Having lost a partner, Malik and I proceeded to the second check. I reminded him not to say anything; the fact that he did not speak Spanish even though his ticket had a Spanish name printed on it would have been suspicious to say the least. As I explained earlier, it is possible to estimate a person's age based on their National Identity Card number. Luck, combined with the officer's negligence, was on our side. Malik and I had tickets with National Identity Card numbers that were close matches with our real ages. Had the officer requested to see some form of identification, he would have discovered that the names on our tickets did not match the names on our identification cards. Not only was my own National Identity Card number a mismatch, but being a foreigner, Malik did not have a local card number at all. Still, the officer was satisfied with a ballpark estimate of the correlation between the numbers on the tickets and the age he thought we were based on our appearance. What was clear, then, was that the security officers were making decisions arbitrarily based on how easy it was to follow the protocol. In other words, they would apply the law whenever it was convenient to do so. Carol was an easy target because it was blatantly obvious that a ticket with a man's name could not belong to her. This circumstance made it easy for the officer to present herself as someone who was simply doing her job.

While Malik and I were fortunate enough to have tickets that originally belonged to people of the same sex who were approximately our age, others were not so lucky. Before we were given the green light, a man who seemed to be in his late sixties had been turned back by the same officer who allowed us to continue to the third and final check. The officer asked the man what his National Identity Card number was, and the man gave him a number that started with 13 million. The officer then told him that his number did not match the one on the ticket. Looking genuinely confused, the man replied with a tone of obviousness that the number on the ticket was not his because he had bought the ticket from some girl he did not even know.

Whether he was aware of the way the ticketing system works is unclear, but it is unfortunate that many fans who simply want to get into the stadium and are not looking to make a profit have to go through so many checks, while *barras* get preferential treatment.

A night at the *Monumental*

Holding our breath, Malik and I proceeded to the third and final security check at one of the stadium's gates. Not being in the mood to conduct an in-depth identity check, especially knowing that we had already been "screened" twice, the officer let us pass through the turnstiles of the *Monumental*, as the stadium is unofficially known, without hesitation. We felt an instant sense of relief knowing that we could finally relax and get ready for what promised to be an entertaining match. In front of us, a few steps that went up to our section blocked our view of the stands and the field. As we climbed these steps, a full view of the illuminated stadium against the darkness of the night sky was revealed to us with an air of solemnity that contrasted with the cheerful chanting of the fans. Without saying a word, Malik looked at me with a big smile on his face, a clear sign that his expectations regarding the stadium's atmosphere had been met. Whether the game would manage to do the same remained to be seen.

The *Monumental*, officially named Estadio Antonio Vespucio Liberti after the club president under whose term the stadium was built, is South America's largest football stadium. At the time of my fieldwork, it had a capacity of approximately 62,000. Having undergone extensive renovations, the stadium now holds 84,567 spectators. It is the most frequently used stadium by Argentina's national football team, although in recent years the Argentinian Football Association has organized friendly and official matches at other stadiums around the country in an attempt to decentralize the game by bringing the national team to fans who would otherwise find it impossible to attend a match in Buenos Aires.

Taking into account that this was an international, South American Cup Round of 16 match, it is not surprising that the vast majority of fans in attendance were River supporters. Only a handful of Paraguayan fans, most of whom probably lived in the Greater Buenos Aires area, had made their way to the stadium to cheer for Libertad. They were in the section directly above ours. Their presence seemed to bother some River fans who were located in the section to the left of the visiting fans' zone, separated by an indentation in the stadium's structure. This indentation – one of many around the stadium – is an empty space

26 Violence in Argentinian football

where a person could fall to their death (see, for example, Télam 2017). Although the empty space acted as a physical barrier, a small group of River fans, leaning forward over it, decided to partially circumvent this obstacle by showering the Paraguayan fans with insults.

Verbal aggression, often euphemized as "folklore" – a fun and harmless way of provoking rivals and allies alike – provides an opportunity for an analysis of the ways in which different types of aggression, be it physical or verbal, have become naturalized in Argentinian society.

Violence and aggression

Before I turn my attention to verbal violence and aggression at football stadiums, I must emphasize that this section will not focus specifically on groups of organized fans and their match day rituals, including their "processions" on the way to the stadium, the strategic positioning on the stands, and the display and use of drums, flags, banners, and flares. Others (Aragón 2007; Garriga Zucal 2010; Gil 2006, 2007) have produced detailed ethnographic accounts of these rituals and the meanings of violence among *barras*.

While groups of organized fans – be it hooligans, *ultràs*, *barras*, or *torcidas*,[4] to name a few – receive considerable attention from social scientists who specialize in football violence, my aim here is to explore the ways in which verbal aggression permeates and influences the behaviour of the vast majority of spectators at football matches. Although *barras* are often demonized for their unrestricted levels of physical violence, the general consensus among spectators seems to be that verbal aggression at football stadiums is harmless, "festive," and fun. Thus, the full weight of the hostility experienced at football stadiums in Argentina rests on the shoulders of the *barras*, who become the easily identifiable and obvious scapegoats. Having said that, it should be noted that it is not my intention in this chapter to provide an impassioned and romanticized account of the reasons behind the *barras'* violent behaviour, nor do I seek to portray them as savage animals (as they often are by the media). The important point here is that *barras* are not the only ones responsible for the propagation of violence and aggression inside the stadiums and beyond. Spectators from every social class play a role in the intensification of aggressive and intolerant attitudes not only in football stadiums but more generally in Argentinian society.

Aggressiveness in Argentinian society is often a consequence of social frustration generated by political and economic uncertainty and instability, as evidenced by exorbitant rates of inflation, to name one example (the price of food, transportation, electronics, clothes, etc. went up several times during my stay in Buenos Aires, while salary increases did not keep up with inflation). Pomer explains that

> in these days when moral restraints lie flaccid and faded, when not reduced to ashes, and frustration explodes and uncertainty pierces the throat, everything

seems to favour the appropriation of what is foreign, the repudiation of any code that gives predictability to civilized relationships between people.

(2004:14; my translation)

Frustration, indignation, and anger sometimes lead people to react aggressively or violently against those who are seen as trying to take advantage of a particular situation at one's expense. This issue gained public prominence with the release in 2014 of the Oscar-nominated Argentinian movie *Wild Tales*, a collection of six short stories that portray a variety of social situations where the main characters lose their temper as a result of feeling taken advantage of. Following the movie's release, newspapers published articles on what they referred to as examples of real life "wild tales." Both in one of the movie's short stories and in real life, people who stand up to the abuse of civil servants, even in cases where verbal aggression and physical violence are used, are seen as heroes.

Definitions

Although sometimes used interchangeably, it is important for the purposes of this section to identify the basic differences between the terms *aggression* and *violence*. Regarding the use of these terms in the context of sport, Atkinson and Young explain that

> the term *aggression* is typically conceived of as behavior that intentionally threatens or inflicts physical injury on another person or thing. The definition of aggression may include assertive behaviors (such as a verbal attack), discriminatory behaviors, or economic exploitations that need not produce physically injurious outcomes.
>
> (2008:28; emphasis in original)

An important omission from this definition is the possibility of psychological harm. The emphasis on physical injury adds some confusion and ambiguity when comparing aggression with violence. Following Olweus' (1993) research on bullying in Norwegian and Swedish schools, Atkinson and Young (2008) identify the use of physical force as the main defining characteristic of violence. Thus, the term *aggression* as defined above overlaps with definitions of violence and is, therefore, too broad and problematic, given its focus on physical injury or, at the very least, the threat of it. Anderson and Bushman provide a more appropriate alternative, emphasizing that

> *human aggression* is any behavior directed toward another individual that is carried out with the proximate (immediate) intent to cause harm. In addition, the perpetrator must believe that the behavior will harm the target, and that the target is motivated to avoid the behavior.
>
> (2002:28; emphasis in original)

28   Violence in Argentinian football

Anderson and Bushman's focus on harm as opposed to physical injury acknowledges and legitimizes the psychological effects of some forms of aggression such as verbal aggression. The difference between these two understandings of the term is far from insignificant, as the presupposition of physical injury seems to negate the existence of other types of harm. Violence, on the other hand, "is aggression that has extreme harm as its goal (e.g., death). All violence is aggression, but many instances of aggression are not violent" (Anderson & Bushman 2002:29). What is meant by "extreme" harm would need clarification, as varying *degrees* of harm – as opposed to *types* of harm – are susceptible to highly subjective interpretations and experiences. Still, violence as defined by Anderson and Bushman revolves around the notion of *physical* harm.

Yet another understanding of violence differentiates between hard violence and soft violence. According to Guilbert (2006), soft violence relies on verbal and psychological actions, while hard violence is meant to produce physical pain and injury. In short, his description of soft violence roughly corresponds to Anderson and Bushman's understanding of aggression. For the sake of simplicity and to avoid confusion and ambiguity, it should be noted that I will be using the term aggression when referring to actions and behaviours that are not meant to cause physical harm, but to elicit feelings of sadness, anger, fear, indignation, humiliation, and/or frustration among those who are on the receiving end. The term *violence* will be reserved for situations where physical harm or injury is the intended goal.

Before turning my attention to an analysis of verbal aggression during the match between River and Libertad, I will describe the historical context that gave rise to the xenophobic chants that can be heard at football stadiums. These chants target immigrants (as well as their descendants) from neighbouring countries.

Civilization and barbarism: On race and class

Buenos Aires is often referred to as the Paris of South America, a comparison that seeks to exalt the city's cultural, ethnic, and architectural European legacy. This legacy is the result of waves of European immigrants that settled in Argentina during the late 19th and early 20th centuries. In the words of Rock, "between 1871 and 1914, 5.9 million immigrants – mostly Italians, but also Spaniards, Ottomans, French, and Portuguese – flooded Argentina" (1985:141). Garguin explains that

> while the idea of Argentina as a white nation can be traced back to the mid-19th century, it was during the 20th century – as an effect of massive immigration – that it crystallized into an undisputable 'myth of origin' and achieved common sense status, expressed in the standing joke that Argentines descend from ships.
>
> (2007:165)

Prior to this massive influx of immigrants, Argentina's population consisted mainly of a white creole Spanish elite and a non-white lower class which included Indigenous, mestizo, and black[5] people (Guano 2003). In the mid-19th century, Domingo Faustino Sarmiento, one of Argentina's founding fathers, described the country's population in terms of a dichotomy that distinguished between *civilización y barbarie*,[6] that is, civilization and barbarism. In the words of Guano, civilization and barbarism "juxtaposed the modernity of urban 'European' whiteness with the premodernity of mestizo and indigenous rural 'Latin Americanness'" (2003:149). In a similar vein, Garguin states that

> the myth of the European origins of the Argentine population is linked to 19th century elite efforts to think of Argentina as different from the rest of Latin America which, according to the ideological tropes of the time, did not fit within the category of 'civilized societies.'
>
> (2007:165)

Although Sarmiento had progressive ideas on education (he is widely regarded as the father of public education in Argentina), his views on race were very much a product of his time. It was through formal education that mestizos, blacks, Indigenous peoples, and gauchos[7] could be saved from the claws of barbarism. Still, if barbarism was to be eliminated, what the country needed was to "implant civilized Northern European immigrants onto Argentine soil. Only the relocation of a superior racial stock, Sarmiento claimed, would correct once and for all the barbarism of Argentina" (idem). His views on the "nature" of the non-European races that inhabited the country are vividly reflected in his work, where he described them as follows:

> The American races live in idleness, and demonstrate an incapacity, even when forced, to apply themselves to hard, uninterrupted work. This prompted the idea of bringing blacks to America, which has produced such fatal results. But the Spanish race has not shown itself to be any more given to action when, in the American deserts, it has been left to its own instincts. In the Argentine Republic, it makes one feel pity and shame to compare the German or Scottish colonies to the south of Buenos Aires with the towns existing in the interior. In the first, the little houses are painted, always clean in front, adorned with flowers and nice little shrubs; the furnishings, simple but complete; the dishes made of copper or tin, always shining; the bed with nice curtains; and the inhabitants in constant motion and action. Milking cows, making butter and cheese, some families have been able to amass colossal fortunes, retiring to the city to enjoy its conveniences. The native town is the disgraceful reverse side of this coin: dirty children covered in rags, living amid packs of dogs; men stretched out on the ground, in utter inactivity; filth and poverty everywhere; a little table and leather chests, the only

30 Violence in Argentinian football

furnishings; miserable huts for habitation, notable for their generally barbaric and neglected appearance.

(Sarmiento 1845/2003:51)

Guano (2003) claims that Sarmiento's racial ideology persists, at least to some extent, to this day. The expansion of the middle class among citizens of European origin during the early 20th century further cemented the idea that non-whites were incapable of prospering and climbing the social ladder if left to their own devices. Although education could help combat the barbarism that was prevalent among non-whites, it was the European immigrants and their children who were the vehicles and guarantors of Argentina's prosperity. When describing the class situation at the turn of the 20th century, Rock states that "since the quickly-growing economy brought about a rampant need for professionals, administrators, and, generally speaking, white collar employees, mandatory public education became the stepping-stone into 'middle classness' for the children of immigrants" (1985:175). The exclusion of the lower classes from discussions around the idea of an Argentinian identity paved the way for the creation of an imagined community (Anderson 1991) that was defined by a "shared" European origin and a common understanding that Argentinians came from somewhere else. This perception encouraged (wittingly or unwittingly) a view of Indigenous populations as the Other. During her fieldwork in Buenos Aires, Navrátilová identified the predominantly white character of the discourse on Argentinian identity. In her words,

> it is interesting that in Argentina the immigrants had become the "locals" and the bearers of national identity.... The newcomers were supposed to create the new Argentine identity based on their white race and the proclaimed "civilization".... The Argentine national identity was replaced by the ethnic white identity of the newcomers, and the indigenous inhabitants had become "the others".

(2014:35)

Guano (2003) and Navrátilová (2014) mention that most present-day Argentinians, unsurprisingly, do not think of Argentina as a racist country. The argument in favour of Argentinian society as an example of an inclusive and welcoming society revolves around the concept of the melting pot. According to Guano, however, Argentina's melting pot is a selective one, to the extent that it tends to exclude Indigenous peoples and mestizos (including immigrants from neighbouring countries such as Bolivia, Peru, and Paraguay) from an idealized Argentinian identity that looks to Europe for inspiration. Put differently, "barbaric" populations have no place in a "civilized" melting pot. Furthermore, it is important to note that the perpetuation of the idea of a national identity that is based on white European characteristics requires a certain degree of maneuvering around ethnic categories. As Guano explains, support for the denial of a racial problem in Argentina came from the transformation of south and east European ethnicities into races: a transformation that, during the first 30 years of the 20th century, refit the dangerously off-white Italians, Spaniards, Ottomans, and Jews into the cast of civilized, modern European people of Argentina, as first prospected by Sarmiento.

(2003:161)

The dichotomy between civilization and barbarism in present-day Argentina, although not always articulated in explicit terms, continues the tradition embraced by Sarmiento with an emphasis on the barbarism of immigrants mainly from Bolivia, Peru, and Paraguay, who represent Indigenous races. Within the Greater Buenos Aires area, these immigrants are often seen as contributing to the growth of the slums, some of which are located around the periphery of the city proper. Moreover, many Argentinians resent the fact that immigrants take advantage of free access to the country's public healthcare and education systems. In the words of Navrátilová,

It has been acknowledged that the most discriminated groups in Argentina are Bolivians, Paraguayans, and Peruvians who represent also the majority of the inhabitants of the *villas*,[8] the slums. Bolivians are often described as *trabajadores*, hard workers, because they often times work at construction sites where heavy manual labour is required, but more commonly they are defined as *inmigrante extractivo*, "extractive immigrants", who steal work from Argentines, send their money back to Bolivia and (ab)use the Argentine welfare such as healthcare and education. Hence, they are contraposed to the former immigrants from Europe who came to *offer* their labour to a country that needed them, as ones who come to *search* for *our* work.

(2014:41; emphasis in original)

According to the 2010 census, there were 76,609 Bolivians, 80,325 Paraguayans, and 60,478 Peruvians living in the Autonomous City of Buenos Aires (i.e. the city proper). Combined, they represented 7.51% of the city's 2,890,151 inhabitants in 2010. The Greater Buenos Aires area (including the Autonomous City of Buenos Aires) had a population of 12,806,866, of which 5.6% were immigrants from Bolivia, Paraguay, and Peru (INDEC 2012). These numbers pose an increasing threat to the idealized and exalted "Europeanness" of middle class Argentinians, particularly considering that demographic growth among immigrants from neighbouring countries is higher than among Argentinians of European background. Furthermore, there were 737,058 foreign residents born in South America living in the province of Buenos Aires in 2010. This figure represents 78.23% of all foreign-born residents in the province. Nearly 51.9% of the total foreign-born population in the province was from Paraguay, while 19.5% was from Bolivia. Compared to the 2001 census, the number of European-born residents in the province fell by 32.6%, while the number of residents born in Paraguay grew by

32   Violence in Argentinian football

83.2% (Cámara Argentina de Comercio 2015). The rapid pace of "Latin Americanization," particularly within the Greater Buenos Aires area, raises concerns among people who blame much of the increase in poverty, crime, unemployment, and drug use on immigrants from neighbouring countries. To some extent, the current demographic trend reignites discussions around Sarmiento's dichotomy of civilization and barbarism.

As previously stated, these racial tensions are sometimes manifested in football chants. In the words of Douglas, "we might think of the audience at a sport event as constituting a particular presence that contains within it the means through which social and racial consciousness and meanings are felt and expressed" (2005:256). Contrary to what happens in other social environments, football stadiums allow fans to explicitly express hostility towards the perceived barbarism of rival fans of Indigenous or mestizo origins through chanting. According to Burstyn,

> the way sport tends to organize around competing identifications, the way it draws lines and divisions, the way its objectives are to dominate and even obliterate the designated Other – all these aspects of sport contribute to the way it often nurtures xenophobia and antisocial behaviours.
>
> (1999:194)

Ironically, however, many of the fans who take part in this practice have mestizo or Indigenous backgrounds themselves.

Although some of the chants presented in the following section target Boca fans of immigrant origin, it should be noted that these chants are not sung exclusively by River fans. Many of the xenophobic chants directed at Boca are also sung by fans of Independiente, Racing, San Lorenzo,[9] and others.

Chants

A few days before our visit to the *Monumental*, Malik forwarded me an email sent to him by Mix Up Exchange with game day tips, directions to the stadium, and other details that foreign visitors might have found useful and informative. In an attempt to provide foreigners with a truly local experience, the email included the lyrics to a few football chants popular among River fans. Needless to say, the intention was to get foreigners to engage with the local crowd by singing these chants during the game. In line with their shady business practices that included illegal ticket scalping, the staff at Mix Up Exchange believed that giving foreigners the opportunity to familiarize themselves with the lyrics of a chant that actively and unequivocally discriminates against Bolivians would "enrich" their experience. Discrimination against immigrants from Bolivia, Peru, and Paraguay on the basis of social class, manners, level of education, and physical appearance is quite prevalent in Argentinian society. Given Boca's origins in an impoverished neighbourhood of Buenos Aires, it is not uncommon for football fans to associate

Bolivian immigrants with the club. Thus, River fans often sing about Boca's immigrant fan base by pointing out their uncivilized customs and behaviour.[10] It is important to note, however, that the dichotomy that states that River represents the educated middle class while Boca represents the uneducated lower class (including immigrants from neighbouring countries) is greatly exaggerated, and at least partially the result of the clubs' geographical location,[11] with River being located in the northern middle class neighbourhood of Belgrano, and Boca being located in the southern lower-class neighbourhood of La Boca. Considering that both clubs have millions of fans throughout the country, there is simply too much variation when it comes to the fans' ethnic, financial, social, educational, and cultural backgrounds. According to sports journalist Alejandro Fabbri, author of a book about the history of Argentinian football clubs, "Boca was a very popular Italian club and continues to be so, but with affluent fans, who used to be closer to River" (Respighi 2006; my translation). Rodrigo Daskal, Sociologist and Director of the River Museum, explains that "like any mythological or folkloric matter, this[12] borrows from some real or historical events, but there is nothing to support these stereotypes in reality" (Pardo 2018; my translation). In a similar vein, Juan Sasturaín, author and fan of Boca, states that "the actual class composition of the fans is much less important than the development of the social imaginary" (idem).

Going back to Mix Up Exchange's seemingly innocent email, it is ironic to note that the lyrics that are meant to insult and provoke Boca fans are in fact directed primarily at Bolivian citizens:

> How ugly to be *bostero*[13] and Bolivian,
> they have to live in a slum.
> The sister spins the purse,[14]
> the mother goes around sucking cocks.
> Bostero bostero bostero,
> *bostero* stop thinking about it.
> Move to Bolivia,
> your whole family is there!

Different forms of aggression have become naturalized and widespread (Plaza Schaefer & Cabrera 2021). This sort of national habitus often relies on the idea of aggression as fun and humorous. Indeed, aggression and humour have become so intertwined in Argentinian society that insulting someone or something is often all it takes to make a "joke." The following chant combines verbal aggression with xenophobia by highlighting the barbarism of Bolivian fans.

> In the neighbourhood of La Boca
> live all the Bolivians
> who shit on the sidewalk
> and clean themselves by hand

34 Violence in Argentinian football

> Saturday at the *bailanta*[15]
> they get drunk
> and they go on vacation
> to the Riachuelo[16] beach
> You have to kill them all
> Let there be no *bosteros* left
> You have to kill them all
> Let there be no *bosteros* left

The following example further emphasizes the precarious social status of immigrants of Indigenous backgrounds:

> They are half plus one[17]
> they are from Bolivia and Paraguay
> I sometimes wonder
> hey, dirty darkie[18]
> if you shower
> Boca you disgust me
> wash your ass
> with turpentine

In the context of football, while it is true that most, if not all, of the lyrics to the chants are authored by *barras*, it is not uncommon for spectators – fans, supporters, and others – to "adopt" the chants, thus legitimizing the practice of verbal aggression at matches and contributing to the spread of intolerance and the perception of the rival as the enemy. The fact that the lyrics to the chant presented above were emailed to foreigners by the staff of an exchange programme as an example of a fun and exciting activity is indicative of an almost naïve inability to distinguish between innocent fun and intolerant behaviour that can potentially escalate to instances of physical violence. It is even more troublesome to think that, from the perspective of the staff at Mix Up Exchange, foreigners would find these lyrics amusing, acceptable, and in line with what cheering at a sporting event should be. It would be surreal to imagine that equivalent exchange programmes in, say, Sweden or Finland, would encourage foreign visitors to join the crowd at football and hockey games in insulting rival fans and players in this racist way.

The four examples that follow point to a common pattern within the Argentinian style of cheering at football matches, a pattern that often prioritizes insulting the rivals over praising one's own team. These chants were sung during the game I attended.

> Sunday arrives, I go see the champion
> River you are my madness
> I take the flags[19] to cheer for you
> I don't give a damn about the cops[20]

I cheer for River because we have *aguante*,
not like Boca, they are all pigs[21]
For ninety minutes,
this terrace won't stop cheering

The chant above provides a rather mild and moderate example of the ways in which River fans attempt to incorporate their archrivals into the lyrics by means of provocation. In this particular case, cheering for River remains the focus of the chant, although this comes at Boca's expense.

The following chant makes little effort to provide encouraging words for River's players, focusing instead on a message of dominance over Boca (the degree to which this message makes reference to clashes and interactions between fans of both teams off the pitch or between players on the pitch is open to interpretation):

This is the chicken coop's gang[22]
    The one that fucks the *bosteros*
    It moves this way
    It moves that way
    This is the craziest gang there is!

On a similar note, the next chant points to a theme of dominance over a rival that must be forced into submission and humiliation. Not only are the rivals' defeats often more important than one's own team's victories, but these defeats seem to be more enjoyable when they are undignified. When it comes to football crowds, dominance is often – although not exclusively, as will become apparent in future sections – imposed by men on other men through chants, mostly by emasculating and feminizing the rivals, who are effectively "tamed" into submission.

The fact that acts of physical violence remain common at football matches in spite of a ban on visiting fans at the national level since 2013 (a point to which I shall return later), points to tensions within the world of football that transcend an analysis of masculinities. As many of my interviewees mentioned, political and economic interests play a prominent role in intra-*barra* conflicts that become public "spectacles" in the form of physical or armed confrontations. Here, power struggles reveal themselves in ways that emphasize personal interests. Taking this into account, it is important to keep in mind the multiplicity of factors that lead fans and *barras* to engage in certain practices. A full picture of the issues that plague Argentinian football must consider the very prominent role of politics as well as the interests and motivations of a variety of actors.

While the previous two chants I discussed point to a particular form of male violence and aggression that reflect the patriarchal values of Argentinian society, the argument I am presenting here is not only about the role of gender in cases of violence at sporting events, but also about the ways in which the figure of the rival in Argentinian football, politics, and society is equated with that of the enemy. In the case of football, clientelist ties between club officials and *barras* directly contribute to the continued, prominent presence of *barras* at football stadiums. As a result, *barras* are granted access to a space where they are free to engage in aggressive and violent behaviour with impunity, sometimes motivated by economic interests, sometimes by the desire to humiliate, overpower, and harm rival fans through displays of aguante. The proliferation of chants that target rival teams highlights the fans' desire to see their rivals/enemies beaten and suffering. To some extent, the degree to which a fan is able to experience unbridled joy as a result of their team winning a tournament is dependent on the rival's perceived level of suffering. When it comes to engaging in the practice of mocking rivals, players and fans become one. Players from different clubs have been filmed by TV news crews in dressing rooms celebrating their team's victory – be it a league or an international or domestic cup – by chanting against their archrivals.[23]

During the South American Cup Round of 16 game I attended, River fans regularly taunted Boca fans by dedicating to them a chant that anticipated a possible clash between both teams at the semi-final stage:

> Boca, Boca my friend
> your mother's cunt[24]
> Boca, Boca my friend
> your mother's cunt
> If you want to do the lap[25]
> don't be left wanting
> There's a carousel
> in Lezama Park[26]
> in Lezama Park

What is perhaps most interesting about these chants is that one may easily forget that they were sung by River fans during a game against Libertad, a team from Paraguay. The fact that three out of the four chants presented here were directed at Boca points to a high degree of animosity between archrivals. It must be noted, however, that fans are much less likely to "compose" chants directed at South American rivals outside of Argentina, as historical connections to these rivals are often weak and frequent encounters with particular clubs are a rarity.

It would be easy to dismiss the lyrics of these chants as trivial and harmless, belonging to a world of football that is grounded on an alternate reality, with little connection to the "outside world" beyond the stadiums. Still, while it would be an exaggeration to claim that chants have the ability to turn most football fans into aggressive and violent troublemakers, it would also be inaccurate at best and dangerous at worst to suggest that manifestations of aggressive (and potentially violent) behaviour at football stadiums occur within microscopic contexts where broader social understandings of violence, morality, and racism either do not apply or are temporarily suspended. I turn my attention to these considerations in the following section.

A grounded and emic approach to interpreting fan behaviour at football stadiums

In his qualitatively oriented and fieldwork-based analysis of football fandom in Buenos Aires, Lyth (2007) makes a distinction between the real world beyond the stadiums and the presumably "less real" world of football inside the stadiums. When it comes to chanting and dancing (to the extent that the mere act of jumping up and down on the spot can be considered dancing), he explains that

> there is something very basic about the beating of a drum that is difficult to ignore, which sets feet moving in dance and bodies swaying in rhythm.... Music provides the soundtrack for football fans.... masking the real world and creating an imagined atmosphere where smiles, laughter, shouts and gestures replace the regular routine of living in the city.
>
> (2007:62)

His statement raises some questions. Without digging too deep into matters that would be more appropriately tackled by philosophers, what constitutes the real world in this case? Whose real world is being analyzed? The observer's or the participants'? In what ways are chanting, jumping, and playing drums during football matches activities that are not part of the real world? While his point about play and performance is an important one, considering that it highlights the ways in which fans let loose in a manner that would perhaps be considered strange or inappropriate in other contexts, it should not be assumed that these performances and displays result in imagined atmospheres. To draw a comparison, a university student showing up for class in the summer wearing nothing but a Speedo or a bikini would probably raise more than a few eyebrows. The fact that this student could then go to a nearby beach straight from class, where they could spend hours without anyone noticing anything that would be considered out of the ordinary in that particular context, does not mean that the beach provides an imagined atmosphere where the expectations of the real world do not apply. The contexts are different and the tolerance thresholds in relation to certain types of behaviours may vary greatly from one context to another, but there is an underlying and shared reality that informs people's actions and interactions in social environments. To be sure, cases of violence inside the stadiums that result in death can hardly be confined to imagined atmospheres, especially considering the finality of death, which defies the dichotomy between imagined atmospheres and the real world.

It could well be argued that football stadiums during matches provide many fans with an opportunity to behave and to express themselves in ways that feel more real to them (i.e. less fake and less restrained) than the "ordinary" world. Put differently, the stadium can represent a space that feels more real than the outside world. Ultimately, whether this is the case or not depends largely on a fan's individual circumstances and experiences. In any case, it is crucial to approach the study and interpretation of football fans (or any other social groups for that matter) from an emic perspective. Having said that, I can easily relate to Lyth's experience from an autoethnographic point of view. Considering that I was not at the match merely as a detached observer, but as an observer *and* as an engaged River fan, I chanted along with the local fans in what could at first glance appear as a festive, high-adrenaline, cheerful – though offensive – and carnivalesque experience. Chanting and jumping during a football match are highly contagious activities that only make sense when they are performed in unison. This is what Herrera calls participatory sounding-in-synchrony, which has the power "to unite people in feelings of bonding and cohesion" (2018:486). Thus, while I found some of the chants questionable, the contagious nature of the melodies produced by tens of thousands of fans was impossible to resist. How else could I cheer for River if not by surrendering to the chants that resonated throughout the stadium? Singing my own tunes would have been weird, out of place, ineffective, and unsatisfying. Carlos, one of the interviewees from Hecho Club Social, agrees that the lure of thousands of fans chanting in unison is impossible to resist. Although *barras* are often the first to start chanting, other fans around the stadium are quick to join them.

EP: The vast majority of people who sing the chants that generate rivalries are not *barras*. I mean, the *barras*, you see them in the stadium, the *barras* are there and they start chanting. You are, let's say, at Boca's stadium, the *barra* begins to chant something against River. They are the ones who start it, but then the chanting reaches the rest of the fans and the entire stadium ends up chanting.

CARLOS: It's because they are the ones, the ones who, uh, how can I put it? The ones in charge of conducting the songs. I'm not going to sing "go Boca! Go Boca!" They (*the fans and spectators*) won't pay any attention to me, because that's the way it is! If I'm not with the *barra*, and I say "hey, let's sing a song!" they will tell me "shut up, moron!"

EP: Okay, but the thing is that the *barra* starts chanting … Let's say that more than 80% of the spectators are not *barras*, but the chants "spread" to them; they are contagious. Now, they shouldn't necessarily have to sing against the rival, insulting and threatening them; they could choose not to, however the vast majority of people who are not *barras* end up singing against the rival.

CARLOS: Weeell… Professional football is complicated. It's not easy in professional football to say "no, I'm not going to sing" because the stadium itself and the fans themselves are calling you to sing.

During the course of the game between River and Libertad, the idea that chanting is a contagious activity was further solidified by Malik's reactions. Being unable to speak Spanish, he looked at me on a few occasions with a wide smile on his face at times when the chanting got louder. He communicated his excitement at what was happening on the field by waving his arms and uttering "ohs!" and "ahs!" whenever there was a well-executed attack, a dangerous play, or a hard foul. Although he had no trouble communicating with me in English, I strongly suspected that he would have liked to become an active member of the crowd by joining in the chanting. I doubt that, had he understood the lyrics, he would have been less inclined to join his "fellow" River fans who were chanting at the top of their lungs.

Following Lyth's notion of play from an autoethnographic perspective that considers my own thoughts, feelings, and reactions in relation to the situations and events in which I am embedded, it is easy to dismiss acts of verbal aggression as examples of harmless fun, particularly in a social environment where these acts have become the norm. An autoethnographic approach, however, risks emphasizing reflexivity at the expense of a detailed understanding of the participants' social, cultural, and economic backgrounds.

Thus, while I might be tempted to claim that offensive, racist, and misogynistic chants pose no real danger to spectators because I know that I do not believe the content of the chants to be true, such a claim would primarily consider my personal upbringing and experiences while ignoring the participants'. It is important, then, to consider the degree to which the lyrics of the chants hold significance beyond the seemingly harmless and carnivalesque performances. Lyth is certainly correct in explaining that most fans and supporters do not take the lyrics too seriously. If they did, we would witness confrontations – some involving firearms, some blunt weapons and knives, and others nothing but fists – between tens of thousands of fans on a weekly basis. Still, although it might be reasonably said that most serious cases of violence inside and around the stadiums are caused by a minority of fans, their influence in terms of the levels of violence within the world of football and beyond is hard to ignore. The lyrics to the chants that resonate in stadiums throughout Argentina are, more often than not, written by these minorities. While most fans adopt these lyrics in the spirit of "fun" by making a conscious choice not to take them seriously, it is safe to say that *some* fans do take them seriously for a variety of reasons that might be tied to their personal circumstances and upbringing.

Cognitive dissonance and role play

I was raised in a middle class family, in a social environment where firsthand, sustained exposure to violence was not a part of my personal life. As I mentioned earlier, I chanted with the fans during the game between River and Libertad even though I did not necessarily agree with the lyrics. Herrera (2018) describes a state of cognitive dissonance by which football fans engage in public displays of fandom in ways that contradict their personally and deeply held beliefs. He explains that

chanting in massive numbers allows the public utterance of slurs, profanity, and violent threats that most people might refrain from using individually.

But voicing ideas about sexuality and violence in a stadium setting is not the same as believing these ideas.

(2018:486)

In the context of football fandom, cognitive dissonance and role play are inseparable concepts. The feelings of bonding that result from participatory sounding-in-synchrony are a manifestation of collective role play, which requires a state of cognitive dissonance in order to allow fans and spectators to perform their roles properly and convincingly. According to Herrera,

> there are aspects of what fans do that resemble role playing.... The genuine excitement that often results from such bonding experiences might create a state of cognitive dissonance, given the inconsistency of the action in relation to the beliefs that most fans hold outside the stadium.

(2018:487)

Still, the fact that Lyth and I – like so many other spectators, supporters, and fans who enter a state of cognitive dissonance – separate the fun of chanting and jumping from the literal meaning of the lyrics does not mean that, for some fans, the lyrics have no meaning other than being an excuse to create a playful and festive atmosphere. Herrera's comments regarding the use of offensive and violent language during football matches is in line with Lyth's description of the stadium as a place where this type of behaviour is tolerated and even expected. Nevertheless, considering the heterogeneous nature of the fans' moral values and beliefs, Bundio states:

> we must ask ourselves about the subjectivity of individual speakers and the ways in which they appropriate the meanings of the message, and how they resist or negotiate them. In this regard, we can find a diversity of views, from adherence to the literal meaning of the message to outright rejection, passing through interpretations that mitigate the gravity of these chants, which indicate that they must be understood within the interpretive framework configured by the act of cheering, in which those practices acquire new meanings and legitimacy.

(2018:207; my translation)

The expectation of "mischief" is tied to what Herrera interprets as role play. Thus, "inside the stadium, many are expected to play the part of fans, screaming, cursing at referees, physically enacting fandom, and releasing aggression that would not be made public otherwise, making it a cathartic experience" (Herrera 2018:487). Although there are certain similarities between his interpretation and Lyth's notion of play, he does not make an explicit distinction between the "alternate reality" of the stadium and the "*real* reality" of the social world beyond its confines. Emphasizing the festive, playful, and recreational nature of fandom in a context where the stands and terraces become a stage, risks turning attention away from the fact that the activities and behaviours that spectators engage in may not always involve role play. When it comes to acts of violence perpetrated by fans, to ignore the significance of their motivations in relation to their upbringing and social backgrounds would constitute a grave omission. A homogenized characterization of football fans and spectators (as well as the police) necessitates an emic "corrective." If the performances put on by fans and spectators during matches were mainly an example of staged role play with little potential for violent conflict, the routine presence of hundreds (occasionally thousands) of police officers at football stadiums would be questionable, as it would not be in the interest of role players to cross the line between role playing and physical violence. Why would a safe environment where "pretend" anger and play fighting are the socially expected norm require the police to keep a close eye on the events that unfold on the stands and terraces? If, on the other hand, stadiums can be described as safe environments *because* of police presence, what does that say about the supposedly playful nature of the spectators? To clarify my point, I am not suggesting that role play is not an important component of the spectators' experience at football matches. Rather, I highlight the stadium as a place where a multiplicity of experiences can be observed. When it comes to Argentinian football stadiums in particular, the current ban on visiting fans as a result of violent confrontations during matches is certainly at odds with the idea that play and recreation result in purely festive expressions of passion and harmless displays of verbal aggression. Thus, while play inside the stadium relies on the spectators' temporarily heightened levels of tolerance, it would be misleading to claim that certain behaviours that are considered unacceptable in public settings are somehow rendered acceptable inside the seemingly controlled environment of the stadium. To be clear, at no point should it be assumed that tolerance turns into acceptance.

In his analysis of play and public performances during football matches and street protests, Lyth establishes a clearly delineated dichotomy between the pretend nature of these performances and the invariably more civilized behaviour of the participants in other contexts:

> During my time in Buenos Aires, I did not otherwise witness the type of vulgar language and lewd gestures performed in the stadium or on the streets during protests. Never did I see someone calling another "A fucking immigrant" as I did during the Boca-River football match. Never, did I see people making lewd gestures towards one another in the subway or at the grocery store as I had witnessed in all of the football matches I attended…. In all of the cases when I did witness these activities, they were reserved for the out-of-the-ordinary world created in the stadium or in the streets during protests. Football fans and street protesters understand that the actions carried out during these specific performances exist outside of the realm of normality and permit them to act and play in a way that might not otherwise be permitted in the city.
>
> (2007:63)

The last sentence raises an important question: do fans and street protesters behave in ways that would be considered play (pointing perhaps to a state of cognitive dissonance) *in spite* of their personal beliefs, or are their behaviours *based* on their beliefs and not fully expressed outside specific contexts because, as Lyth says, they are *not permitted* in the city? His statement hints at the possibility of fans and street protesters behaving aggressively and offensively beyond street protests and football stadiums if only it were permitted. This is not to say that play and cognitive dissonance do not inform the behaviours of fans and protesters in some cases. Rather, I argue that, given the multiplicity of experiences, values, and beliefs, the dichotomy that separates public performances at football matches and street protests from the normality of the "real world" is a fragile one. It would hardly be surprising to witness more acts of aggression and racism inside the stadiums than outside, but although in some instances this may have something to do with role play and putting on a performance, in others it may be the result of the protection and anonymity provided by large gatherings. A person on the street yelling racist remarks at an immigrant in broad daylight and in full view of passersby would be easy to single out. Furthermore, it might not be in this person's best interest to compromise their physical integrity by risking a violent backlash from people who might want to "teach them a lesson." Stadiums, on the other hand, allow spectators who mean what they say to utter offensive and racist remarks without fear of retaliation. This is often, although by no means exclusively, done in unison with other spectators in the form of chanting. Even a small crowd of, say, 2,000 spectators suffices to provide a sense of security and anonymity.

Taking into account that part of the fun of chanting lies in creating a loud atmosphere by getting the crowd to chant in unison, it is important to note that chants are more prone to instances of cognitive dissonance than insults uttered by individuals. Thus, a spectator might feel compelled to engage in chanting – in spite of the offensive and racist lyrics of some chants – because of the excitement and rush produced by the shared experience. The same spectator, however, might very well refrain from making offensive comments on the basis of gender, nationality, race, and socioeconomic background due to their values and upbringing.

Although it is true that manifestations of racism, verbal aggression, and physical violence become amplified and are more prevalent in and around football stadiums on game days, the comparatively peaceful interactions that one can witness on the streets should not be attributed solely to the fact that, outside the stadiums, people no longer engage in role play and return to their "civilized" ways. As I mentioned earlier, there are spectators for whom the stadium represents a space where they can express their true feelings freely and without the constraints of the outside world. In fact, their interpretation of role play might revolve around the ways in which they negotiate their behaviours *outside* the stadium, in settings where public scrutiny and social norms impose a level of tolerance that they might not otherwise display.

The internet provides good examples of cases where people express their views on issues related to gender, race, nationality, and religion, to name a few, usually from the comfort of a private setting and without the fear of public backlash. Online newspapers in particular provide a forum for readers to express their unfiltered thoughts, opinions, and feelings behind the veil of anonymity. Unlike football chants, which often rely on spectators "going with the flow," comments posted online require some degree of premeditation. By reacting and responding to the content of online newspaper articles in the form of written comments, readers communicate their views through varying degrees of introspection, reflexivity, and self-awareness. Expressing opinions online is an individual task that contrasts with the group mentality of spectators who temporarily suspend their values and opinions at football stadiums in favour of a shared sense of identity.

Although the readers' comments in online newspapers are moderated, moderators do not often delete what some readers might consider inappropriate and/or offensive comments. As I said, it might be uncommon for someone to make openly racist remarks in public settings and within hearing distance from strangers. On the other hand, given their (optional) anonymity, online newspapers' comments sections sometimes include racist rants, usually aimed at Bolivians, Paraguayans, Peruvians, and "Indigenous-looking" Argentinians. It is worth noting that many of the online newspaper articles that include racist and offensive readers' comments are in no way related to football, which reinforces the idea that the world of football is not an isolated social entity with a special status that transcends the expectations of the broader social, cultural, legal, and political contexts in which it is embedded.

The comments sections of online newspapers are far removed from the feelings of bonding and cohesion generated by participatory sounding-in-synchrony at football stadiums. These sections offer a public forum where readers are much more inclined to express their opinions and beliefs in ways that are not restrained or contradicted by the collective and public performances at stadiums that often require them to enter a state of cognitive dissonance.

In an article about a teenager who could have played in Club Almagro's[27] first team but ended up in jail instead, accused of having murdered a woman, a reader by the name of Rudy Hess wrote the following comment: "A shitty darkie, like all those who play slum football" (Gallotta 2016; my translation). In line with this less than favourable view on people – and, in this particular case, football players – who live in slums and impoverished neighbourhoods, another reader wrote: "shitty darkie, burn him at the stake. The only thing they want with these little darkies is to profit so that coaches and player agents can make money! Let the good, decent kids play!" (idem). These comments, typed in anonymity from undisclosed locations, represent a continuation of the sentiments that are often expressed in football stadiums. Still, it is crucially important to note that these types of comments are not confined to football-related articles. In an article on an Argentinian family's ordeals during a holiday trip to Bolivia, a commenter wrote: "THESE CUMIN-SMELLING BOLIVIANS ARE SHIT, ARGENTINA'S CANCER" (Que Pasa Salta 2018; my translation, all caps in original). Echoing these sentiments, another reader added: "Argentinian fools when you see a

44 Violence in Argentinian football

Bolivian, spit on the ground and treat him like crap; make him feel like what they truly are, SHIT!" (idem). Although it would be simplistic and sensationalistic to conclude from these examples that most people tend to be racist and aggressive when given a chance to express their true feelings and opinions, unfiltered on-line comments do offer a counterpoint to a view of society that simultaneously romanticizes people's civility outside the stadiums and dismisses acts of violence and aggression inside the stadiums as play. When it comes to football spectators in particular, I propose a more nuanced approach to an analysis of their behaviour in different contexts, a middle ground that acknowledges the role of play and cognitive dissonance during football matches while recognizing instances of violent and/or aggressive behaviour that transcend notions of collective play and are informed by personal circumstances. Although much has been said about specific – often organized and clearly delineated – groups of violent fans in different countries in relation to social class and political ideology (Aragón 2007; Armstrong 1998; Armstrong & Harris 1991; Frosdick & Marsh 2005; Garriga Zucal 2010; Gil 2006; Grabia 2009a; Kennedy 2013; Scalia 2009; Spaaij 2007; Testa & Armstrong 2010; Tsoukala 2009), my interest in the Argentinian case is not restricted to *barrabravas*. Rather, I consider the ways in which spectators in general contribute to the creation of hostile environments at football stadiums by wittingly or unwittingly validating the actions and discourses of the *barras*.

In a conversation I had with Hugo, the former leader of the *barra brava* of one of Argentina's most important clubs, he highlighted the positive and supportive attitude that some supporters have towards *barras*.

EP: How is it that you first joined the group in the stands?[28]

Hugo: In Argentina, you are born with the folklore of football fandoms. You are born with the love for a club and the desire to belong there. What happens is very strange, *very* strange. A *barra*[29] arrives at the stadium, goes to the terraces and the entire crowd cheers for them. But also when your team plays in other countries, the fans[30] are the ones who protect the people who go there. It has happened many times. It has happened in Bolivia, it has happened in Peru, it has happened in Paraguay. I could tell you that thanks to that group of people[31] that goes everywhere, the regular members are looked after.

Although he did not directly answer my question – he expressed his desire to be a part of the *barra*, but the actual steps and logistics required to accomplish his goal remain a mystery – his statement raises questions regarding the degree to which *barras* are admired by some fans. Although I would dispute the claim that *the entire crowd* cheers for them, it is certainly true that some fans celebrate the arrival of the *barras* and their drums, flags, flares, and banners. Is this reaction merely an exaltation of the folkloric aspects of football fandoms, with an emphasis on the sensory experience of cheering for a team, or does the admiration professed by these fans point to a desire to belong to those "elite" groups? Whatever the case may be, it seems that a dichotomous conceptualization that places the world of football and the ordinary world in separate camps creates an artificial barrier by overlooking the social conditions that inform and shape people's beliefs, attitudes, and behaviours. Ontologically, the social interactions and manifestations of support, passion, animosity, racism, misogyny, hatred, joy, and despair that take place inside the stadiums as well as in their vicinities do not belong to a parallel reality.

At the risk of generalizing, it should come as no surprise that many of the fans that contribute to the lyrics and participate in acts of violence are often (although not exclusively) raised in hostile environments where exposure to drugs, alcohol, shootings, and physical confrontations is much higher than in middle class neighbourhoods. This is not to say that marginalized populations are invariably responsible for the "evils" that afflict Argentinian football, nor that the middle class remains blissfully isolated from violent incidents. Rather, the point is that, from an interpretive perspective, grounded observations must be coherent with the backgrounds and experiences of the people whose interactions one seeks to analyze and understand. Observing the behaviour of spectators from the relative comfort of a section of the stadium that is mostly occupied by casual middle class fans might lead to a different conclusion regarding the importance and seriousness of the occasion when compared to an analysis of the fans' reactions and behaviour conducted in a section that is dominated by *barras*. Although it is true that, as Gil (2007) explains, no section of a stadium is completely free from the potential threat of physical violence, it would be misleading to assume that all fans and spectators experience football and its various meanings and manifestations through the same lens. According to Gil,

> violence exceeds – to a greater or lesser degree – what happens on the terraces and the supporters' chants, sometimes considered as one of the fundamental causes of the violent behaviours of 'those few'.[32] No section of any stadium (and outside of it) constitutes a safe refuge to guarantee, for example, people's physical integrity. Thus, it is not convenient to forget that many supporters who do not belong to groups of fans are often involved in small scale acts of violence, such as assaulting a rival who walks alone wearing their club's jersey in enemy territory. Neither the stands that are commonly populated by middle class individuals, nor the official suites where leaders and influential personalities meet, constitute a refuge against the possibility of being physically assaulted.
>
> (2007:231; my translation)

The claim that no section of a stadium can guarantee people's physical integrity seems almost obvious and banal. Indeed, the same can probably be said about any sports stadium in the world. It would be unwise and perhaps equally obvious, however, to suggest that the probability of being caught in a confrontation that might cause physical injuries is the same in all sections. Although it is not my intention to demonize *barras* (nor to sanctify them), I would certainly avoid watching games from their sections.

46 Violence in Argentinian football

For the purposes of this discussion, which revolves around the notion of play and football stadiums in Argentina as sites for innocent, harmless chanting and carnivalesque expressions of joy that defy the rules of the so-called outside world, the point is that ethnographic observations that rely solely on an etic approach risk trivializing interactions by inadequately contextualizing the social environments in which they take place. Gil's warning regarding the inability of stadiums to guarantee the physical integrity of spectators is somewhat at odds with Lyth's perception of stadiums as fairly secure environments. In his words:

> For many fans, Sundays are reserved for going to the stadium, where for a couple hours they can play with friends, strangers and competing fans in a relatively controlled and secure environment.[33] This setting and the security provided by fences, police and other fans of the same team, enable play to occur in the stands in a fashion whereby fans are allowed to shout profanities, make gestures, light fireworks, dance and literally play in ways that would otherwise be frowned upon or prohibited within the real world that exists outside of the stadium.
>
> (Lyth 2007:61)

Although it is easy to understand how a stadium that has fences and a strong police presence might at first glance give the impression of being a secure environment, Lyth's observations seem to be grounded on a foreign conceptualization of the role and reputation of the police and the assumption that being surrounded by fans of the same team guarantees a certain level of protection and safety. As a football fan growing up in Buenos Aires, I attended about a dozen River games at the *Monumental* stadium. In most cases, the atmosphere was comparable to what I observed during the game between River and Libertad. Far from thinking of stadiums as secure and controlled environments, my reluctance to attend games on a regular basis stemmed from the unpredictability and volatility that I ascribed to them. One afternoon during the course of my fieldwork, I passed by the main street that leads directly to the *Monumental* – the same street I walked with Malik and Carol when we attended the game – while riding a bus on my way to visit a relative. River was playing a home game that day. From the bus, I was able to see part of the personnel that had been assigned to the security operations. Standing guard approximately five blocks from the stadium were officers from the Federal Police, the Metropolitan Police,[34] the Military Police, and the Navy Police. Most of them were wearing helmets and holding shields. For a game where visiting fans were not allowed, it would be ironic to think that such heavy police presence could signal that a fun, family-friendly, and carnivalesque spectacle was about to take place.

Going back to the game I attended with Malik, and taking into account the bad reputation that police forces have in Argentina, the presence of Military Police officers standing in formation along the length of one block on our way to the stadium, looking ready for battle, created a tense atmosphere. I could not help thinking that one sign of aggression or confrontation from a fan could trigger a disproportionate response from the officers, creating a rapidly escalating situation where fans who simply want to get to the stadium get caught in a fight.

The idea that stadiums are secure places *because* of heavy police presence is contradicted by the conflicting and ambiguous relationships that supporters and different groups of organized fans have with police authority, as discussed by Galvani and Palma (2005) in their analysis of the spectators' perception of violence at football stadiums in Argentina. When asked about the levels of violence exhibited by the police, *barras bravas*, club officials, and fans, 50% of their survey respondents placed the police under the "very violent" category, while 35.5% placed it under the "somewhat violent" category. *Barras bravas*, on the other hand, received a rating of "very violent" by 43.4% of respondents, while 38.2% considered them "somewhat violent."

When it comes to the relative safety of being surrounded by fans of the same team, it should be noted that in Argentina visiting fans have been banned from stadiums since June 2013. The ban was implemented at the national level after a fan was killed by the police during a first division match played in the province of Buenos Aires (Plaza Schaefer & Cabrera 2021). The ban applies to all professional divisions and remains in effect even though there have been attempts to remove it. This is a clear sign that, under "normal conditions" (i.e. no ban) the threat of physical violence, which is usually accompanied by displays of verbal aggression, is palpable and beyond what could be considered a playful and innocent expression of passion. More interesting, perhaps, is the fact that fatal acts of violence have not decreased since the ban was implemented. According to the list of victims of violence in Argentinian football created by the non-governmental organization Salvemos al Fútbol or "Let's Save Football" ("Lista de víctimas," n.d.), there have been 347 deaths since 1922. Seventy-two of these occurred *after* the ban on visiting fans took effect. This points to a shift from acts of violence directed at fans of rival teams, which are often motivated by passion and *aguante*, to acts of violence directed at fans of the same team, usually motivated by political, territorial, and financial interests. It is not uncommon for a club's *barra brava* to become fragmented into factions that clash over the distribution of money and the control of specific sections of the stadium.

In contrast to the comparatively cheerful picture of the stadium painted by Lyth, Uliana and Godio describe Argentinian stadiums as spaces where the elements that are meant to provide a sense of security end up exacerbating the conditions under which acts of violence occur:

> The polarized spatial configuration of the stadiums contributes to the reproduction of forms of violence, because it reproduces the symbolic confrontation that any football match between two teams implies, taking to the extreme the idea that football fans are irrational beings (vandals or barbarians) who could not coexist without assaulting the rival. The division between "sides" is reproduced in the spatial reconfiguration of the stadium

by the security operations teams, the stadium with its fences and spatial divisions contributes to reproducing confrontations between fans, it deepens them because, through physical separation, it sends the fans a message that in some way affirms the impossibility of coexisting with the other, it transforms the rival into an enemy.... This is about installing and producing – dividing, separating, and mortifying – the subjects' interaction at a football event in an intrinsically risky, menacing, and violent space.

(2013:318–319; my translation)

Although Uliana and Godio present an interesting argument that highlights the ways in which spatial configurations and security measures can backfire by increasing tensions between rivaling fans and creating a militarized environment that unwittingly encourages confrontations, I remain highly sceptical about the possibility of creating heterogeneous spaces where fans can interact peacefully by tearing down physical barriers. Such a scenario is particularly hard to imagine when one takes into account the sometimes mild, sometimes brutal, and sometimes fatal confrontations that take place between fans of the same team. When intragroup clashes are motivated by interests that have very little to do with passion, pride, or a strong sense of identity, the absence of physical barriers does nothing to de-escalate tensions and promote peaceful interactions.

Similarly, the idea that the removal of physical barriers would signal to the fans the authorities' trust in their ability to coexist without assaulting each other seems to be based on a somewhat idealized and romanticized view of football fans.

Stadiums are often described by scholars as spaces where displays of violence under controlled circumstances allow the actors involved to release the stresses of daily life in ways that are deemed socially acceptable to football crowds (Miller 2014). The degree to which this conceptualization of violence inside football stadiums can be readily and universally applied to performances by individuals and groups of supporters and organized fans is unclear and problematic. To assume that most acts of violence are triggered by the actors' socioeconomic-related stress would be misguided. Power struggles, identity building, and displays of *aguante* are examples of triggers that are not necessarily related to social strains. This is not to say that the socioeconomic status of the fans, which may in some cases cause frustration and social resentment, does not inform their actions. Miller raises the question: "at what level violence and disorder cease functioning as a safety valve and, instead, become a genuine threat to society" (2014:233).

There is an abundance of cases of violence that defy the idea that stadiums are spaces where social actors engage mostly in playful and carnivalesque displays of pseudo-violence/aggression. These cases keep football stadiums firmly grounded in the reality of the social and cultural context of which they are a constitutive part.

On September 12, 2022, Manuel Alejandro López died after being shot in the neck as a result of an internal confrontation between *barras* of a club from the city of Tucumán (Perfil 2022a). In July 2022, Joaquín Coronel, an 18-year-old fan of Club Luján, a fourth division club from the province of Buenos Aires, was found lying on the ground with a bullet wound a few metres from the stadium. He later died in hospital. An investigation revealed that Joaquín had been shot by members of Club Leandro N. Alem's *barra brava*. Luján and Alem are rival clubs (idem). On July 30, 2023, Jonathan Leonel Borda, a fan of Club Atlético Lanús, a first division club from the Greater Buenos Aires area, was shot in the temple during an internal confrontation between two factions of the club's *barra brava*. He died in hospital the following day (Clarín 2023).

Words can kill: The case of Emanuel Balbo

As I mentioned in a previous section, cases of violence inside the stadiums that result in death pose a challenge to interpretations of fan behaviour that define stadiums as controlled environments where fans can engage in physical confrontations in "socially acceptable" ways. More importantly, dismissing the role of verbal aggression as a mere component of cognitive dissonance during role play risks downplaying the effects that words can have beyond the realm of the carnivalesque. As I will show in this section, words can have fatal consequences when used maliciously. The key point here is that all it takes for a tragedy to occur is that people take words seriously, reinforcing the idea that for some fans, the rivals are *real* enemies. Far from being spaces where people *only* engage in playful provocations devoid of ill will, stadiums are places where the social and personal realities of the spectators manifest themselves in varying ways depending on individual circumstances. Displays of role play and real animosity take place simultaneously, highlighting the heterogeneous nature of football crowds. Thus, although instances of role play involving cognitive dissonance are widespread among spectators, to conclude that stadiums are safe environments based on the perceived playfulness of the interactions would be misguided. Furthermore, such a conclusion would be methodologically detached from the multiplicity of backgrounds, experiences, and motivations that inform the spectators' actions and interactions.

Emanuel Balbo was a fan of Club Atlético Belgrano, a club from Córdoba, Argentina's second largest city. On April 15, 2017, he attended Córdoba's derby between Belgrano and their historical rivals, Club Atlético Talleres. The ban on visiting fans was enforced during this match, meaning that only fans of Belgrano were allowed to enter the stadium. Although Belgrano has its own stadium, the match was played at the provincially owned Mario Alberto Kempes stadium. With a capacity of approximately 57,000 spectators, the Kempes (as it is popularly known) almost doubles that of Belgrano's stadium, and is mostly used for important or high profile matches.

Prior to the match, 22-year-old Emanuel had crossed paths outside the stadium with Oscar Gómez, a fan of Belgrano who had killed Emanuel's 14-year-old brother in a car accident in 2012 while street racing. After recognizing each other, a verbal altercation ensued. Although according to journalistic sources (BBC Mundo

2017; La Nación 2017; La Nueva Mañana 2017; Zatat 2017) there were no signs of a physical confrontation at the gate, the altercation continued and escalated inside the stadium during the halftime. Emanuel and Oscar were following the match from the highest point of the stadium's upper level, in a section with no seats (i.e. a standing section). At one point during their verbal exchange, Oscar uttered the words that resulted in Emanuel's death: he told the surrounding Belgrano fans that Emanuel, who was wearing a Belgrano-themed t-shirt, was in fact a fan of Talleres in disguise. Almost instantly, the fans started attacking Emanuel by hitting and kicking him. In despair, he tried to reach one of the section's exits as fans continued to attack him along the way. Once he reached the exit that would lead him to a lower level, he attempted to jump to the level below him. Just as he was climbing the railing, two fans pushed him over the edge. The approximately four-metre fall proved fatal. As he lay unconscious on the steps that led back to the upper level, one fan seized the opportunity to steal his shoes, while dozens of fans gathered around the perimeter formed by the Military Police, chanting:

> *Olé olé,*
> *olé olé,*
> He who doesn't jump,
> cheers for the T[35]

In an age of increased public scrutiny and surveillance due to the widespread use of smartphones with video-recording capabilities, it should come as no surprise that video footage of the attack and of the fans chanting around a shoeless Emanuel is available on popular internet websites such as YouTube.

According to Maximiliano Tittarelli, the Director of the *Hospital Municipal de Urgencias*, the hospital where Emanuel was admitted, he arrived with "parietal fracture and collapse, with cerebral edema and a very low state of consciousness" (La Nación 2017; my translation). Emanuel was declared brain-dead shortly after being admitted.

On March 28, 2019, Oscar Gómez was sentenced to 15 years in prison for instigating the events that resulted in Emanuel's death. The judge explained that

> Gómez encouraged a group of people directly and with clear intention – knowing how they would react – to violent behaviour, one of the possible consequences of which was the death of the victim…. He fell because he was violently beaten in his desperate attempt to flee.
> (La Nueva Mañana 2019; my translation)

Similarly, Martín Darío Vergara received a prison sentence of 11 years and seven months, while Matías Ezequiel Oliva Molina was sentenced to ten years and eight months. They are the fans who pushed Emanuel. Regarding their role, the judge said,

> the defendants could have anticipated a possible fatal outcome, since the remarkable violence with which they acted against (Emanuel) Balbo consisted

in throwing him from a height greater than four metres, with fury and impulse. It is not possible to accept that they did not foresee that a possible outcome was his death. A generalized violent reaction, in this context, is uncontrollable and none of the contributors can claim that they did not know that the episode could end in unpredictable ways, even in the death of the attacked person.

(idem)

Emanuel's case provides a good synthesis of some of the issues I have discussed in relation to violence and aggression at football stadiums. As I mentioned earlier, the finality of death is at odds with the notion of the stadium as a place where spectators can engage in verbally offensive but ultimately playful and harmless interactions under relaxed rules of behaviour. Emanuel's death was the culmination of a conflict that had begun outside the stadium and had no relation to football. This poses a problem when conceptualizing stadiums as bubbles that remain isolated from the "real" world. Rather, stadiums act as fairly fluid and permeable extensions of life beyond their gates. Put differently, they represent a continuation of the spectators' lives, and even though role play informs the spectators' behaviour to varying degrees, it would be an exaggeration to say that their beliefs and personal circumstances are put on hold every time they watch their teams play.

Emanuel's case challenges the image of football as carnival and stadiums as spaces where fans engage in "cartoonish" displays of aggression in one crucial way: his conflict with Oscar over the death of his younger brother had no connection to football, but it was football that was used by Oscar to instigate his fellow Belgrano fans to attack him. This brings me to the role of verbal aggression. As I have discussed, instances of cognitive dissonance where spectators verbally attack their rivals – particularly when chanting in unison – are not uncommon, but as this case shows, it is dangerous to assume that verbal exchanges between fans always revolve around fun and play. Oscar's intentional, untruthful, and malicious choice of words had fatal consequences. He understood that his colleagues would take his words seriously; his intention was never to make fun of Emanuel in the spirit of play. Moreover, he uttered those words knowing that his colleagues would identify Emanuel as an enemy – one that did not pose a threat – without bothering to verify the truth of his claim (i.e. that Emanuel was a fan of Talleres in disguise).

Spectators

In everyday common parlance, the term "fans" is often used to refer to all people in attendance at a football match, regardless of their level of interest in the match, personal attachment to the clubs, and physical and emotional involvement. Here, I will differentiate between four categories of people who go to the stadiums. These categories are, by necessity, at least partially arbitrary, as it is simply not possible to draw a clear, impermeable line between one category and another. Still, they are useful in articulating the most salient features that characterize stadium-goers and the degrees to which they might participate in cheering, role play, chanting, acts of verbal aggression, and displays of physical violence.

Throughout my writing, I use the term *spectators* to refer to all members of the crowd. This includes people who might have very little interest, if any, in football in general. Granted, it may be difficult to find many uninterested spectators at a match, but the odds of this should not be underestimated. It is far from uncommon to come across people who attend matches in the company of a reluctant relative, boyfriend, girlfriend, or close friend who knows little about the sport, its rules, and its protagonists but agrees to spend an evening at the stadium motivated by the lowest level of curiosity imaginable. To name an example, a few years ago I attended a Toronto Blue Jays (of the American-based Major League Baseball) game that was played at the stadium known at that time as the SkyDome, currently called Rogers Centre. It is safe to say that my role during the game was purely that of a spectator. I was somewhat curious about people's behaviour and the style of cheering at a baseball game, which made me much more of an observer than a supporter. I did not – and still do not – know the rules of baseball, but my level of interest in the match itself was, for the most part, incidental. At this point I should mention that I had gotten a free ticket, which was the single most important factor in my decision to experience a slice of "baseball culture." Another excuse to attend was the fact that the match afforded me the opportunity to visit the SkyDome, much like a tourist in Barcelona might feel compelled to experience the atmosphere at FC Barcelona's Camp Nou stadium, or a tourist in Buenos Aires might be tempted to experience a match at Boca's *La Bombonera*. In short, the spectator's experience is emotionally detached from what happens on the field, and the reasons for attending a match might have little to do with *who* is playing or *what* the teams are playing for (e.g. points, promotion, and a title).

Supporters

Supporters fall somewhere between spectators and fans. This category is arguably the most fluid one in terms of boundaries, as supporters might gravitate slightly to one of the "neighbouring" categories depending on the level of emotional investment in the sport and the teams they cheer for. Unlike spectators, however, supporters cheer for specific teams and are not indifferent to the action on the field. In this sense, then, they are more closely related to fans, although they might not be as well informed about a league and its teams or as familiar with the rules of football as most fans. A classic example is that of the offside rule. I have been in many situations where supporters who were genuinely concerned about the fate of their teams would ask for clarification regarding the offside rule, as they did not understand the conditions under which a player could be caught offside. Most fans, on the other hand, would not have a problem understanding the rule (although, admittedly, exceptions to the rule or special circumstances can get tricky at times, even for fans). Further differentiating between supporters and fans is the fact that it is not uncommon for supporters to cheer for a team and follow its progress when conditions are favourable. Put differently, a supporter might actively cheer for a team and express an increased interest in the team when it is doing well. This includes cases where the team is, for instance, in the final stages of a cup competition or well on the way to becoming league champions. Conversely, an active interest in football might be almost nonexistent during times when the team falls from grace and wanders aimlessly at the bottom of the table or fails to win titles. To be sure, supporters are not unconditional in their degree of involvement. This is not to say that their feelings for a club are insincere; rather, they tend to be manifested at particular times and under specific circumstances.

Fans

Fans are deeply attached to their clubs. They are the ones who initiate the chanting outside and inside the stadiums, the ones who loudly cheer for their teams when things on the field are not going well. They tend to be well-informed about their leagues and have an active interest in football that often exceeds an exclusive focus on their domestic competitions. To a lesser or greater extent, football plays an important role in their lives for a variety of reasons. Some fans identify with a club based on the club's ties to a neighbourhood or city, while others enjoy the respite from the stresses of daily life provided by football on a weekly basis. In the case of Argentina, this category can be somewhat problematic, as there are different interpretations regarding the appropriate use of the term *fans*. Alabarces and Garriga Zucal, for example, use the term to refer to *barras* as a nod to the label preferred by the members of the *barras bravas*. In their words,

> 'fans' is one of the native names used to identify one of the groups of organized spectators that follow a football club. These groups are called '*barras bravas*' by common sense and the media. We will not use this term, but will use the native ones instead: 'fandoms', 'the kids' or 'the gang.' Similarly, we will refer to the members of these groups as 'fans', differentiating them from the rest of the spectators.
>
> (Alabarces & Garriga Zucal 2008:288; my translation)

Although it is true that members of *barras bravas* often prefer to be known as fans, to refer to them by this name simply because it is their preferred term can be simultaneously condescending to *barras* and offensive to fans who have no ties to *barras bravas*. To clarify, Alabarces and Garriga Zucal propose using the word "fans" to refer *exclusively* to *barras*. There are certainly members of *barras bravas* who should be considered fans to the extent that they personify at least some of the features I have described above. *Barras bravas*, however, are not homogeneous in terms of their members' love of football and level of support and emotional investment. Thus, some *barras* might well be considered supporters; one might even find the odd spectator among them who joined a *barra brava* for reasons that have little to do with football itself, such as the sense of belonging generated by a shared group identity, or "business opportunities." Additionally, in the case of Alabarces and Garriga Zucal, referring to *barras* as fans has the unfortunate side effect of "downgrading" fans who are not members of *barras bravas* to the category of spectators in an attempt to avoid confusion. There is a conflict here, however, when it comes to the use of the Spanish word *hincha* (meaning "fan" when used in the context of football), presented as a native term. I question the validity of the claim that *barras* should be addressed simply as *hinchas* because that is their preferred native term. The problem with this claim is that it confounds *native term* with *preferred term*. To be sure, *hincha* is not a native term to the extent that members of *barras bravas* did not come up with it. According to Soca (2010), the origin of the use of the word *hincha* in football can be traced back to the early 20th century in Montevideo, Uruguay. He explains that Prudencio Miguel Reyes, an employee at Club Nacional de Fútbol[36] (popularly known as Nacional) who was in charge, among other things, of inflating the balls (the Spanish verb *hinchar* means to inflate), would passionately cheer for the team during matches. As a result, spectators began to notice and comment on "the inflator's" (i.e. the *hincha's*) loud demonstrations of support for Nacional. Over time, *hincha* became the word used to refer to Nacional's fiercest supporters, and eventually its use became widespread in some South American countries. To sum up, nowadays the term *hincha*, when used in relation to football, means fan, while the verb *hinchar*, also in the context of football, means to cheer for or to support. Crucially, *hincha* has never been reserved for *barras*, and its meaning is not directly related to the characteristics that define *barras*. In fact, *hincha* is the common term used by virtually everyone in Argentina to refer to anyone who supports a team, regardless of his or her level of support. It is easy to understand, however, why *barras* would want to appropriate the term and claim exclusivity over its use by describing themselves as the "real" fans, the ones who follow a team unconditionally, rain or shine; the ones responsible for providing the entertainment during matches with their chants and colourful displays of flags. Appropriating the term *hincha* would mean diverting attention from the negative connotations of the label *barra*. It could be seen as an attempt to renew the image and improve the reputation of *barras* by highlighting the festive aspects of their behaviour while setting aside their more questionable practices.

From a methodological perspective, Alabarces and Garriga Zucal risk romanticizing their research participants by uncritically assigning them a label on the basis of their stated preference, ignoring the fact that the label has been historically applied to all football enthusiasts and has never implied violent behaviour or political and economic interests, unlike the term *barra*. Equally concerning is the suggestion that everyone who is not a member of a *barra brava* should be referred to as "spectator" to accommodate the *barras'* request to be known as fans (*hinchas*). This raises questions regarding the role of the researcher in the field, as it is not unusual for researchers to empathize with their participants to a degree where it might become difficult to maintain a critical distance. In Argentina, people state the teams that they cheer for by saying "*soy hincha de...*" ("I'm a fan of..."). Under the usage proposed by Alabarces and Garriga Zucal, where "*barras*" become "fans" and people previously known as fans become "spectators," this would mean that anyone claiming to be a fan of a team would be saying that they are members of that team's *barra brava*.

An argument in favour of replacing the term *barra* and all of its variants with more benign alternatives would likely point to the stigmatizing effect that the current vocabulary has on fans who are members of particular groups. Indeed, *barra* has negative connotations, although, as Hugo mentioned during our interview, some fans look up to *barrabravas*. In any case, I use the commonly used terms – *barra, barras bravas, barrabravas*, etc. – for the sake of simplicity and as a way of differentiating between organized groups of fans and "regular" fans. To be abundantly clear, my intention is neither to stigmatize nor to romanticize these groups. It would be simplistic and reductionist to think of *barras* as dangerous criminals who take pleasure in causing chaos. Having said that, I have yet to find someone who does not think that *barras bravas*, as a social entity and independently of individual cases, are a real and tangible problem. As a researcher, I do not feel obligated or inclined to avoid the use of the term *barra* on the basis of an emic approach that seeks to understand a particular social context from the perspective of its participants. Put differently, understanding is not the same as agreeing. In this case, the origin of the word *hincha*, combined with its meanings and widespread use in common parlance, indicates that the term is not native to the *barras*. Thus, the *barras*' claim to exclusivity over its use is a weak one. Furthermore, examples of members of *barras* who refer to the groups as *barras* are not uncommon, which suggests that the rejection of the term is not universal.

Barras bravas

Barras bravas are groups of organized fans that create festive environments at the stadiums through their chants, drums, and carnivalesque displays of flags, banners, and flares. Although, as previously discussed, they do not hold a monopoly on violence at football stadiums, they are generally responsible for the most serious acts of violence, including cases involving the use of knives and guns, many of which have ended in death. Parallel to their role as "entertainers," *barrabravas* are often in charge of profit-making operations such as the sale of food and merchandise around the stadiums, to name two examples. Prominent members of the *barras* maintain clientelist ties with club officials, either through friendly relations or intimidation. These ties allow *barras* to navigate their clubs' facilities with absolute freedom and grant them access to illegal businesses such as ticket scalping. Furthermore, *barras* are sometimes employed by clubs and, as Mónica Nizzardo, co-founder of the NGO Salvemos al Fútbol, explained in relation to her experience as Press Secretary at Club Atlético Atlanta,[37] participate in meetings held by club officials.

In some cases, club officials rely on *barras* for political support within and beyond the clubs. In the words of Gaffney,

> The *barrabravas* are hierarchical organizations of primarily young, economically and socially disenfranchised men[38] that are paid by the club in a variety of ways. Some members are given fictitious jobs[39] in the companies of directors, others are given tickets to sell on match days,[40] while others have relationships with the stewards of the clubs and collect money from spectators who are then slid under the turnstiles. The *barrabravas* can also act in a more sinister fashion in the service of the club directors by disrupting rival club director's businesses, causing political disruptions, or engaging in violent acts against other *barrabravas* and the police. They are in essence professional fans, operating within an institution of their own creation, financed by club management to act in the service of club directors. On the other hand, the *barrabravas* influence the decisions and internal politics of the directors in regards to team managers and club initiatives.
>
> (2009:170)

The fact that *barras* are "professionals" means that their actions inside and outside the stadiums are often guided by their economic and, in a few cases, political interests. Put differently, their passion for their clubs sometimes takes a backseat to the economic relations that allow their businesses to thrive. In this regard, Alabarces states that

> from the point of view of the rest of the fans, these actors are 'not in the least interested in the club'.... The emotional contract with the club and 'the club's colours' disappears only to be replaced by an economic contract.
>
> (2004:57; my translation)

This observation is in line with the opinions of three interviewees, who believe that business and passion are incompatible. Alabarces also explains that a *barra brava*,

> viewed from the perspective of its own active or militant fans, is defined by a political or economic relation – or both at the same time – that they maintain with the club or with some of its officials, which leads them to alternately occupy official and opposition roles: although, ultimately, every *barra* is official because a club's governing body ends up entering into an agreement sooner rather than later.
>
> (idem)

His definition makes reference to the use of intimidation that allows *barras* to "negotiate" profitable deals with club officials. Still, it is important to note that some officials and politicians (such as Marcelo Mallo, founder of the NGO United

Argentinian Fandoms) have an active interest in establishing and maintaining relationships with *barras*, as the *barras* are able to mobilize political support during elections, political rallies, and protests. They also serve as "task forces" that can be deployed at rallies and political demonstrations to confront and disperse members of the opposition. Unsurprisingly, as I mentioned in the previous section, many *barras* reject the use of a label that identifies them as members of a group that is characterized by the use of violence and intimidation and operates as a criminal organization. This became apparent when Hugo got defensive about my use of the term *barra brava* during our interview, in which I asked him about the role of *barras*.

EP: What would be, if there is one, the role of a *barra brava* within a club?

HUGO: (*He thinks about it*). Being politically correct I would have to say that it's not a *barra brava*, it's a group of... What everyone says... You already know that...

EP: I sometimes refer to it as a group of organized fans.

HUGO: It's a group of organized people.

EP: Right, exactly, that's what we are getting at.

HUGO: That has its hierarchies. There's the first line, the second line, and the foundations. To become a member of the first line you have to go through different stages, mainly of knowledge, time, and leadership.

EP: How did the name *barra brava* become popular?

HUGO: It was due to many violent episodes that happened and still happen in football. What happens is that those episodes got distorted. During my time there weren't so many economic interests. Now there are *many* economic interests.

EP: And political as well.

HUGO: Yes, as a springboard to reach higher places.[41] It was very useful for Mauricio Macri to be the president of Boca, which later allowed him to become the Chief of Government (*of the Autonomous City of Buenos Aires*). I'm going to give you this example; you *know* who the president of Boca was during Mauricio's time: Macri. But if I ask you who was the education minister, you might not know the answer, because being the president of a prominent club like River or Boca gives you more influence than being, say, a provincial senator.

Even though Hugo avoided mentioning the specific activities that *barras* participate in, he explained that economic interests gradually became more important than manifestations of passion and support for the *barras'* clubs. This coincides with Alabarces' description of *barras bravas* as groups that are defined, at least in part, by economic relations. Although Gil (2007) and Murzi and Segura Trejo (2018) emphasize that acts of violence are not confined to specific groups and particular areas of the stadiums, Hugo believes that most of the football-related violence that can be observed today revolves around intra-*barra* confrontations over economic interests.

58 Violence in Argentinian football

HUGO: Nowadays, acts of violence take place between different factions of the same *barra* over the loot.

EP: That's the other type of violence that people refer to. One is based on the love for the club colours, the jersey, and the other revolves around economic interests …

HUGO: Yes, but it's not like you fall from the sky and become the leader of a group of fans. You were also a genuine fan who gave your life for the club colours, but later things become distorted.

EP: Yes, I'm not saying that one thing excludes the other, but that they are two types of violence that are intertwined, and sometimes a fan starts from one place and ends up in another …

HUGO: Where money appears, passion dies. Money comes in through the door and passion comes out of the window. It's impossible for them to go hand in hand, it's like water and oil. Either you have economic interests, or you have ideological interests.

The argument that claims that passion and economic interests are mutually exclusive is a popular one among my interviewees. Nevertheless, for many *barras*, physical confrontations with rival *barras* and the police remain important ways of exalting their passion for their clubs. In fact, these confrontations encapsulate notions of passion and belonging that are hard to detangle.

When it comes to doing business, economic interests take precedence over club allegiances. Miguel, a lawyer who represented a famous *barra*, agrees with Hugo and emphasizes the *barras'* economic interests as well as their corrupt arrangements with politicians and the police as the main source of violence in football.

MIGUEL: Football in Argentina has tremendous social relevance. In other words, if there is a football-related strike, if a football club disappears, a lot of people would go mad. The incorporation of politics created the other side of football,[42] which involves the protection of the *barrabrava*, because the *barrabrava* is no longer that stereotyped individual who is somewhat ignorant or with a low cultural level, who saw his team as a, a, a projection of his masculinity, and cheered for his team on the weekends, and handled the drums, and the flags, and handled all of those things that some people call football's "party." Um, he started doing business. You have the merchandising of the jerseys, the sale of tickets to international matches, the trips; here we have an NGO called Hinchadas Unidas Argentinas that plans trips to other countries with the intention of becoming the official *barra brava* of Argentina's national team. So, the leaders of different *barras bravas* began to unite to build Argentina's *barra brava*. It's all business. That business is often maintained by journalists and players. All of that became mixed up and it is now a tangle, a tangle that is very, very, very, very difficult to take apart. The *barrabrava* is the hand that does everything. Everything that you see around the stadium, be it the sale of flags, the sale of jerseys, you will see one, two, four, ten hot dog and hamburger carts; the *trapitos*[43] who guard the parked cars around the stadiums... All of that is an arrangement between the *barra brava* and the police. Because here you get to the degradation of what it means to be a public official in Argentina who starts to generate a business, and part of the business is shared between the police and the *barrabrava*. *Barrabrava*, police officer, politician, why? Because during the week, I (*the* barrabrava) am the tough guy, the heavyweight, the one who looks after the politician, and on the weekends I am the one who runs the stadium in connivance with the police. That means that you have to move fortunes in police operations supposedly so that there are no confrontations. That degrades the clubs' economies even more, because opening a football stadium today is not profitable due to the costs of "running the show" and the security operations. This means that nowadays, for example, you witness the incredible truth that *barras* go from one place to another protected by a police escort so that in theory they don't cause any trouble. They are escorted by the police until they reach the stadium.[44] They have priority over you in transit; they travel in buses that cannot possibly have any type of authorization because they are all beat up. To top it all off, we have reached the point where visiting fans cannot attend matches. And now there are *barras* within *barras*, because business is so good that the leaders of different factions of a *barra* confront each other to decide who runs the business.

Leonardo, a police commissioner and Head of Security at Club Barrial,[45] further supports the argument that violence in football is largely a consequence of the internal conflicts between members of a *barra*. He emphasizes the highly profitable[46] nature of football-related businesses.

LEONARDO: Here, today the *barras* don't fight anymore with the rival *barras*; the fights are internal. Why are they internal? Because of the drug business on the stands, the merchandising business around the stadium, the *trapitos* around the stadium. I always say, if they give me the extra income of a game, of a Boca – River played at Boca's stadium, I... My family, my grandchildren, and I would live comfortably for ten years, because there are fortunes involved. All the merchandising, all the tourism, all the *trapitos*, parking, sale of hot dogs on the street, all of that at Boca, for example, is managed by the *barra*. So, we are talking about astronomical figures, *astronomical*, what they earn from one game. You may say, "look, I don't have a job, I'm going to go to Once[47] and I'm going to buy thirty jerseys, twenty Boca hats, three little flags and I'm going to stand on a corner to sell them"... Two minutes later you are thrown into the Riachuelo[48] if you are not a member of the *barra*!

EP: Do they get merchandising from the club?

LEONARDO: No, no. Generally speaking, the clubs have their own official stores. What the *barra* sells on the street is all knockoffs. They get their stuff from the guys who sell at Once, and they set up their little shops on the street. The official jersey, bought at an official store, costs, let's say, 500 pesos, but you can get it on the street for 100... That's what the guys sell. And they have a certain status. At Boca, tourists pay to go to the terraces, to stand on the guard rails. They have a tango club in front of the stadium where they take the tourists; they make fortunes. The club gets nothing more than the money from ticket sales.

As Leonardo mentioned, *barras* turn passion into a lucrative business. Thus, far from being defined primarily by their role on the terraces, *barras bravas* are groups that have adapted themselves to the reality of Argentinian football and politics by taking advantage of the opportunities afforded by clubs. Their illegal activities, as well as their status within the clubs, reinforce the idea that Argentina's culture of impunity perpetuates corrupt practices. These practices represent an obstacle to the country's socioeconomic development to the extent that they create relationships that revolve around the political and economic interests of particular groups, such as politicians and club officials. Although my focus here is on the social, cultural, and political implications of football, the system of organized chaos that characterizes Argentinian politics permeates all spheres of society.

Keeping in mind what Hugo said earlier regarding the admiration that fans feel for the *barras* (a fact that he may have overgeneralized), it is important to note that, far from being condemned, manifestations of passion are often celebrated even when they include instances of physical violence and verbal aggression. In 2012, during a speech introducing a biometric ticketing system that would facilitate the identification of violent fans,[49] the then President of Argentina, Cristina Fernández de Kirchner, stated that violence in football is not confined to small, easily identifiable groups of fans. Indeed, as I mentioned above, it would be simplistic to blame all cases of violence and aggression on *barras*. Still, the general consensus seems to be that small groups of organized, violent fans ruin the spectacle of football for the vast majority of peaceful, civilized fans (Gil 2007). As a result – and to reiterate a previous point – although far from having no responsibility in acts of violence, *barras* serve as a scapegoat. In the words of Fernández de Kirchner,

> the issue of violence in football does not... If we confine ourselves only to a small group, um, we are going to make a mistake and we are not going to give a real solution to the problem. The problems with some small groups, more than with violence in football, have to do with other things that happen outside the stadiums and not inside. The most serious things don't happen inside the stadiums, they happen outside.... Another thing that I also have to say, when fights break out, they don't break out only where the *barras* are.

I've seen fist fights between fans from the same club because they have differences with respect to the referee's call, what they think of the coach, what they think of football.

(infobae 2017; my translation)

Gil (2007) mentions that no stadium is free from the small-scale acts of violence perpetrated by fans who have no ties to the *barras*. Even though it would be a mistake to ignore the role that fans play in the creation and perpetuation of hostile environments, it would be equally irresponsible to elevate *barras* to the status of national icons. In an attempt to appeal to the masses by painting a colourful picture of the manifestations of passion in Argentinian football, Fernández de Kirchner proceeded to praise the *barras* during her speech, emphasizing their "heroic" demonstrations of support for their clubs:

I wanted to really do justice to thousands and thousands of people who have a passion that has made them a true icon of Argentina. You know that there are tours for tourists who go specifically to the stadiums... They enter with the flags, it's a whole, a whole mystical experience carrying the flags, defending them, then deciding where they keep them and so on.

(infobae 2017; my translation)

It is interesting that she would consider the act of defending the flags (an act that includes physical confrontations with members of rival *barras*) a mystical experience. In other words, violent confrontations over flags are desirable incidents. She then said:

I don't understand much about football and I don't like football, but when I went to the stadium, because they took me, or when I went with Néstor,[50] do you know what I would look at? The stands, because what amazed me the most were the stands. Those guys standing on the guard rails, with the flags, haranguing... They are wonderful... And I know some of them... I know one from Boca[51] who occupies an important position in the National State – I will not say his name – who is impeccable.... Now he's more serious, but at the stadium, hanging from the guard rail with the flag, never watching the game because they do not watch the game, they harangue, harangue and harangue... They have my respect, because the truth is that feeling passion for something, feeling passion for a club, is also, you know what? It's also being alive. Those who have no passion for anything... The truth is that I always distrust those who have no passion for anything.

(idem)

As an example of impunity, her comments, which make reference to a *barra* who became an important member of the national government, indicate that, at times, *barras* enjoy friendly relations with club officials and politicians. Furthermore, she

62 Violence in Argentinian football

talks about passion as an emotion to be celebrated regardless of its manifestations. In the next chapter I will argue that passion in the context of Argentinian football serves as an antagonizing force that creates enemies.

Aguante

Aguante is arguably the single most important term used to describe acts of violence perpetrated by *barras*. In its most basic form, the term can be translated as endurance. In football, it refers to the physical, emotional, psychological, and financial endurance displayed by fans during adverse conditions. According to Parrish and Nauright, "the essence of *aguante* is not only an expression of physical strength in terms of support, but also mental strength. Possessing the ability to withstand challenging times requires resilience and an intangible inner strength linked to pride" (2013:6). Although the term can be applied to fans in general, it has a strong association with the collective identity of the *barras*. *Aguante* is considered a native term, one that is used by *barras* to describe their own actions, to differentiate themselves from other fans, and to signal their sense of belonging to a *barra brava*. Indeed, *aguante* can be claimed individually or collectively according to the circumstances. As a marker of group identity, it is common for *barras bravas* to claim that they have *aguante* while their fiercest rivals do not. Thus, saying that a particular *barra brava* does not have *aguante* is considered an insult, a taunting affront that ridicules its members by portraying them as weak, cowardly, and unmanly. Those who have *aguante* do not run away when confronted by rivaling *barras* or the police; they stand their ground against all odds, facing adversity and defending their club's honour. Alabarces et al. (2008) base their interpretation of *aguante* on the *barras'* conceptualization of the term as one that includes violence and confrontation as its distinctive features. According to them, spectators experience *aguante* in ways that avoid acts of violence, which they consider responsible for ruining the festive atmosphere of football matches. A *barra brava*, on the other hand, "creates a 'community' of belonging which is defined by being the bearer of *aguante*, the one that fights" (Alabarces & Garriga Zucal 2008:277; my translation). This interpretation leaves out a view of the group as an organized "business" entity. *Barras* define themselves publicly and proudly as the carriers of *aguante*. Some of them, although certainly not all, lead a sort of double life whereby public demonstrations of *aguante* and passion are encouraged while illegal profitable activities are not to be mentioned.

Figure 2.2 depicts an expression of *aguante* in support of Club Atlético Defensores de Belgrano, a club that played in the fourth division at the time of my fieldwork. The poster says:

> Thursday November 20, everyone to the Juan Pasquale (*stadium*). We will gather at the club at 12 to welcome the team; if you are a fan of DEFE[52] you can't miss it. We have the balls that YOU don't have…

Although it is unclear who the last sentence refers to, it is interesting to note that it was placed inside a photograph of Defensores' *barra brava*, known as *La Barra*

Violence in Argentinian football 63

Figure 2.2 A poster depicting an expression of *aguante*. Photo by author.

del *Dragón* ("The Dragon's *Barra*"). Thus, the club's *barra* is proudly represented as the legitimate carrier of *aguante*. To have balls is to have *aguante*, to stand one's ground, to face adversity head on. In this sense, *barras bravas* are the epitome of *aguante*.

As seen in Figure 2.2, *aguante* often serves a double function: it is as much about emphasizing a group's or an individual's mental and physical strength and

64 Violence in Argentinian football

resilience as it is about provoking and belittling the rivals. Thus, to claim that Defensores' *barra* has the balls that its rivals do not have, is to invite a reaction from the intended targets. According to Hugo, the culture of *aguante* has turned many football fans into fans of the *barras bravas*. Bearing in mind Hugo's past as the leader of a *barra*, I would argue that he has a tendency to exaggerate the levels of support and admiration that fans express for the *barras*. In any case, his comment sheds light on the prominent role of *aguante* as a symbol of pride, honour, strength, and resilience.

HUGO: (*Regarding the fans*) They became fans of the *barras* some time ago. Their chests expand with pride when their *barras bravas* fill the stadiums, but not when their teams play well, because we arrive at the same issue, the culture of *aguante*.

From his perspective, *barras* act as unofficial "club ambassadors." Put differently, the *barras* on the stands take precedence over the teams on the field as representatives of the clubs' values. Hugo explains that it is the *barras*, in their capacity as the bearers of *aguante*, who get the fans' attention and respect. Indeed, Branz et al. state that fans often celebrate and legitimize their *barras'* bravery by, for example, filming their actions with the intention of posting videos on internet websites as proud evidence of their *barras' aguante* (2020).

In this chapter, I have described my experiences and observations attending a game at River's stadium. After unwittingly buying illegal tickets from Mix Up Exchange and being subjected to three lax security checks on my way to the stadium, the game afforded me the opportunity to analyze the fans' displays of passion from an emic perspective that takes into account the diverse reasons for participating in offensive and discriminatory chanting. Although role play and cognitive dissonance are important concepts to consider when trying to make sense of performances that go against the fans' values and beliefs, it would be unwise to assume that instances of verbal aggression in the form of chants are in all cases expressions of innocent, harmless, and playful taunts that hold no real meaning. With this in mind, I have argued that football stadiums do not represent "alternate realities" where certain practices are permitted and celebrated as part of carnivalesque performances. Stadiums represent different things to different fans. Given the diversity of life experiences, values, and beliefs among fans, it is impossible to reduce their motivations for engaging in certain practices to a common cause. As the case of Emanuel Balbo shows, hostilities between fans are sometimes all too real and far removed from playful manifestations of cognitive dissonance. The words uttered by Oscar Gómez, which ultimately resulted in Emanuel's death, were chosen with the intention to cause physical harm.

After identifying the four categories of people who attend football matches, I have described the features that characterize *barras bravas*. Far from being confined to providing entertainment during matches by chanting, playing drums, and displaying colourful banners, flags, and flares, *barras* play various roles within the clubs. As self-proclaimed "real" fans, they engage in acts of verbal aggression and physical violence inside and around football stadiums through displays of *aguante*. Although some acts of violence are motivated by a culture of *aguante* and an antagonizing form of passion, others are related to economic interests, as evidenced by the frequent intra-*barra* confrontations between factions that seek to monopolize the control over certain businesses such as the sale of tickets they receive from club officials, drug trafficking, parking around the stadiums on match days, etc. The political role of *barras* will be examined in future chapters.

Notes

1 Some *barras bravas* sell packages through tourist agencies. These packages allow tourists to mingle with the *barras* during a match by granting them access to sections of the stadiums that are usually off limits to regular fans. The packages often include transport from and to the tourists' accommodations. This is a profitable business for *barras*, who receive free tickets from club officials. In 2006, a newspaper reported that Boca's *barras* kept 60% of the profits from their "Pure Adrenaline" tour (Yarroch 2006).

2 Even club members who paid a monthly fee were too often unable to procure tickets because they would sell out minutes after being made available online. This was especially true in 2014 due to the fact that River was performing well in the South American Cup under the guidance of coach Marcelo Gallardo, a former River star player.

3 It is possible, based on the National Identity Card number, to estimate a person's age. For example, based on a number that starts with 26 million, someone who is familiar with the correlation between year of birth and card number may estimate that that number corresponds to a person who was born in 1976 or 1977. A higher number means a younger person; thus, a card number starting with 32 million corresponds to someone who was born in 1985 or 1986.

4 These are names that groups of organized fans receive in different countries. Apart from the English hooligans and Argentinian *barras*, other well-known groups are the Italian *ultràs* and the Brazilian *torcidas*.

5 Most of the black population succumbed to diseases and wars (Afro-Argentinians participated in the War of Independence during the early 19th century). In the 2010 census, only 149,493 people self-identified as descendants of Afro-Argentinians, a number that represents 0.37% of the country's total population (INDEC 2012).

6 *Facundo: Civilización y barbarie* is the title of his most famous work, published in 1845.

7 Gauchos are skilled horsemen and cattle herders of mestizo origin.

8 In Argentina, the word *villa* (pronounced *visha*) means both a large and expensive country residence and a slum. Although slums are called *villas* for short, the full expression is *villas miseria*, which roughly translates to misery towns.

9 Club Atlético Independiente, Club Atlético San Lorenzo de Almagro, and Racing Club are three of Argentina's five biggest clubs.

10 In spite of this, many Bolivians, Paraguayans, and Peruvians are River fans.

11 River was founded in 1901 in the neighbourhood of La Boca. In 1906, the club relocated to the city of Sarandí, a few blocks south of La Boca in the Greater Buenos Aires area, before returning to La Boca in 1907. In 1913, the club was evicted and rented a stadium until 1915, when it returned to La Boca once again. In 1923, River

relocated to the Buenos Aires neighbourhood of Palermo. On May 26, 1938, the inauguration of the *Monumental* stadium in the neighbourhood of Belgrano marked the club's last move (Hasicic 2016). Boca was founded in 1903 in La Boca. The origin of the Boca – River rivalry is tied to intra-neighbourhood competition.

12 The misconception surrounding the socioeconomic backgrounds of River and Boca fans.

13 *Bostero* (feminine: *bostera*) is the nickname given to Boca fans. It comes from the word *bosta*, meaning dung.

14 The expression "to spin the purse" refers to prostitutes. More specifically, it evokes the stereotypical image of a prostitute "spinning the purse" while looking for clients.

15 A *bailanta* is a nightclub that plays various genres of tropical music. *Bailantas* are associated with the lower classes and are generally looked down on by people from middle and upper class backgrounds.

16 The Riachuelo (officially called Matanza-Riachuelo) is a river that runs west to east and serves as the southern border of the Autonomous City of Buenos Aires. The neighbourhood of La Boca (La Boca means "The Mouth") takes its name from the fact that it is located at the mouth of the Riachuelo. The Riachuelo is infamous for its high levels of contamination from industrial waste.

17 Boca fans say that Boca is "half plus one," a phrase that highlights that Boca is Argentina's most popular club in terms of its total number of supporters.

18 In Argentina, "darkie" is used as an expletive referring to brown-skinned Indigenous and mestizo people.

19 *Trapos*, the slang word used in Spanish, literally translates to pieces of cloth or rags, but is used to refer to flags and banners of all sizes.

20 This line points to the complicated and often conflicting relationships that fans have with the police.

21 In this case, *pigs* is used as the derogatory term that refers to the police.

22 "Chickens" (*gallinas*) is one of the nicknames used to refer to River fans. Originally intended as a derogatory nickname, River fans have adopted it and turned it into a symbol of pride. It is not uncommon for River fans to introduce themselves in conversations about football as chickens. River's stadium, popularly known as *El Monumental*, is sometimes, though not often, referred to as the chicken coop (*gallinero*).

23 This practice, however, is not confined to Argentinian football.

24 A very common insult in many South American countries.

25 This refers to the victory lap that players do around the field when they win a league, cup, or tournament.

26 Lezama Park is a popular park located in the tourist Buenos Aires neighbourhood of San Telmo, approximately ten blocks from Boca's stadium. In Spanish, rather than going for a *spin* on a carousel, one goes for a *lap* on a carousel. Thus, the chant's joke about doing a lap on Lezama Park's carousel as a consolation prize for not being able to do a victory lap is lost in translation.

27 Club Almagro, simply known as Almagro, plays football in the Argentinian second division.

28 "The group in the stands" is a euphemism for *barra brava*. Hugo had mentioned that he preferred talking about organized fans, as *barra brava* is a non-native term loaded with negative connotations.

29 Interestingly enough, in this case he used the term *barra* in spite of his previously stated aversion to it.

Violence in Argentinian football   67

30 Here, he used the term *fans* to refer to the same group of people that he had referred to as *barras* in the previous sentence.

31 In this case, "group of people" means *barra* or organized fans, depending on one's perspective.

32 When discussing football-related violence, media outlets often refer to "those few," i.e. small groups of what they describe as "savages and social misfits" who are seemingly responsible for the vast majority of acts of physical violence.

33 The argument that describes football stadiums as secure and controlled environments where fans are able to perform cathartic rituals is a common one. Tuastad (1997), for example, explains that the Jordanian government attempted to "pacify" Palestinian refugees living in Amman by allowing them to externalize their political frustrations while cheering for Wihdat under controlled circumstances. Wihdat is a Palestinian football club from the Wihdat refugee camp in Jordan. The club symbolizes Palestinian nationalism.

34 The Metropolitan Police was dissolved after my return from fieldwork. Within the city of Buenos Aires, the Federal and Metropolitan Police forces were combined to create the new City Police.

35 "The T" is short for Talleres.

36 Nacional is one of Uruguay's two biggest and most successful clubs.

37 At the time of writing, Atlanta plays in the second division.

38 This is not always the case. Some *barrabravas* belong to the middle class, while very few might even belong to the upper-middle class. The Schlenker brothers at River are the most famous example. These are, however, exceptions to the rule.

39 Gonzalo Acro, a *barrabrava*, received a monthly salary of 5,763 pesos while working as a maintenance agent at River Plate's Olympic-size swimming pool (Buzzella 2007). Although impossible to corroborate, it is generally believed that Acro was paid for doing very little work, if any at all. Most of the club officials (including the then-president José María Aguilar) knew that he was a *barrabrava*. Aragón describes a similar scenario at San Lorenzo de Almagro, one of the most important first division clubs. When talking about the club's *barrabravas*, he states that "some members work for the club....without actually performing any specific task" (2007:70).

40 Raúl Gámez, ex-president of Vélez Sársfield, another important first division club, told me that he used to give tickets to the club's *barrabravas*, who would then sell them. He explained that this was a way of avoiding trouble with them, but in retrospect regrets his actions and urges club officials to stop financing the *barrabravas*.

41 See Duke and Crolley (2001).

42 Beyond the clubs' typical function as social and sports clubs.

43 In Buenos Aires, people who drive to concerts or sporting events are often extorted into paying protection money for their cars when they park on the street. The so-called *trapitos* (*trapito* means small piece of cloth) charge drivers a fee that is arbitrarily set by them. Although drivers can refuse to pay the fee, they do so at their own risk, as their cars may be vandalized as a result. *Trapitos* often work for *barras bravas*.

44 Former federal judge Mariano Bergés also described this scenario, stating that more often than not, the buses that take the *barras* to the stadiums are not authorized.

45 Club Barrial is a fictional name.

46 Although I do not have access to specific figures regarding the profitability of the *barras'* businesses, it is probable that only a few *barras bravas* from the country's most important clubs are able to run *highly* profitable operations.

68 Violence in Argentinian football

47 Once is an area within the neighbourhood of Balvanera in Buenos Aires famous for its shopping malls with stands that sell trinkets and knockoff goods.

48 As previously stated, the Riachuelo is a river, infamous for its high levels of contamination from industrial waste.

49 The system was never implemented.

50 Néstor Kirchner was President of Argentina from 2003 to 2007. He died in 2010.

51 Although here she avoided using the term *barras*, she was indeed talking about *barras* when she said "some of them" and "one from Boca." She did, however, use the term *barras* at another point during her speech.

52 Short for Defensores.

Chapter 3

Corruption in Argentina

In this chapter, I provide an explanation of the approach to the understandings and conceptualizations of corruption that inform my study. From an anthropological standpoint, my focus is on the local interpretations of corruption that emerge from field observations and semi-structured interviews I have conducted with research participants. In the case of the semi-structured interviews, I have refrained from asking participants to provide an explicit definition of corruption. Considering that the term is often an ambiguous one with many ramifications, I have found it more useful and productive to let their views on the subject emerge candidly as our conversations unfolded. Having said that, my questions encouraged participants to provide details regarding the ways in which corruption was manifested.

Definitions and approaches

Although clear, concise, and universally applicable definitions of corruption remain elusive, a macroscopic consideration of some of the most salient structural factors that lead to acts of corruption in different settings may pave the way for an analysis of the local conditions that help encourage and perpetuate these very same acts in Argentina. The point here is to establish a comparison between global and local understandings of corruption in an attempt to elucidate the political mechanisms and cultural characteristics that sustain Argentina's culture of impunity.

In the words of Sissener, corruption refers to "the abuse of public office for private gain" (2001:1). Keeping this broad and concise definition in mind, it is useful to consider some of the causes of corruption that have been examined by scholars from a variety of disciplines.

Bull and Newell (1997) point to the political opportunities afforded by the state to private and public actors to become involved in corrupt dealings while taking into account the actors' willingness to participate in these exchanges. More importantly, however, they highlight the impossibility of identifying objective causes and definitions given the plethora of locally produced understandings and evaluations. This is problematic, to say the least, because it makes attempts at

DOI: 10.4324/9781003458937-3

70 Corruption in Argentina

measuring levels of corruption on a global scale heavily reliant on the social and cultural norms, values, and beliefs of the people or organizations (e.g. Transparency International) that conduct research on corruption.

On the other hand, "there are those analysts who give up the attempt at objective definition altogether and who, in effect, make the characterisation of behaviour as corrupt dependent upon their own values" (Bull & Newell 1997:173). While making one's own values explicit when talking about corruption is a step in the right direction, this approach fails to adequately integrate the views of the research participants into the analysis by privileging the analyst's perspective. Put differently, it does not suffice to recognize the decidedly ambiguous and context-specific nature of corruption.

Resolving this ambiguity by resorting to the researcher's values does little to advance a proper understanding of the specificities that come into play in different settings. In his study on corruption in Argentina, Pomer advances an interpretation of corruption that considers the multiplicity of factors that inform its definition.

> Corruption is a consciousness, a way of thinking and feeling, a culture that is defined in relationships with others, a lifestyle with its justifications and myths, a practice that uses a wide range of material and verbal disguises protected by discourses that legitimize, pamper, and accept it as an inherent fatality of a supposed, definitive and unalterable human condition.
>
> (2004:13; my translation)

From a political science perspective, Hopkin (1997) recognizes the limited reach of definitions that are strictly legalistic but offers an alternative that, while broader in scope, falls short of taking into account the ambiguous and morally convoluted relationship between public and private interests. His approach, based on analyses of European democracies, is informative to the extent that it takes into consideration legal, ethical, and public norms (what he means by public, however, and the ways in which public norms differ from legal ones, is not entirely clear). Still, matters become more complicated when public and private interests coincide.

Clientelist networks often serve as examples where the private interests of a patron promote the common good by providing clients with illegally obtained benefits that they would otherwise not receive. These benefits are one of the "perks" of holding public office. Thus, while redistributing public money – money that would originally have been assigned to other areas – among clients without the legal consent of the pertinent national, provincial, or municipal office could easily be seen as an act of corruption, a moral approach might well be able to justify the act by pointing out the higher quality of life for the clients that results from a more equitable distribution of public resources. As I will discuss later, this is especially true in what O'Donnell (1993) and Goldstein (2003) refer to as "brown zones," areas where the state is largely absent. Hopkin also explains that the 'political economy' approach to the study of corruption takes the economic assumption that political actors act rationally in order to maximise their utility (generally defined in terms of material self-interest), and analyses acts of corruption as hidden exchanges between two actors.

(1997:256)

Indeed, this political economy approach stems from the assumption that acts of corruption take place almost exclusively in private settings and between people of a similar socioeconomic status. Furthermore, it takes for granted a relation of reciprocity whereby the actors involved offer something in exchange for something else.

An analysis of clientelism offers an alternative understanding of the conditions under which acts of corruption can be carried out. These acts need not take place in private settings. As Auyero's studies on clientelism in the Greater Buenos Aires area show (1999, 2000, 2001, 2007), the settings where clients receive goods and services from political brokers are far from private. In fact, many of the physical settings (such as a broker's house) where resources and services are distributed are clearly marked and advertised. These buildings, called *Unidades Básicas* or "Basic Units," are easily identifiable by their signs or their painted walls, which show the names of the *Unidades Básicas* as well as their political affiliation. Visibility is therefore desirable, as the populist and paternalistic/maternalistic character of the *Unidades Básicas* thrives on extended networks of clients. More importantly, in cases involving two or more actors, reciprocity is not a defining feature of corruption and should not be presupposed. While it is expected that clients will reward their patrons' "generosity" with their votes, the fact remains that in societies where voting is a private, anonymous act, patrons and brokers may have to rely on trust when it comes to their clients' professed loyalty. Put differently, the clients' votes are not guaranteed, at least in theory. In practice, however, things are more complicated. Still, even though clientelist networks rely on mechanisms of social control in an attempt to monitor the clients' voting behaviour (Stokes 2005), the point here is that reciprocity is not an inherent component of corruption. Furthermore, in some cases where there *is* reciprocity, exchanges may be coerced rather than mutually agreed upon. This will become apparent in my analysis of clientelism in football.

Contextual understandings of corruption must be framed in terms of the participants' experiences, values, and opinions. This is not to suggest the often romanticized idea of the moral obligation of the researcher to take on the role of an activist who acts in the interests of those they seek to "represent"; rather, my emphasis on contextualization and on prioritizing local insights and perspectives has more to do with the accuracy and validity of the data generated with the research participants. Following Heeks' (2007) distinction between context of design and context of use, it becomes apparent that attempts at defining and analyzing corruption by dissociating one context from the other can only produce partial or inaccurate understandings and interpretations. Heeks explains that a system of tools, processes, values, and resources designed in one context can carry with it inscribed assumptions – values drawn from designers' backgrounds; assumptions about the skills, values, and resources of the user context; requirements needed for the proper implementation of the initiative – which may undermine its suitability, or which contain elements that may be appropriated by local users.

(2007:258)

Thus, Heeks points to the failure of interventions that do not address the economic, social, and cultural gaps that exist between the designers' contexts and the contexts in which supposedly sophisticated anti-corruption models are applied.

Needless to say, this is also true of interventions aimed at reducing corruption and violence in football that apply a rigid set of measures universally and uncritically. Still, the distinctiveness of local conceptualizations of corruption must not be overstated. Mény and Rhodes argue that

it is…no longer possible to consider corruption as a peripheral phenomenon in the analysis of politics, or as a culturally specific 'syndrome' found only in particular places at certain times. To a greater or lesser extent it infiltrates the political process and relationships of all countries and poses special problems for political reform and regulation.

(1997:96)

Thus, corruption might not be *entirely* culturally specific; however, my fieldwork data suggests that culture plays a role in the form corruption takes in different places and at different times. From an interpretive perspective, the key is to adopt a comparative middle ground in order to identify the differences and commonalities that inform the ways in which corruption is thought about, practiced, and experienced. While arriving at a value-free definition of corruption seems implausible (Bull & Newell 1997), the unattainability of such goal need not be an obstacle to its study. In fact, the context-dependent nature of its representative characteristics affords opportunities for an examination of people's mentality at the individual and social levels. Although not "culturally specific," the reasoning behind Bull and Newell's (1997, 2003) enumeration of some of the factors that help perpetuate acts of corruption can easily be applied to the Argentinian case. Considering the opportunities for corruption afforded by the country's well-established and widely distributed clientelist networks, it comes as no surprise that the government's inability to deal with the issue results in the lowering of the "moral and material costs of corruption" (Bull & Newell 1997:176). In other words, people who engage in acts of corruption come to believe that their actions will go unpunished. Once corruption becomes endemic, a generalized sense of impunity follows. This, in turn, leads some people to believe that not taking advantage of the opportunities one is presented with is simply dumb (Jiménez & Caínzos in Bull & Newell 2003).

Recent surveys indicate that Argentinians are distrustful of politicians and judges. The National Survey on Media and Justice found that 66% of the 1,000 respondents above the age of 16 does not believe that the judiciary is independent when it comes to cases related to corruption (Perfil 2022b). Similarly, another survey shows that 80% of respondents think that politicians are corrupt, while 70% think that judges are corrupt (infobae 2022). A third survey, conducted among 1,133 respondents above the age of 16, found that 81.2% of respondents believe that the state is incapable of tackling the main problems that affect society, including corruption, insecurity, poverty, and inflation, while 88.4% believe that the state is absent (El Cronista 2023). These factors could certainly contribute to the "success" of clientelist networks to the extent that these informal networks fill the gap left by the absence of the state.

A culture of impunity often serves as a powerful motivator for corrupt behaviour. Bull and Newell's conclusion regarding the perpetuation of corruption fits the Argentinian case: "where *systemic* corruption develops, then not participating is no longer a sign of honesty but rather lack of power, weakness or incompetence" (1997:179; emphasis in original). More importantly, the argument presented above assumes a best-case scenario where the state seeks to reduce the levels of corruption but fails to implement effective measures or lacks the funds to develop anti-corruption programmes and agencies. Needless to say, the social and economic interests of politicians at the municipal, provincial, and national levels in Argentina are often – though not necessarily always – at odds with those of the general population. This exacerbates the problem because clientelist networks of exchange are functional to the patrons' and brokers' political careers and economic prosperity. It should be noted, however, that for a clientelist regime to work, patrons and brokers *must* provide some sort of social assistance in the pursuit of their personal interests. As a result, clients whose most pressing needs are fully or – as it is most likely the case – partially satisfied might come to think of clientelism as a type of social welfare programme that tackles corruption by distributing goods and services rather than contributes to it.

Girling's statement on the relevance of morality in critical analyses of corruption highlights the difficulties in arriving at a universal consensus regarding what constitutes corrupt behaviour:

> neither the existence of 'checks and balances' nor insistence on ethical performance necessarily leads to 'honest' government serving the 'common interest'. Yet the moral aspect is....crucial to the explanation: corruption is defined normatively, as a 'deviation' from the public good.
>
> (1997:2)

This explanation poses some problems. In his view, "normative strengths" (Girling 1997), understood as the values and moral obligations that ought to inform and guide a person's actions, serve as an "antidote" to political corruption. It is thanks to these normative strengths that some societies are able to

74 Corruption in Argentina

prosper economically in spite of the politicians' selfish and often illegal use of resources. What Girling means by normative, however, remains unclear. While he does mention that the normative understanding of corruption discussed in his book stems from Aristotle's distinction between public and personal interests, the universal applicability of this perspective is debatable. Furthermore, the idea of normative strengths seems to have its foundations on moral absolutism. Indeed, Girling suggests that high moral standards help keep corruption in check. The problem here is that talking about a predefined scale of moral standards is comparable to attempts at measuring corruption exclusively in terms of statistical values and numerical data, with little regard for context. Are the notions of corruption and public good mutually exclusive? Could a political patron who uses public resources illegally, for example, have a genuine interest in helping clients on top of advancing their own career? Girling explains that according to Aristotle, "the true purpose of the political community....is that each member attain a share in the good life" (1997:2). Could corruption help fulfill this goal by taking on the role of the state as a social safety net in areas where the state is largely absent?

In Auyero's studies (1999, 2000, 2001, 2007), the clients might think of clientelism/corruption as a means to gain access to the "public good." Thus, clientelism as a form of "benevolent" corruption might not necessarily represent a deviation from the public good, but rather a way to channel goods and services to those who need them most. Indeed, Girling admits that "corruption can be understood as a functional, if not generally acceptable, way of overcoming the systemic misfit" (1997:23). It could be argued that, from a client's perspective, the dyadic relationships that characterize informal networks of exchange help to mitigate the government's – be it national, provincial, or municipal – inability or unwillingness to redistribute goods and services fairly and equitably. Put differently, the state deviates from its duty to ensure the public good, while clientelist networks "correct" the state's shortcomings by allocating public resources to impoverished areas through personal ties.

Corrupt behaviour on the part of politicians represents, according to Girling, a perversion of power: "the abuse of political power for private ends, or 'power corruption'" (1997:3). When it comes to the particular form that corruption takes under clientelism, the idea of a "perversion of power" or "power corruption" is complicated by the fact that this alleged perversion often – and ironically – results in increased social, medical, and financial benefits for the poor, regardless of the actor's selfish intentions. This is not to suggest that clientelism is indeed a form of social welfare that provides opportunities for social mobility, but simply that it may be seen as such by clients. One could well argue that the conditions that lead to the poor's reliance on the short-term and often limited benefits of clientelism are themselves a consequence of endemic corruption. Thus, the workings of clientelist networks pose a challenge to normative and legal interpretations of corruption. Clientelism's dual role as an extension of systemic corruption and as a remedy to the most pressing needs of the poor – that is, as a remedy to the very same corruption that often characterizes it – highlights the subjective and contextually sensitive understandings and interpretations of the actors involved. Thus, the question remains:

> why does corruption occur on a massive scale in some countries and much less so in others? Again, the narrower approach does not provide an answer. For legal prohibitions of corruption exist both in countries where corruption is widespread and where it is much less significant. The question is why such prohibitions are effective in some cases and not in others: this question is posed by the broader, social approach rather than by the narrower, legal one. These two factors alone –first, electoral funding and lobbying, which are undeniably conducive to corruption; and second, the existence of large-scale corruption throughout the world – strongly support the case for a broad systemic, and not narrow legal, definition.
>
> (Girling 1997:7–8)

Here, Girling calls for a holistic examination of the sociocultural conditions that provide opportunities for and encourage corrupt behaviour. In his view, the strictly legalistic definitions advanced by some scholars (Grondona 1993; Lancaster & Montinola 1997) are ill-positioned to account for the multiplicity of possible interpretations that a variety of social actors may offer based both on their personal circumstances as well as on their understandings of the social and cultural contexts of which they are a part and in which corrupt practices are embedded. Girling seems to contradict himself, however, by adopting the concept of normative strengths, which relies on a rigid view of morality that is more in tune with Grondona's (1993) positivist perspective than with Sissener's (2001) grounded theory approach. He goes on to say that

> Supporters of modern legalistic definitions of corruption....face in addition two serious problems. The first is the difficulty of coping with 'sharp practices' that have the same effect as legally defined corruption – such as using indirect 'influence' rather than outright bribery – but are not actually illegal. The second follows from the first. Corrupt behaviour, on the one hand, and lawful behaviour, on the other, are not so much polar opposites (as the narrow definition insists) but represent stages on a continuum.
>
> (Girling 1997:8)

From an interpretive perspective, Girling emphasizes the ambiguity and elusiveness inherent in intellectual exercises aimed at arriving at a concise, satisfactory, and "ready-made" definition of political corruption. As stated above, the never-ending search for an all-encompassing definition might seem futile, but the conceptual differences found in a variety of settings has the rather fortunate effect of forcing researchers to seriously consider and think about the local factors that give rise to these differences.

76   Corruption in Argentina

Following this line of thought, clientelism in Argentina may well be identified as a "sharp practice," to borrow Girling's term, as opposed to a clearly delineated form of corruption with boundaries that conform to legalistic definitions. Assessing the legality of clientelist practices can be a complicated matter, especially since it is nearly impossible for researchers/social scientists who are without direct access to municipal, provincial, or national political offices to identify the ways in which public funds are assigned, distributed, and accounted for. Still, even in cases where the legality of the transactions and exchanges between patrons/brokers and clients is unquestionable, Girling's social approach (1997) takes into account the *influence* that patrons have over their clients. Putting aside the notion of normative strengths, this adds a layer of ambiguity, to be sure, as claims of corruption will be judged according to differing and sometimes competing moralities.

In *La corrupción* (1993), Mariano Grondona, a renowned Argentinian journalist with a background in law, sociology, and political science, focuses on corruption in the public sector by emphasizing the impossibility of regulating and controlling state corruption. While the state is often able to control and punish acts of corruption in the private sector, Grondona asks, "who could control or punish the state? If the state mechanisms are infiltrated by corruption, the system is left without appeal" (1993:5; my translation). A system that is left without appeal, then, poses a serious challenge to structural reforms. According to Grondona, acts of corruption can be classified according to degrees of corruptness. His approach to the study of corruption also makes reference to different levels of moral advancement. Countries where levels of corruption are kept to a minimum are referred to as "morally advanced." In his words, "the different degrees of severity of acts of corruption.... depend on the degree of moral evolution attained by the societies that sanction them" (1993:5). While Girling's perspectives on moral standards and normative strengths are not as explicitly evolutionist as Grondona's, their views share some similarities. Contrary to Grondona's universally homogenizing conceptualization of morality, however, Girling's (1997) normative strengths are specific to particular countries, a fact that does not negate a rather inflexible and overgeneralizing approach to the links between morality and corruption. Ironically, Moreno Ocampo, a lawyer and prosecutor of the International Criminal Court who contributed a chapter to Grondona's book, states: "I have a great objection against those who seek to impose their personal morality on others: their intolerance is dangerous" (1993:44). His statement stands in opposition to Grondona's moralizing reactions. Going back to the idea that corruption and morality are closely linked, some questions arise. What constitutes an act of corruption? Who determines the severity of each of the proposed types of corruption? *How* is it determined? Is it useful to classify acts of corruption, or is there an overarching issue that transcends classification, rendering it obsolete? Grondona's explicitly anti-relativist perspective is based on a homogeneous conceptualization of morality that all societies should ascribe to.

Corruption and violence in Argentina: A brief background

Corruption has been a prevalent feature of Argentinian society since the second founding of Buenos Aires in 1580.[1] As historian Felipe Pigna explains,

> during those centuries from 1580 to 1810, a corrupt state was being developed. At the same time, under its protection, a society that would learn empirically that laws can be flexible, that rules can be violated and that, in general, the law follows one path and people another was being consolidated.
>
> (2004:101; my translation)

The Spanish Monarchy established a commercial monopoly between Spain and its American colonies. Goods coming from Spain arrived in the colonies at the port of Veracruz, in present-day Mexico, while raw materials and products going from the colonies to Spain were to depart exclusively from the port of Habana, in Cuba. To reach Buenos Aires, all goods had to travel from Central America by sea to Lima, in present-day Peru, and from there they made their way to Buenos Aires by carriage. The approximately 4,000-kilometre trip between Lima and Buenos Aires took months to complete, and the price of the goods being transported rose excessively by the time they reached Buenos Aires. As a result, smuggling became an alternative to the oppressive economic policies imposed by the Spanish Crown. The silver from Potosí, in what is now Bolivia, was carried south to Buenos Aires and smuggled into Rio de Janeiro (Brazil) via Colonia del Sacramento (Uruguay) (MacLeod 1984). In addition, foreign ships, mostly British, officially stopped at the port of Buenos Aires for repairs, covering up the smuggling of all kinds of merchandise. Under the restrictive conditions imposed by Spain, smuggling became the most important commercial activity in Buenos Aires. Within the town, those who had been assigned the responsibility of eliminating smuggling were in fact active participants in the practice (Moutoukias 2000).

During his voyage aboard the *HMS Beagle*, Charles Darwin visited Argentina in 1832.[2] After observing people's behaviours, he stated the following:

> During the last six months I have had an opportunity of seeing a little of the character of the inhabitants of these provinces.... Police and justice are quite inefficient. If a man who is poor commits murder and is taken, he will be imprisoned, and perhaps even shot; but if he is rich and has friends, he may rely on it no very severe consequence will ensue. It is curious that the most respectable inhabitants of the country invariably assist a murderer to escape: they seem to think that the individual sins against the government, and not against the people.... Sensuality, mockery of all religion, and the grossest corruption, are far from uncommon. Nearly every public officer can be bribed. The head man in the post-office sold forged government franks. The governor and prime minister openly combined to plunder the State. Justice, where gold

78 Corruption in Argentina

came into play, was hardly expected by any one. I knew an Englishman who went to the Chief Justice (he told me that, not then understanding the ways of the place, he trembled as he entered the room), and said, "Sir, I have come to offer you two hundred (paper) dollars (value about five pounds sterling) if you will arrest before a certain time a man who has cheated me. I know it is against the law, but my lawyer (naming him) recommended me to take this step." The Chief Justice smiled acquiescence, thanked him, and the man before night was safe in prison. With this entire want of principle in many of the leading men, with the country full of ill-paid turbulent officers, the people yet hope that a democratic form of government can succeed!

(1913:165–166)

From 1860 to 1930, liberal pro-European governments modernized the country with capital provided by Great Britain. The construction of a railroad network, the installation of meat processing plants, advances in agriculture and the introduction of improved cattle breeds led to massive exports of wool, grains, and meat that resulted in a significant rise in GDP. As Mundlak et al. explain,

during this period, Argentina grew more rapidly than the United States, Canada, Australia, or Brazil, countries similarly endowed with rich land, which also accommodated large inflows of capital and European immigration. During the first three decades of this century,[3] Argentina outgrew the other four countries in population, total income, and per capita income.

(1989:12)

The middle class grew significantly, although the actual size and living conditions of the lower classes are still being debated (Rocchi 2000). In spite of the rise of the middle class, government corruption, clientelism, electoral fraud, and political violence continued unabated. The British newspaper *The Times of London* published articles denouncing corruption during the presidency of Argentinian lawyer Miguel Ángel Juárez Celman, which lasted from 1886 until his resignation in 1890. Juárez Celman was involved in cases of bribery, nepotism, and the allocation of public funds for private use (Giordano 2000).

From 1973 to 1983, the country endured the most violent years of its recent history. In 1978, two years after a military junta rose to power in what was Argentina's bloodiest dictatorship, known as the Process of National Reorganization, the FIFA World Cup took place in Argentina. This period is particularly important in relation to the present-day role of *barras bravas* in football and politics. Although groups of fans who fought against rival fans over who had more *aguante* had existed for years, most of these groups had no connections to political figures or club officials. During the dictatorship, however, the *de facto* government began employing *barras* as henchmen tasked with eradicating the perceived threat of communism. On the one hand, *barras* were asked by military leaders to behave well during the course of the World Cup; on the other hand, they were instructed to confront those who opposed the dictatorship. The ties that the *de facto* government established with the *barras* set the precedent for the political and economic ties that present-day *barras* maintain with club officials, politicians, and the police. The 1978 FIFA World Cup was "the dirtiest world cup of all time" (Hersey 2018). The head of the event's organizing committee, General Omar Actis, was assassinated in circumstances that were never clarified. Admiral Carlos Alberto Lacoste, who took General Actis' place, spent 517,000,000 American dollars on the organization of the tournament, 400,000,000 more than the money spent by Spain in preparation for the 1982 World Cup. Author, journalist, and university professor Gustavo Veiga states that Admiral Lacoste was never able to explain how his personal assets increased 443% between 1977 and 1979 (Veiga 2004). Furthermore, there were strong allegations of match-fixing that allowed Argentina to win the Cup (Herbert 2018). Although these allegations have never been officially confirmed, the final score in the game between Argentina and Peru does not help to dispel them. The Argentinian national team needed a win against Peru by a difference of at least four goals in order to reach the World Cup final. The fact that Argentina beat Peru by a score of 6-0, which allowed the team to move on to the final against Holland,[4] raised suspicions regarding the role of the country's *de facto* President General Jorge Rafael Videla in the outcome of the match, taking into account that the dictatorship was eager to use the 1978 World Cup to promote a positive image of Argentina to the world. As Herbert explains,

> Videla's visit to the Peru dressing room before kick-off was the most suspicious part. He was accompanied by Henry Kissinger, who had recently concluded his four-year term as US secretary of state. The encounter left the Peruvians feeling worried, as the message to them had been how important a win was to Argentina.
>
> (idem)

Since 1983, Argentina has been enjoying a succession of democratically elected governments. The return to democracy, however, did not result in a radical socio-political transformation when it came to the role of corruption in all areas of government. Corruption under the administration of President Carlos Saúl Menem (1989–1999) was rampant. Domingo Cavallo, Minister of Economy from 1991 to 1996, denounced political control of judges and illicit activities of high-ranking officials in most areas of the state (Cavallo 1997). To name a well-known example, Menem was involved in the illegal export of weapons to Ecuador and Croatia between 1991 and 1995. At the time, Ecuador was at war with Peru. As one of the guarantors of a peace agreement the two nations had signed after an earlier war that took place in 1942, Argentina was banned from selling weapons to either side. Menem was found guilty in 2013 and was sentenced to seven years in prison (The Telegraph 2013). However, due to his old age and position as Senator, he was granted immunity, thus avoiding imprisonment.

80 Corruption in Argentina

Néstor Kirchner served as President of Argentina from 2003 to 2007, while his wife, Cristina Fernández de Kirchner, served two consecutive terms as President from 2007 to 2015. They increased their wealth by 4,500% between 2005 and 2010. Their presidential terms were marked by several allegations of bribery (Lanata 2014) and a new plague in Argentina, association with drug dealers (Keep 2014). Cristina Fernández de Kirchner served a term as Vice President of Argentina from 2019 to 2023. The position granted her immunity from prosecution (Dubowitz & Dershowitz 2019). She is facing at least six indictments of corruption including illicit association, money laundering, concealment, and fraudulent administration (Centenera & Rivas Molina 2018). Former President Mauricio Macri (2015–2019), a political rival of the Kirchners who had been elected at least in part as a result of the exorbitant levels of corruption experienced during the Kirchners' presidencies, accumulated at least ten indictments related to corruption and conflicts of interest (Medina 2020).

The succession of catastrophic administrations over many years led to a severe economic decline. In the words of Glaeser et al.,

> Argentina began the 20th century as one of the wealthiest places on the planet. In 1913, it was richer than France or Germany, almost twice as prosperous as Spain, and its per capita GDP was almost as high as that of Canada.
> (2018:2)

According to the International Monetary Fund, in 2019 Argentina ranked 71st in the world in terms of per capita GDP (Statistics Times 2020). By the end of 2019, 53% of children and adolescents lived in poverty, and it is predicted that the number will increase to 58.6% as a consequence of the COVID-19 pandemic (Soria 2020).

The Nobel Prize laureate economist Simon Kuznets reportedly said that there are four kinds of countries: developed countries, underdeveloped countries, Japan, and Argentina (Yglesias 2012). This classification implies that Japan was able to thrive economically in spite of having few valuable natural resources, whereas Argentina's economy shrank in spite of having access to plenty of resources.

Argentina's social and political history has been marked not only by corruption but also by violence. The last military dictatorship (1976–1983) created a social environment in which violence became privatized. Following Alabarces' (2004) definition, the "privatization of violence" refers to the illegitimate use of violence which is both uncontrolled and implicitly encouraged by the state. Romero claims that the political discourses of the dictatorship

> divided the world into two opposing camps: friends and enemies.... Because everything stemmed from power, the sole purpose of political action was to capture it.... By one or another route, everything led to an interpretation of politics as an extension of war.
> (2006:189)

The privatization of violence, coupled with the privatization of the economy and the erosion of the judicial system as a result of the neoliberal policies of the 1990s, enabled different social actors (such as *barrabravas*, club officials, and politicians) to gain political and economic power through illegal arrangements, extortion, and the use of unregulated violence.

In spite of the state's apparent intention to restore its monopoly on violence, Alabarces explains that

> the violence of the dictatorship means.... a perverse prolongation: the rupture of the modern contract through which the only legitimate violence is monopolized by the State, which must use it rationally and democratically. That rupture creates a frame of interpretation in which violence is privatized and can be legitimized by different actors for particular goals. Also, State violence not only loses legitimacy as a result of the dictatorship: its anti-democratic practices are prolonged to the present-day in the form of police violence. And all of this can be seen, amplified, in football.
>
> (2004:27; my translation)

Thus, as Alabarces shows, the privatization of violence during the dictatorship permeated the world of football. It was not until 1976, when the military junta took power, that groups of football fans organized around political and economic interests emerged. The Process of National Reorganization provided the social conditions that allowed these fans to privatize the use of violence by copying (to some extent) the behaviour of the *Grupos de Tarea*.[5] As previously mentioned, during the 1978 World Cup many football fans were used by the *de facto* government to patrol the stadiums. Shortly after, this relationship evolved to the point where fans and politicians became interdependent actors. Since then, some groups of fans have organized themselves and carried out acts of violence with impunity as a result of their association with power.

As Gaffney explains, the relationships between the actors that make up the world of football "are marked by corruption, 'gentlemen's agreements' and mutual exploitation" (2009:166). In his article, he summarizes many of the issues discussed in this book:

> The president of Chacarita Juniors,[6] Luis Barrionuevo, also a senator in the national congress, refused to answer the questions of a federal judge regarding violence in soccer because he claimed he was being persecuted by ex-president Menem. Macri, Barrionuevo and others like them are often life-long members of the clubs they head up and as such have a vested personal interest in their sporting, economic and political successes. The involvement of high-level political figures in the running of social clubs, soccer teams, stadiums and associated violence frequently involves conflicts of interests, claims of corruption and a lack of transparency in local and national governance. The exact nature and extent of most of these relationships are not clear, but

82 Corruption in Argentina

the effects of widespread corruption and continued violence are increasingly evident in the inability of the clubs to prevent or control violence.

(2009:167)

While Gaffney rightly claims that the clubs are often unable to control violence, I would add that in many cases, they are unwilling. This is not to say that all club officials and employees have a personal interest in maintaining close relationships with *barrabravas*, but many influential officials would lose their political and economic privileges if their ties to groups of organized fans were to be severed. According to a 2007 Transparency International report, Argentina held the unflattering title of "most corrupt judicial system," a title the country shared with Russia (Press TV 2007).

An exhaustive account of specific cases of political corruption and violence in recent Argentinian history is beyond the scope of this book. Pomer (2004) and Alconada Mon (2018) provide detailed descriptions of cases of corruption, including high-profile cases involving politicians and unionists, among other actors. Alconada Mon in particular describes no less than 15 cases that point to the relationships that exist between football and politics.[7]

A culture of impunity

Corruption and clientelism in Argentina are directly related to what I refer to as a culture of impunity. MacLachlan makes a similar point. In the following passage, worth quoting at length, he summarizes many of the features that make up Argentina's culture of impunity:

> Civic values are reflected in social and political behavior.... Such values may be more directly pertinent to an explanation of how a society actually works than any other element.... As Niccolò Machiavelli observed, everything depends on the civic virtue of the citizenry.... In Argentina, few would make the case for equality or trust. Suspicion that others are taking advantage of the situation to gain an unfair advantage converts [society] into a self-serving system and, consequently, civic virtue becomes naiveté. If wealth cannot be achieved through hard work and merit, then it must be wrested from those who have it. A sense that one has been shortchanged sets off a "grab what you can" mentality, outright theft, systemic corruption, and totally self-serving political and union careers. A negative approach to the law further undermines predictability and trust and sets off a race at every level of society to get what one can before the opportunity passes. It negatively colors social relations, politics, economic activity, and ethics.... An intense focus on personal survival subordinates collective issues not directly connected with an individual's well being. Understandably, the direct personal impact on individuals and their families pushes all else aside and it becomes a situation in

which it is *"sálvese quien pueda"* (everyone for themselves). An implosion of empathy results in "amoral familist" behavior that strives to maximize advantage for the individual family unit, and overrides guilt with the assumption that everyone is doing the same. People contact their representatives, not over broad public issues, but to ask for favors, jobs, permits, tax matters and other specific personal needs. The understanding that their political representatives will exchange favors in return for personal loyalty creates clients rather than citizens.

(MacLachlan 2006:197)

As a self-sustaining mechanism, corruption effectively blocks attempts at producing social change and prevents the development of viable solutions. This is in part due to the fact that it is not in the best interest of those who have the power to implement laws and control corruption to give up the benefits they obtain by perpetuating the system of organized chaos. The fact that Darwin described the elements that make up Argentina's culture of impunity in 1832 points to the difficulties in disrupting a system that favours politicians and public officials in positions of authority. Darwin's comments resonate to this day. His observations signal that the ways in which public institutions operate have changed little since the time of his exploratory voyage. The scenario he related nearly two centuries ago contributed to the "everyone for themselves" attitude described by MacLachlan. Indeed, the general consensus among people in positions of power seems to be that one would be a fool not to take advantage of one's privileged position. Thus, rejecting certain "benefits" (such as bribes) on moral grounds is not considered a laudable act; rather, it is seen as a missed opportunity. The early Roman playwright Plautus made similar remarks in his comedy "Trinummus," written over 2,000 years ago: "Why, nowadays the 'custom' is to disregard what's proper and do what's pleasing. And corruption is sanctioned now by 'custom' and legal loopholes.... It's become the 'custom' to be a rotter and then stand for office" (1952:201). A culture of impunity permeates Argentina's politics and informs people's perceptions of authoritative figures. In an interview I conducted with Miguel, a lawyer who represented one of Argentina's most infamous *barras*, he explained that it is difficult to break the cycle of corruption given the country's levels of impunity:

MIGUEL: Corruption is a round trip. It is the corruption of an active subject that corrupts and a passive subject that receives it, but there must be an active subject that corrupts. And then when you see that the one above you does what he wants and nothing bad ever happens to him… You wonder, why not me?

In a similar vein, Hugo, the former leader of Ferreteros'[8] *barra brava* and former vice president of the club's security (roles that were not considered incompatible

84 Corruption in Argentina

by the club officials who offered him the position, even if he did not perform them simultaneously), told me that there is no incentive to behave like a model citizen: "Here (*in Argentina*) you behave well and you have no reward; you behave badly and you have no punishment." To take this one step further, it could be argued that those who behave badly get rewarded, to the extent that not only are they not punished, but they get away with the benefits of whatever legally and morally questionable activities they participate in.

Corruption in football

A survey conducted in Buenos Aires among 170 people between the ages of 17 and 35 revealed that football clubs were perceived as the second most corrupt institution in Argentina, with a score of 8.09 out of 10 (10 being the highest level of corruption). The top "honour" went to the police, with a score of 8.50 (Estévez 2016). Although these scores are significant, an ethnographic approach based on semi-structured interviews and casual conversations is better able to shed light on the ways in which corruption and impunity are thought about and experienced. According to Gupta,

> Corruption's infatuation with storytelling might be revealed by asking a simple question: where would a good analysis of corruption be without its stories? Even when these stories are not narrated in the text, as in economics papers, they often underlie the analysis: despite the fact that they are seen as 'illustrating' the theory or providing 'case studies' or 'examples,' they do much more. One can easily invert the relationship and argue that the stories are the bedrock on which the superstructure of analysis is often constructed.
>
> (2005:174)

Indeed, far from acting merely as examples, the analytical relevance of stories should not be underestimated. Taking into account that stories are grounded on people's actions, interactions, and exposure to particular social and cultural contexts, to produce an analysis that minimizes lived experiences in favour of abstract interpretations that are largely detached from the field would be unwise.

During a meeting I had with Javier, a journalist and politician from the city of Córdoba, we talked about corruption in the Argentinian Football Association (AFA). Julio Humberto Grondona, president of the AFA from 1979 until his death in 2014, had died exactly one month before our meeting (incidentally, on the day that Grondona died, I overheard my neighbour through the wall saying that nobody liked that son of a bitch). Given Grondona's multiple, consecutive, and uninterrupted presidencies, it is perhaps unnecessary to explain that indefinite re-elections were allowed during his time. I was intrigued by the fact that no club officials had succeeded in proposing changes to the AFA statute that would limit re-elections. Javier explained that officials had no particular interest in changing the statute, as the way it was set up seemed to benefit them.

EP: The curious thing about the AFA is that, less than 24 hours after Grondona's death, many club officials said, "well, let's see if we change the statute, this thing about indefinite re-elections" when it had not been considered during Grondona's 35-year presidency.

JAVIER: The AFA... The AFA is a liberated zone,[9] a liberated zone for money laundering and for any type of business that minorities do for political and economic power. Nobody messes with the AFA, because there you have a great business, both economic and symbolic. The symbolic capital of football is enormous.

EP: However, the question remains. Beyond the ties of political power, what prevented member clubs within the AFA from being able to achieve a change in the statute?

JAVIER: Because they don't want to do it. Most of the political leadership of the clubs were ok with Grondona's businesses because these businesses somehow benefited them. The clubs are broke, the AFA is rich...[10] This has to do with a high level of complicity and a phenomenal cowardice of the presidents of the football clubs, who take refuge in the fear they feel for the *barrabravas* to continue feeding the same business. Football has a safe-deposit box that must have ten times the money that is reported by accountants due to money laundering, and that's not only within the AFA but within each club. So there is this mysterious issue where the balance sheets always show a deficit, the debts are getting bigger and yet the clubs continue to function, they continue to hire players, they continue to hire people, how is that? This clearly demonstrates the falsity of the system.

Javier's comments echo Gaffney's description of the financial situation of football clubs:

> There is growing concern that while many clubs are falling inextricably into debt, in part due to declining memberships and increasing violence, the governing members of clubs are maintaining a level of wealth and privilege at the expense of the club, a situation many see as a reflection of Argentine society at large.
>
> (2009:167)

Javier went on to explain that *barras* often have a privileged position within the clubs, being in charge of player transactions and fees, which allows them to conduct businesses under the table. Furthermore, he believes that football clubs generate impunity, although his argument would need clarification.

86 Corruption in Argentina

EP: When I was at Oeste's[11] Olympic Village I met with Pedro Tala and asked him – because he had been a Sojeros player during Navarro's presidency – I asked him what the atmosphere was like at Sojeros, and he told me that all decisions would go through the *barra*.

JAVIER: The *barras* managed both Ferroviario's and Sojeros'[12] Academy players.[13] And of those players who for years disappear from the Academy, which can be as many as 20 in a year, a lot of money went directly to the *barra*. That's why they were so powerful, both Pereyra's *barra* at Sojeros and Fusile's[14] *barra* at Ferroviario. And then they entered the drug business thanks to the place they occupy in the *barras bravas*. That gives them symbolic power to control neighbourhoods.

EP: In the case of player percentages,[15] how do you get to that point? Because I think that also depends on the club. There are some clubs where the *barras* reach that level (*i.e. they own percentages of players' transfers*) due to intimidation, and others where they get a say because they are functional to the political aspirations of club officials.

JAVIER: Yes yes yes, Navarro would tell you "talk to Pereyra." There was no intimidation at Sojeros. It went like this: as a young player, you would be selected by the Academy at Sojeros or Ferroviario, and right from the start they would tell you "to play here you have to close a deal with Fusile or with Pereyra."

EP: What was the political benefit for Navarro, for example? Was it something that remained within the club? Was he looking for something beyond football, on a political level?

JAVIER: What football gave Navarro was impunity. Nothing gives you more impunity than being an official at a football club, so the club generated impunity for whatever he wanted to do outside the club.

EP: And why does football generate so much impunity?

JAVIER: Because of what we were saying before, the symbolic power that football represents. Grondona was never going to be touched, he could say anything but nobody touched him, why? Because he was football's main leader. It is a symbolic and cultural power; nobody messes with football.

The issue of symbolic power remains unclear to me. In the cases he described (e.g. players who have to reach a financial agreement with the *barras* to be able to play in the Academy), the power seems to be real and tangible, with clear, observable, and sometimes measurable consequences. I was left wondering what the "symbolic" component of this type of power is. In any case, he was very clear regarding the role of the judicial system in maintaining a culture of impunity.

EP: Beyond the symbolic power that it generates, if there is a supposedly independent judicial system that remains apolitical, what is it that prevents it from getting involved?

JAVIER: The judicial system is part of the same system.

Corruption in Argentina 87

EP: Right, sure, but what does the judicial system get out of this? What does a judge get out of not getting his hands dirty on the subject of football?

JAVIER: The judiciary in a capitalist system is a class-based judiciary that will always judge against the impoverished sectors and always in favour of the rich sectors. White-gloved criminals will never step on the courts; they will be summoned, but they will never be convicted, because the system works like that. Justice is an inverted fisherman's net, the big fish pass by and the small fish get caught. And that's the justice of the system. That's how it works in Argentina for the most part, unless someone stops supporting a certain official and he can be condemned.

A judicial system that generates impunity combined with a corrupt police force creates ideal environments for *barras* to conduct their operations. In line with the survey results presented at the beginning of this section, Dr. Mariano Bergés, former criminal judge and co-founder and president of the non-governmental organization Salvemos al Fútbol (SAF for short), believes that the police are extremely corrupt.

BERGÉS: There is a lot of corruption when it comes to the police, much more than people imagine... I believe that the police, basically because of their activity on the street, have a great chance of being contaminated. Much more than those of us who work in an office. I believe that the Argentinian police are corrupt, *very* corrupt! And, and, and, I am not one of those people who criticize the police authority on an ideological basis. On the contrary, I try not to do that, however, I have verified it on many occasions, and I keep verifying it. I have experienced it inside the Courts[16] and outside... I do not agree for example, when people bring up the famous argument that says "most police officers are good but there are some who are the, the, the, let's say the bad apples." I would say no; I would dare to say that it is the other way around. There are very few police officers who are not corrupt. It might be hard to admit it, but it is like that, it is a very ugly situation... But they (*the police*) are the ones who have to prove me wrong. In other words, it is very common for the police to ask for money (*i.e. bribes*). That is why we have drugs where we have them, that is why we have prostitution where we have them, and when it comes to football, the police are also corrupt.

On June 26, 2011, the case of a referee who received a death threat during the half-time of a game between River and Belgrano made national headlines. This case highlighted the ties between officials, *barras*, and the police. The game, played at River's stadium, was the second leg of the promotion playoffs.[17] Having lost by a score of 2-0 in the first leg, River needed a very good result at home. The first half ended with a score of River 1 – Belgrano 0. CCTV[18] footage revealed that, during the half-time, eight River *barras* were allowed to enter referee Sergio Pezzotta's dressing room.

88 Corruption in Argentina

According to Pezzotta, the *barras* told him that unless he awarded River a penalty kick in the second half, he would not get out of the stadium alive (La Nación 2011). The game ended in a 1–1 draw, relegating River to the second division for the first time in club history. The investigation following the halftime incident determined that there was a security camera pointing at the referee's dressing room door. However, at the time of the incident, the camera was pointing in the opposite direction (Olé 2011). It is important to note that the club's private security and the Federal Police were in charge of the CCTV equipment. The footage collected during the investigation showed that River's Head of Security communicated with an associate via two-way radio. This associate was later seen escorting the *barras* to Pezzotta's dressing room. Members of the police's Sporting Events division were seen talking with *barras* (idem). Although the police officers and security officers in charge of the CCTV cameras saw the *barras*' movements and interactions, they did not make arrests.

When I asked Leonardo, the police commissioner and Head of Security at Club Barrial,[19] about the security operations involving CCTV equipment, he explained that all cameras are thoroughly checked to confirm that everything is in order before a game.

EP: Are the cameras checked before a game, to make sure that they work?

LEONARDO: Yes! There is a direct link with the police department, apart from what you are seeing in the stadium. The police, the operating room can also take control of the cameras and see.

EP: So in cases where there is a camera that doesn't work and it's precisely the one that was supposed to capture some crime…

LEONARDO: Before the game starts, they make you file a report if a camera doesn't work.

EP: But it *has* happened, that a camera doesn't work. It happened, for example, at River.

LEONARDO: What happens is that the police have to be in collusion, because the system is managed by the police.

EP: Right, so… If there is a case like this, where the camera doesn't work… That's why I asked if they did a prior check. Because if they check things, and if it's known that they check things,

LEONARDO: They do.

EP: And still there is a malfunction or a camera that doesn't work, that tends to point to some previous contact with a *barra*, a police officer, or someone else.

LEONARDO: A preliminary report is written, stating that everything is in operation. Now, if later something broke down, or if there was a failure at a particular moment, doubts remain, but the checks are done. And the handling of the equipment is reserved, it's in a place… I tell you more, the entrance to the video surveillance room has a passcode. The door has a passcode, and only police personnel and the chief of the operation can enter, plus a maintenance man from the company that has the cameras installed. And those cameras record during the entire match... During the entire time that the stadium is open, they record, and on top of this, they have a link with the police department. The police department can see... There are four or five matches being played simultaneously, "I want to see River," and they ask to look at the cameras.

Although it is certainly possible for a camera to malfunction after a check has been conducted, it seems curious that spontaneous failures tend to affect *precisely* the cameras that could have recorded violent incidents where *barras* could have been identified. When it comes to preventing acts of violence, investments in technology and personnel will never suffice as long as the actors involved (politicians, club officials, *barras*, and the police) prioritize their interests. As Pezzotta's case shows, the corruptness of those in charge of monitoring suspicious activities and acting on them makes any technology inefficient. More often than not, security cameras are only as good as the interests and motivations of the people who control them.

In line with what happens in other spheres of politics and society, football perpetuates the cycle of corruption and impunity that has existed in Argentina since colonial times. In his book *Los árbitros del soborno* ("The Referees of Bribery"), former professional referee Humberto Rosales provides an impassioned account of the workings of a culture of impunity that lures people into becoming active participants in a system that perpetuates corruption. Rosales explains how, in spite of his initial reluctance to become involved in what he explicitly recognized as illegal activities, which included match fixing among others, he eventually succumbed to the temptations of a system that offered opportunities for financial gains through illegal deals without the fear of legal punishment. In an opening note, he says: "this book aims to alert the public about a phenomenon of social importance that I consider widespread: the bribery of football referees" (Rosales 2013:11; my translation). It is interesting to note that he emphasizes the *social* importance of this phenomenon, hinting at the fact that bribery among referees serves as one example of endemic corruption in Argentina. In his introductory chapter, he presents the reader with a "Decalogue," a set of ten rules that referees must adhere to if they are to become successful referees of bribery. The second rule states that the referee

must know his place. Who are the officials who control his league or association, which are the clubs with more and less power.... Remain aware of the political fluctuations of the environments. And not stop having contacts with the *barras*.

(Rosales 2013:19; my translation)

Here, Rosales explicitly mentions the ties that exist between football and politics, as well as the *barras'* participation in illegal deals and clientelist networks, activities that have little to do with their role as fervent supporters of a club during

90 Corruption in Argentina

match days. Crucially, Rosales describes his experiences as a referee in a provincial league. In other words, he did not officiate first division matches of the AFA's Liga Profesional de Fútbol (Professional Football League), which includes the country's biggest and most important clubs. In spite of this, a relatively small provincial league afforded him plenty of opportunities for illicit and profitable deals. He recounts how he was approached by officials of one of the provincial league's second division clubs, who offered him to act as a broker between them and the referees with the intention of fixing matches. In Rosales' words,

> they offered me a monthly payment and a fairly high figure if they were champions or promoted. By way of example, the figure per month was like a good salary for a bank employee, and the 'prize' for the championship, the same figure multiplied by ten.
>
> (2013:29; my translation)

It should come as no surprise that Rosales expresses remorse and regret for his actions. Still, it is thought-provoking to consider that Rosales is currently a criminal lawyer. At the time he was approached by the officials mentioned above, he was a student.

In this chapter, I have discussed the difficulties in arriving at a universal understanding of what constitutes corrupt behaviour. Legalistic interpretations as well as rigid moral categories do a poor job of accounting for the fluid, malleable, and context-dependent circumstances that shape people's actions and interactions. Thus, corruption must be interpreted not only in relation to particular legal systems, but also in relation to the social, cultural, moral, and economic specificities that inform people's lived experiences in particular contexts. As noted in a survey mentioned above, people between the ages of 17 and 35 identified the police and football clubs as the two most corrupt institutions in Argentina. On a similar note, the consensus among my interviewees is that Argentinian football clubs provide ample opportunities for engaging in corrupt behaviour. This is further confirmed by Rosales' experience as a referee in a provincial league. More importantly, the examples presented in this chapter revolve around local understandings and interpretations of what constitutes corrupt behaviour.

Considering Argentina's extensive history of corruption and impunity, it is perhaps unsurprising that a culture of impunity that fosters a "grab what you can" mentality continues to prosper. In the world of Argentinian football, corruption and clientelism are often inseparable. I now turn to an analysis of the practices that characterize clientelist relationships.

Notes

1 Pedro de Mendoza, a Spanish explorer and conquistador, founded a settlement in 1536 where the present-day city of Buenos Aires is located. This event is known as the first founding of Buenos Aires. The settlement was attacked by Indigenous populations

and abandoned in 1542. Juan de Garay, another Spanish explorer and conquistador, returned to the site in 1580 and established a permanent settlement.

2 By this time, Argentina had become an independent nation. The Declaration of Independence from Spain was signed in the city of San Miguel de Tucumán on July 9, 1816.

3 The 20th century.

4 Argentina won the World Cup after defeating Holland 3–1 in the final played at River Plate's Monumental stadium.

5 The *Grupos de Tarea* ("Death Squads") were clandestine paramilitary squads that fought against leftist guerrilla groups called *Montoneros*.

6 Club Atlético Chacarita Juniors is a third division football club located in the district of San Martín, in Greater Buenos Aires.

7 For a look at the ties between high-profile politicians and *barras* in cases of corruption and violence, see pages 115–117 of his book. For an in-depth historical look at political violence in Argentinian society, see Marcelo Larraquy's (2017) *Argentina. Un siglo de violencia política* ("Argentina. A Century of Political Violence").

8 Ferreteros is a fictional name.

9 In this context, "liberated zone" refers to the fact that legal authorities turned a blind eye when it came to investigating the AFA's finances.

10 Similarly, Rosales claims that Córdoba's Football League (a provincial league) "has been and will continue to be a rich father with very poor children called football clubs" (2013:175; my translation).

11 Oeste, Sojeros, and Ferroviario are fictional names.

12 Ferroviario and Sojeros are city rivals.

13 This was confirmed by Leonardo, another interviewee.

14 Pereyra was the leader of Sojeros' *barra*, while Fusile was the leader of Ferroviario's.

15 In Argentinian football, it is common for percentages of a player's transfer value to be owned by different actors. Thus, to name an example, a club might own 50% of a player's transfer, while an investment group might own 35% and the *barras* the remaining 15%.

16 Bergés co-authored a book with Adriana Galafassi in 2014, titled *Acá no pasa nada: La corrupción del sistema judicial argentino contada desde adentro* ("Nothing to see here: The corruption of the Argentinian judicial system told from within").

17 Belgrano was a second division team looking to be promoted to the first division, while River needed to win the series to avoid relegation.

18 CCTV stands for closed-circuit television.

19 Club Barrial is a fictional name.

Chapter 4

Anthropological perspectives on clientelism and politics in Argentina and beyond

Definitions

Roudakova describes clientelism as "a form of social and political organization where access to public resources is controlled by powerful 'patrons' and is delivered to less powerful 'clients' in exchange for deference and other forms of service" (2008:42). Alternatively, Gay defines it as "the distribution of resources (or promise of) by political office holders or political candidates in exchange for political support, primarily – although not exclusively – in the form of the vote" (in Auyero 2000:57).

Roudakova's anthropological analysis of clientelism introduces an interesting perspective that places culture at the heart of the mechanisms of exchange that characterize patron-client relations. In her view, clientelism is a cultural feature,

> a belief that formal, universalistic rules are less important than personal connections. The exact reverse is true in political science of clientelism's analytical opposite, rational-legal authority, defined as a form of socio-political order where access to public resources is transparent, impersonal and merit-based, where the notion of the public good is strong, and where adherence to formal, universalistic rules of procedure overrides particularistic interests and personal connections.
>
> (2008:42)

Her view of clientelism as a cultural feature can be applied to Argentina, where personal connections and interests are often seen as the most effective way of dealing with social and economic hardships (in the case of the poor), or increasing political support (in the case of politicians and public officials). Some clients choose to reciprocate as a result of the emotional bonds they form with brokers, in spite of the fact that they believe that they would still receive goods and services from brokers even if they would not attend political rallies or vote for them in municipal elections. Other clients, on the other hand, believe that the implicit rules of the game place them in a subordinate position.

DOI: 10.4324/9781003458937-4

As a form of exchange that is characterized by the unequal status of patrons, brokers, and clients, clientelism relies heavily on face-to-face interactions that have immediate and tangible implications for those involved in patron-client relationships. Although clientelism in Argentina has not always been confined to the Peronist *Justicialista*[1] Party, the spread of the *Unidades Básicas*, which, as has been mentioned earlier, are places where people can obtain goods and services directly from a local broker, has solidified its monopoly on patron-client relationships. Lemarchand and Legg (1972) believe that the greater the difference in social status between a patron or a broker and a client, the higher the level of affectivity entering into the relationship. This stems from the fact that, "pushed to its limit, equalization of status logically spells the dissolution of patron-client ties and their replacement by bargaining among equals, as individuals or as groups" (1972:152). Lemarchand and Legg emphasize the need to take into account the social and cultural specificities that inform patron-client relationships. They also claim that, in particular cases, clientelist models can sometimes promote economic and social development. This does not seem to be the case in Argentina, where ethnographic studies such as those conducted by Auyero (2001) show that clientelism functions simultaneously as a problem-solving network that allows the poor to deal with their most pressing needs and as a mechanism for social control that prevents them from coming out of poverty. In those cases where clientelism does generate economic and social development, its very success leads to its disappearance (Lemarchand & Legg 1972). In other words, if the poor in Argentina were to come out of poverty as a result of clientelist practices, the need to rely on patron-client relationships would be eliminated. This is not always in the best interest of patrons and brokers, who perpetuate clientelist practices in ways that minimize the impact of collective agency and impede social change.

Clientelism in Argentina: A brief background

When Argentina became independent from Spain in 1816, a type of clientelism emerged under the form of *caudillismo*. *Caudillismo* refers to a social system structured upon the interdependence between the head of a political faction, called *caudillo* (often a military leader) and his followers (Safford 1985). In the newly independent state, known at the time as Provincias Unidas del Río de la Plata (United Provinces of the Río de la Plata), the lack of a central power and formal rules, combined with the agrarian structure of a society made up of landlords who owned vast territories and the people working in their estates, contributed to the emergence of patron-client relationships (Lynch 1992). *Caudillos* would hand out money and favours to their followers as a reward for their faithful service (Wolf & Hansen 1967). Furthermore, Haigh (1964) describes another type of patron-client relationship in which the *caudillo* himself was the client of powerful patrons who "created and controlled" him for their own political and/or economic purposes.

After a long period of autonomous provincial governments, the construction of what would become the Argentinian Republic took place from 1860 to the controversially called "Conquest of the Desert"[2] in 1879–1880, which integrated the isolated southern region of Patagonia with the rest of the nation. During this period, there were no modern political parties but political clubs whose members represented mostly the landowning elite. Elections were usually held with electors voicing their votes under the intimidation of *compadritos* (henchmen hired by local political *caudillos*) (Eggers Brass 2006).

The period from 1880 to 1916 was characterized by governments composed of members of the oligarchy. Positions of power were determined in advance and routinely confirmed through electoral fraud to keep the newly founded Radical Party, which represented the lower classes, out of power. In the words of Lobato, "the *electoral machine* (control of the lists of voters and of the voting stations, as well as the use of various fraud mechanisms) guaranteed the election of official candidates and the political control of the elite" (2000:192; my translation; emphasis in original). Gallo describes this period as follows:

> recruitment in politics had to be carried out with an eye to the possibility that recruits would be involved in fighting at great risk to their lives. It was for this reason that strong bonds of loyalty had to be formed between the leaders and their followers. Those responsible for cementing these bonds were not the national leaders, but the *caudillos* (bosses) of the rural districts or the urban areas. Such people held a key position in the political mechanism, because they were the real link between the regime and its clientele. The loyalty of this clientele was not freely bestowed, but was based on a complex system of reciprocal favours. The political boss provided a series of services which ranged from the solution of communal problems to the less altruistic activity of protecting criminal acts. Between these two extremes, there were small personal favours, among which obtaining jobs was paramount.
>
> (1986:380)

The *caudillos* were men of varied origins (small landowners or merchants and, more often, former military officers of the disbanded provincial militias) and, even though at times they held minor political appointments as justices of the peace or deputies, to name two examples, they were usually content to exercise informal power within their regions.

In 1912, mandatory secret ballot elections were introduced by law. The electoral reform coincided with important changes in the make-up of Argentinian society due to a massive wave of European immigration, mostly from Italy and Spain, but also from France, Poland, Russia, Turkey, Germany, and Great Britain. The previously sparsely populated country experienced an unprecedented increase in the size of its urban populations, particularly in Buenos Aires, which served as the port of entry for ships arriving from Europe. The Radical Party, now reinforced by the sons of these immigrants, who had the opportunity to vote and to obtain positions within the government, won the elections and took power in 1916 (Romero 2004).

Through an extended net based on the organization of committees at the national and provincial levels, as well as within cities at the ward and precinct

Anthropological perspectives on clientelism and politics 95

levels, the Radicals established permanent ties between the leaders and the voters. As Rock explains,

> In the major cities, especially in Buenos Aires, a system of ward bosses emerged similar to that in the United States. Although the Sáenz Peña Law[3] ended the open purchase of votes, the Radicals quickly established a party patronage system which served equally as well to buy electoral support. In return for a biennial vote, the ward bosses, the *caudillos de barrio*,[4] performed numerous petty services in the city and rural neighbourhoods. By establishing this close link with the *caudillos de barrio*, the original nucleus of the Radical Party, the landowners, were able gradually to escape the consequences of their lack of direct contact with the urban environment. Although the landowners had no control over urban jobs, many of the middle class sub-leaders were able to acquire sufficient influence and prestige in their local areas to overcome this weakness. They had some control over the allocation of housing, for example, through their association with the owners of the tenement blocks. Their relative affluence allowed them to provide loans for needy businessmen. Their own positions as lawyers or physicians brought them into close contact with different groups of the new electorate. They were also known for having some contact with the local police, and this allowed them to dispense immunities for all sorts of petty transgressions against the law. Along with the parish priest, the ward boss became, particularly in the city of Buenos Aires, the most powerful figure in the neighbourhood and the pivotal figure upon which the political strength and popularity of Radicalism depended.
>
> (1975:56)

In 1930, a military coup overthrew the democratically elected Radical government. It was the first of several coups that would permeate Argentinian politics in the years to come. The period between 1930 and 1943 became known as the *Década infame* (Infamous Decade). The Conservative Party seized power by overt electoral fraud, popularly referred to as the "patriotic fraud." The period was marked by rampant corruption and scandalous deals (Galasso 2006; Pigna 2006). The Conservative Party developed a strong populist tone and used state resources to maintain power drawing on the tradition of clientelism (Macor 2001).

In 1943 the military took power once again. Colonel Juan Domingo Perón took several positions within the government that allowed him to establish the foundations for the formation of the future Peronist Party. During the preceding years, industrialization around the major cities (especially Buenos Aires) resulted in the migration of new workers from the provinces. As a result, Perón took control of the workers' unions, which would become the "spine" of the Peronist Party (Waldman 1986). Three years after the coup, Perón became a democratically elected president. During this period, in order to compete with the Radical committees, the Peronists established neighbourhood centres called *Unidades Básicas* (Basic Units). The emphasis at that time was to show that no clientelist relationships were to be encouraged, in opposition to the old Radical practices. While the government's political ties with the people were conveyed through the unions, the Basic Units flourished within the neighbourhoods in matters related to the recruitment of party members, distribution of pamphlets and posters, and the organization of electoral campaigns, sporting events, and political rallies.

In 1955, the so-called *Revolución Libertadora* (Liberating Revolution) deposed Perón. Argentinian politics alternated between military and civil governments until 1973. From 1973 to 1976 the Peronist Party briefly returned to power. Perón died while holding office in 1974; he was replaced by his widow, Isabel Martínez de Perón. As discussed earlier, in 1976 a military junta headed by Admiral Emilio Eduardo Massera, Lieutenant General Jorge Rafael Videla, and Brigadier-General Orlando Ramón Agosti seized control of the government. The dictatorship was marked by the "disappearance" of tens of thousands of civilians (Romero 2012).

After the fall of the dictatorship in 1983, the Peronist Basic Units were re-organized. Each Basic Unit became a cell within a clientelist system. In 1989, the Peronist Party returned to power under the leadership of the democratically elected President Carlos Saúl Menem. At this time, ties between the government and the people were mediated by political brokers (known as *punteros*) through clientelist networks of exchange and favours at the expense of the weakened unions (Levitsky 2005). This brand of clientelism, characterized by brokers who establish personal ties with members of the lower classes by operating out of their Basic Units, persists to this day.

In the following section, I consider the role of clientelism in ancient Rome as an example of clientelism's resilience throughout history as a type of problem-solving network that relies on both state resources and personal ones depending on the context.

Clientelism in ancient Rome

The passage cited below provides an informative account of clientelism in ancient Rome as well as in the town of Pompeii. This example from Rome and from a town that was buried in ashes and pumice nearly 2,000 years ago points to similarities across time:

> archaeologists have re-imagined how one characteristic Roman social ritual might have taken place in this Pompeian setting. That ritual is the early morning *salutatio*, at which 'clients' of all sorts would call on their rich patrons, to receive favours or cash in return for their votes, or for providing more symbolic services (escort duty, or simply applause) to enhance the patron's prestige. From Rome itself, we have plenty of complaints about this from the client's point of view in the poetry of Juvenal and Martial, who – as relatively well-heeled dependants – predictably enough made the most noise about the indignities they had to suffer in return for a modest handout. 'You promise me three *denarii*,'[5] moans Martial at one point, 'and tell me to be on

duty in your atria, dressed up in my toga. Then I'm supposed to stick by your side, walk in front of your chair, while you go visiting ten widows, plus or minus...' .... We are also in danger of over-simplifying the social dynamics of the relationships involved, whether in Rome or Pompeii. The anxieties and humiliations of those waiting to be admitted to the presence of their patron are one thing. We can all imagine what it must have been like waiting to put one's case to some bigwig who could choose whether to help you or not (with a job for your son, a loan, or a blind eye to the unpaid rent). There must have been anxieties on the other side too. For, in this world of status and show, patrons needed clients almost as much as clients needed patrons. Imagine the anxiety and humiliation on the other side, for a patron installed in his *tablinum*[6] waiting for clients – and not a single one shows up.

(Beard 2008:102–103)

It is thought-provoking to consider how little clientelist practices have changed over the course of 2,000 years. Certainly, the persistence of such practices points to an institution of patronage that is decidedly effective at maintaining and replicating itself. For the purposes of this book, the similarities between the Roman and Argentinian cases highlight the resiliency of patronage politics. The current relevance of Beard's example points to the prominent role of clientelism as a mechanism that relies on personal relationships in order to solve people's problems. It is easy to recognize and identify many of the features that characterized ancient Roman clientelism in present-day Argentinian society. Not only do Argentinian clients receive favours in the form of goods and services such as medicines, food, mattresses, and casual employment, but they also provide brokers and patrons with symbolic support by attending political rallies, a practice that finds a parallel in Beard's mention of applause as a common way of showing support for Roman patrons. The *tablinum* finds its modern Argentinian counterpart in the Basic Units. While it is safe to say that the Basic Units lack the luxury of the *tablinums*, they serve a similar purpose; they act as the local "headquarters" where clients can meet with their patrons (in the case of Rome) or, more probably, with their brokers (in the Argentinian case) in order to discuss their most pressing needs. In Argentina, it is not uncommon for a broker's house to double as a Basic Unit.

Given the often populist tone of clientelist discourse in modern times, it is easy to understand why the ties between brokers and clients tend to be defined by emotional friendships (Wolf 2001). Far from being seen as *"some bigwig who could choose whether to help you or not"* (Beard 2008:103; emphasis added), a broker might instead be seen as a benevolent, caring person who has a genuine interest in the well-being of their clients beyond their economic and/or political goals. While the role of emotional friendships in the ancient Roman context is not clear from Beard's description, it is nonetheless indisputable that patronage politics across time and space are characterized by dyadic and symbiotic relationships that create ties of interdependence. Still, to claim that brokers (or patrons) and

98 Anthropological perspectives on clientelism and politics

clients need each other *in equal measure* would be an exaggeration, but unlike the hypothetical scenario described by Beard, I would find it hard to imagine a situation where a present-day broker in Argentina would stress over a lack of clients.

Clientelism in anthropological studies

Many ethnographic and qualitative studies on clientelism (Auyero 1999, 2000; Golden 2003; Hallin & Papathanassopoulos 2002; Lopes 2007; Magazine 2004; Roudakova 2008; Sissener 2001) point to the importance of personal interactions between researchers and the people who are directly affected by the clientelist practices that are observed on a daily basis in specific contexts and at particular times. While detailed ethnographic accounts of clientelism do not abound, the available literature provides concepts that are potentially useful in thinking about the ways in which patrons, brokers, and clients relate to each other. Keeping this in mind, I will relate the terms described in this section to the Argentinian social and cultural context in an attempt to assess their suitability and applicability.

James' (2008) distinction between welfare and well-being is of interest in the context of clientelist relationships. She explains that

> 'Welfare' can only be imagined, and put into practice, in the context of a very clear social whole, where responsibility can be located for the ongoing lives of persons to whom some obligation is publicly acknowledged…. The provision of welfare is always recognisably a political matter, entailing the redistribution of resources between the 'parts' of a wider social world, on more or less consensual principles relating to need. On the other hand, 'well-being' as a concept is not geared to the needy…. 'Well-being' in this sense is difficult to regard as an obligation on the part of the wider society. A handy test is to ask how the benefits of welfare or well-being are actually funded; who pays? By and large, I think a crucial difference will be found between the public funding and the private purchase of these 'goods' or benefits.
>
> (69–70)

It could be argued that brokers offer clients goods and services that promote "well-being." The difference with welfare here is that goods and services are provided through personal interactions between the broker (*not* the state) and the recipients. Granted, brokers have access to state resources, but as Auyero (2000) points out, clients think of these resources as personal favours that are made available through the generosity of the broker, who is often – though not always – seen as having a personal interest in the "well-being" (as defined by James) of each of the individuals in any given community.

In a slight modification of James' argument, I would argue that clientelist practices offer well-being disguised as welfare. In other words, the concept of well-being *is* indeed geared to the needy, at least to the extent that clients pay for it with votes. Still, the ethnographic data provided by Auyero suggests that many clients conceptualize the transactions involved in terms of what James calls welfare because there is no explicit obligation to reciprocate. There are, of course, conflicting points of view regarding this matter.

An ethnographic approach to the exchanges that take place in different contexts is illuminating: "from the outside, what appears as an exchange of votes for favors is seen from the inside in many different (and, sometimes, antagonistic) ways: manipulation *versus* caring, interested action (politics, calculative exchange) *versus* disinterested actions (friendship)" (Auyero 1999:305; emphasis in original). From a microscopic perspective, it is important to note that "national contexts" are by no means the smallest divisible unit of analysis. Put differently, clientelism in Argentina in the context of the poor neighbourhoods examined by Auyero differs from clientelism in football. Auyero's clients represent a more vulnerable population compared to many of the organized fans who participate in agreements with club officials. These fans may or may not belong to the lower classes, and have a power of negotiation (often through collective action and intimidation) that Auyero's clients lack.

The role of friendship in clientelist relationships is also found in Wolf's (2001) work. He explains that "the primary bond in the friendship dyad is not forged in an ascribed situation; friendship is achieved" (2001:174) and distinguishes between two types of friendship

> I shall call the first expressive or emotional friendship; the second, instrumental friendship. From the point of view of the friendship dyad, emotional friendship involves a relation between an ego and an alter in which each satisfies some emotional need in his opposite number. This is the obviously psychological aspect of the relation. Yet the very fact that the relation satisfies a need of some kind in each participant should alert us also to the social characteristics of the relation involved.
>
> (2001:174–175)

Emotional friendships seem to play a prominent role in patronage politics. In Auyero's study, however, clients seem to exhibit feelings that combine aspects of emotional and instrumental friendship. It is hard to determine which type of friendship precedes the other, as the actors involved may experience and interpret their social environments in vastly different ways. Generally speaking, the evaluation of a broker's activities seems to be directly related to the degree of closeness in relationships between clients and brokers. Some parallels can be established with the organized groups of fans found in Argentinian football. Those who are closer to the *barras*' leaders (*la primera línea* or "the first line") have positive things to say about them, while "regular" fans (*hinchas*) will often see them as manipulative and corrupt.

Wolf (2001) believes that when the instrumental aspect surpasses the emotional aspect, the relationship runs the risk of disruption. While this might be the case in situations where socially and economically disadvantaged individuals have few opportunities for collective action, I would dispute his argument based on the often instrumental ties that pervade clientelist relations in Argentinian football, where club officials, organized fans, politicians, and the police exchange goods and services in spite of the often negative opinions they hold of each other. Wolf explains that once it reaches a point of imbalance, an instrumental friendship turns into a patron-client tie. This situation arises when one partner "is clearly superior to the other in his or her capacity to grant goods and services" (Wolf 2001:179). It is interesting to note that the exchanges observed in Argentinian football can be classified under clientelism in spite of the fact that the balance of power is fairly even. In this case, the groups involved establish relationships that allow them to negotiate.

In her article on patronage politics in postwar Italy, Golden (2003) borrows the term "bad government" from studies that had been previously conducted in the United States to account for high levels of corruption. Her interpretation differs from the political culture and the principal-agent arguments that have been developed in an attempt to throw light on the issue of clientelism and corruption in Italy. In her words,

> 'Bad government' provided reasons for members of parliament to offer voters compensatory constituency services. It also enhanced the partisan political loyalty of civil servants, who were typically appointed on a patronage basis, by providing them with extensive opportunities to engage in bureaucratic corruption. While the overall system that emerged was not itself planned, the interactions and behaviours that underpinned it were strategic and self-serving.
>
> (2003:189)

From a comparative perspective, the Argentinian case seems remarkably similar to the Italian case. Golden might be right in claiming that the political system that developed in Italy was not planned, but once established, politicians and public officials with personal interests seek to perpetuate it. In other words, the system that emerged was unintended and probably undesirable, but ironically, little is done to modify it. Perhaps the situation is not so ironic if we consider that those who have the power to modify the current system are the ones who have gained access to material and economic resources that place them in a position of dominance over large sections of the population. Culture here plays a big role.

In the case of Argentina, it does not make sense for politicians and public officials to conform to normative rules and laws for the welfare of the population, as this would mean giving up benefits that someone else would be ready to collect. As MacLachlan (2006) explains, Argentina's culture of impunity revolves around self-serving political careers. I agree with Golden in that the political culture and principal-agent arguments are unable to account for the establishment of patronage politics in Italy and, from a comparative perspective, in Argentina. The

Anthropological perspectives on clientelism and politics   101

political culture argument claims that "poor institutional performance is an out-growth of a weak civic culture and a low level of social capital" (Golden 2003:190). An analysis of collective organization within Argentinian football clubs reveals that poor institutional performance cannot be reduced to a weak civic culture. Clientelism in Argentinian football persists in spite of the fact that fans who become registered members of clubs become actively involved in the social, political, and cultural activities organized by the clubs. Given the fact that *barras* have access to club politics, it could be argued that in this particular case, a rather strong civic culture has facilitated the development of clientelist ties by providing opportunities for unregulated cooperation between different social actors. This is ironic to say the least, and I am not suggesting that a hermetically closed system where fan participation in the life of a club is suppressed would be a better alternative.

The principal-agent argument states that "bad public administration is a technical defect accountable to poor institutional design and/or inadequate political monitoring, which can be remedied by greater and better control by politicians of bureaucratic agents" (idem). As a manipulative strategy, clientelism succeeds in providing individuals with the basic goods and services that they need to make it through the day, but offers no real opportunities to come out of poverty, as it is not in the best interest of patrons and brokers to lose clients. Golden emphasizes the relations of domination that permeate clientelist practices in Italy:

> Citizens value both the collective benefits they receive from legislation and the individual benefits they collect through facilitation, or what in the Italian context is made manifest as patronage. Because the latter depends specifically on the retention of office on the part of the individual legislator, voters (and their extended families) who are recipients of patronage are effectively trapped into voting for the incumbent regardless of how they evaluate his party's performance nationally. Moreover, voters opposing the system cannot co-ordinate their actions effectively with those located in other electoral districts, and so are largely powerless.
>
> (2003:210)

Her analysis coincides with Auyero's (1999) ethnographic material, although Auyero explains that many clients do not think of the ties they share with their brokers in terms of domination and subordination.

One of Golden's main contributions to the study of clientelism is her emphasis on comparative approaches that take into account social and historical specificities. In her words: "I am interested in offering a new interpretation of ostensibly disparate, country-specific 'facts' and fitting them into a theoretically-grounded comparative framework" (2003:191). As a political scientist, Golden's focus on ethnographic data and microscopic studies of communities is understandably weak, but this is mostly a matter of disciplinary background.

In line with Roudakova's, Golden's, and Auyero's emphasis on specificities, Sissener's (2001) study on corruption provides ethnographic examples of the

102 Anthropological perspectives on clientelism and politics

ways in which clientelism operates in different cultural contexts. She begins by arguing that

> people's own assessments of courses of action do not arouse from a set of culturally universal, invariable norms that helps to decide if certain actions are to be classified as 'corrupt' or not. Rather, what is seen as corruption varies from one context to another. Given such variations, explorations of how the actors themselves evaluate social practices are required.
>
> (2001:1–2)

This is a decidedly anthropological approach to the assessment of different definitions of corruption, which in Western contexts tend to focus on illegality. The culturally and morally relativist approach adopted by Sissener stands in sharp contrast to positivistic approaches such as Lancaster and Montinola's (1997). Sissener seeks to understand definitions of corruption at the grassroots level by taking into account people's values, opinions, and experiences. Challenging the notion that corruption – including clientelist networks of exchange – is inherently "bad," Sissener argues that in some contexts corruption has positive effects because "it 'humanises' the workings of bureaucracy" (2001:4). This means that the informal and unofficial rules regarding the (re)distribution of goods and services adopted by particular actors are often better suited to local conditions than the official rules. This becomes apparent in the case of *blat*, a term used in Russia to define a set of informal relationships based on close personal contacts that allows people to gain access to goods and services by bypassing official rules. The following ethnographic account illustrates the workings of *blat*:

> My mother worked as head of a Soviet farm buttery. She could sell really good meat and at much cheaper prices, or other foodstuffs in short supply. For example, when there was a shortage of butter she could obtain some. Naturally, she had good connections, and worked hand in glove […] with shop assistants from the clothes store. My father worked in construction all his life, and construction materials were always in demand. When he retired and became a gas-supplier, he could offer a bigger gas cylinder in exchange for a small one. And city gasmen gave him more of the bigger cylinders because his wife would sell good meat to them. He also obtained fuel for his car by *blat*. He knew the tanker drivers and received an unlimited supply from them, normally for a bottle of vodka or 'moonshine'. He also paid, of course, but they did not offer this to everyone, only those whom they trusted. For him it was cheaper and free of queuing. Another example: a meat storekeeper in the village was a good acquaintance from long ago. Every year when she went on holiday she left him in charge. She trusted he was not going to cheat, whereas he was happy to help and to have this opportunity to buy meat for all his family. My father also helped my brother with dacha construction. You know how expensive it became. And he hardly spent any money. Contacts,

Anthropological perspectives on clientelism and politics 103

old contacts. They allocated him cut wood for free or for a few kopecks. And he gave them fresh eggs or dung.

(Ledeneva in Sissener 2001:16)

In the above example, Wolf's concepts of emotional friendship and instrumental friendship are clearly at play. *Blat* is not seen as a form of bribery because, according to Ledeneva, it involves a reciprocal exchange of favours between members of a close-knit group. Contrary to what happens in the poor Argentinian neighbourhoods where Auyero conducted fieldwork, *blat* does not revolve around unequal relationships where one person has considerably more wealth and leverage than the other. It could be said that *blat* works *against* the government to the extent that those involved in networks of exchange bypass official regulations without the knowledge or consent of public officials. In Argentina, the poor work *with* the government at the municipal level, meaning that the exchange of goods and services is "officially" (notice the irony) endorsed by politicians who rely on public resources obtained directly from the state.

In her discussion of gift giving in the Philippines, Co (2007) provides an example of a widespread and widely accepted cultural practice that is adopted, modified, and "perfected" by politicians to fit their interests and advance their careers. When combined with the political power to mobilize resources and influence voters, the respected and highly regarded practice of gift-giving becomes a tool for establishing clientelist networks that many see as a manifestation of corrupt behaviour, although some might think of them as social safety nets, depending on their personal circumstances. When it comes to academic research on corruption and clientelism, the (admittedly problematic) interpretive differences that emerge from observation and conversations are better able to provide clues about ways of thinking and experiencing corruption on a daily basis than the rigid, homogenizing, and purely legalistic explanations. In the Philippines, the culture of gift giving and reciprocity is molded by politicians and clients in ways that encourage the establishment of instrumental and emotional friendships. What is important to consider here is the variety of local specificities that give rise to clientelist practices in different social and cultural environments. While these specificities point to contextual differences, clientelism often manifests itself in remarkably similar ways across countries where it plays a prominent role in politics. Thus, even though Argentina does not have a culture of gift giving like the one described by Co (2007), the practice of clientelism – beyond the locally dependent factors that give rise to it – seems to be virtually indistinguishable from the brand of clientelism observed in the Philippines. The motivational similarities are certainly present. Co explains that

a widespread view among aspiring politicians and candidates is that public office is an employment from which money, cars, travel abroad, wealth, a privileged lifestyle and social mobility result.... Public office is therefore seen as an opportunity to reward one's self rather than as an apex of responsibility and public service.

(2007:129)

104   Anthropological perspectives on clientelism and politics

Indeed, her statement applies not only to the Argentinian brand of clientelism at the national, provincial, and municipal levels, but also to the opportunities that Argentinian football clubs provide club officials and *barras*. It is this constant dialogue between specificities and generalities that informs my analytical framework. When compared with the Argentinian case, the Philippine case serves as one example of the general features that characterize clientelist networks across space.

The Chinese term *guanxi* (meaning social relationships or social connections) can also be compared to Auyero's analysis of clientelist practices. More specifically, *guanxi* refers to the practice of gift giving. As in the case of *blat*, it involves close personal connections between friends, neighbours, coworkers, colleagues, and relatives. Gift giving in China creates the implicit obligation to reciprocate. This is similar to what Auyero has observed in Argentina. Yang claims that "the art of guanxi cannot be reduced to a modern western notion of corruption because the personalistic qualities of obligation, indebtedness, and reciprocity are just as important as transactions in material benefit" (in Sissener 2001:13). These qualities, however, are also present in Western contexts. Auyero's and Golden's accounts of patronage politics in Argentina and Italy show that, similar to what happens in China, personalistic, face-to-face interactions create ties of interdependence based on obligation, indebtedness, reciprocity, and even gratitude.

While the terms *bribery* and *corruption* have negative connotations in China (as in most other places), Yang explains that *guanxi* evokes positive images of people helping each other in a context where those involved in the practice of gift giving are either relatives or close acquaintances. In other words, the difference between *guanxi* and an act that would be considered corrupt is established in terms of the quality of the relationships. As Yang explains,

> there is a good side of guanxixue which bribery does not have. For example, if you and an official do not have a prior personal relationship already, such as shared native homes, kin relationship, and so on, and he is seen to help you, then other people will surmise that there is bribery going on between you.
>
> (idem)

This is not necessarily the case in Argentina, where a pre-existing bond between brokers and clients is not a prerequisite when it comes to exchanging favours, although both brokers and clients have an interest in developing and maintaining relationships that revolve around emotional ties to varying degrees. It is interesting to note that Yang's distinction between insiders and outsiders in networks of *guanxi* finds a parallel in what Auyero calls "inner circles"

> Brokers usually do favors such as distributing food and medicine for their potential voters and others. They are not alone in their work, however, because they almost always have an inner circle of followers. A broker is related to the members of his or her inner circle through strong ties of long-lasting friendship, parentage, or fictive kinship.
>
> (2000:64)

Anthropological perspectives on clientelism and politics 105

The differences and similarities between clientelism in Argentina, *blat*, and *guanxi* become apparent. Compared to what happens in Russia and China, Argentinian networks of exchange seem to be more flexible when it comes to accommodating people who do not have strong personal ties to brokers who are in a position to provide goods, jobs, and services. Being part of an inner circle, however, has its advantages. Auyero reveals the workings of an inner circle in the following ethnographic account of an exchange network in a city he calls Cóspito:

> Matilde[7] has a circle of men and women who visit her on a weekly basis. For example, forty-five-year-old Lucía used to be Matilde's cleaning lady. Two years ago, Lucía had a stroke, and Matilde (then the Secretaria de Acción Social[8] of Cóspito), obtained a pension of 110 dollars a month for her. Lucía now receives daily medicine for her high blood pressure from Matilde. She spends almost every afternoon at the neighborhood's Centro Cultural (where Matilde's son Paco serves as the president), in the front part of Matilde's house, a half-block from the UB.[9] There Lucía makes puppets that the Cultural Center sells or gives away on special occasions among the children of the slum. Adolfo (Matilde's husband and the Under-Secretary of Public Works) got Lucía's husband a job at the municipality. Lucía and her *comadre*[10] Antonia fashion puppets with a sewing machine belonging to the Plan País. Launched almost ten years ago, this state-funded program is intended "to strengthen community organization" in poor neighborhoods through the subsidized development of productive micro-enterprises. In Cóspito the brokers captured part of the funds of the program, thus acquiring an extra source for their inner circles. Matilde obtained one of the subsidies and organized a group of women to work with (and for) her at the Cultural Center. Lucía considers herself a friend of Matilde: "She always lends you a hand." Lucía has known Matilde since 1984 and is a *manzanera* (block delegate) of the state-funded Plan Vida. Matilde also provides her with food.
>
> (2000:64–65)

The emotional aspect of the types of relationships described above seems to be at least as important (if not more so) as the instrumental aspect. Still, not belonging to an inner circle does not prevent people from participating in networks of exchange, as relying on "problem-solving networks" (Auyero 2000) that do not require strong personal relationships does not carry the stigma that seems to pervade similar cases in China. Weak ties (Auyero 1999) are established whenever clients who belong to the outer circle seek help to deal with a particular problem or when they need a favour from a broker.

From a comparative perspective, a close look at different types of exchange networks highlights the relevance of in-depth, microscopic studies of specific social contexts through qualitative methods such as participant observation and semi-structured interviews. The ways in which people in different places conceptualize clientelism are of the utmost importance when it comes to thinking about possible solutions to issues related to corruption within and beyond networks of exchange. *Whose* definition of corruption are we talking about? How can researchers approach an issue that is not perceived as such by the people who are directly involved in everyday practices that they consider beneficial? In the conclusion to her article on corruption, Sissener states that

> the intention has not been to excuse illegal actions by providing an explanation by 'culture', but to show that the borderline for acceptable behaviour is not universal. Knowledge of people's own views and their discourses of corruption provided by anthropologists will bring to light possible discrepancies between official and practical norms and practices. Unless practices are seen as unacceptable to the practitioners, reformations may prove hard to implement.
>
> (2001:18)

In Argentina, the difficulties associated with the development of viable solutions to the issue of corruption are exacerbated by the fact that different actors have different views on what constitutes corrupt behaviour. While many of the people interviewed by Auyero see clientelism as a legitimate way of dealing with their most pressing needs, others see it as a corrupt mechanism aimed at maintaining power imbalances. On the one hand, patrons and brokers accumulate political and economic power while the poor are effectively prevented from coming out of poverty, but on the other hand, the poor often think (perhaps rightly so) that without "problem-solving networks," they would be worse off. The personalistic ties that pervade patronage politics create relationships where the poor are grateful for the help they receive from generous brokers. In many cases, clients provide brokers with political support without having a clear knowledge of the broker's party's political inclinations.

In Argentina, patronage politics are closely associated with populist governments. De la Torre offers various definitions of populism in relation to the Latin American context. The most relevant definition for the purposes of an analysis of clientelism describes populism as "a type of political party with middle or upper class leadership, strong popular base, nationalistic rhetoric, charismatic leadership, and lacking a precise ideology" (Angell in De la Torre 1992:386). Llach and Lagos define it as "the implementation of economic and social policies that, in the short term, improve the situation of vast sectors of the population – generally, but not always, low-income sectors – but that are unsustainable in the medium or long term" (2014:102; my translation). Angell's definition is particularly interesting in relation to Peronist political strategies. At the national level, Peronism, a decidedly populist political movement, fits Angell's definition well to the extent that the movement is variously associated with extreme left-wing and right-wing leanings, pointing to a lack of a clearly defined ideology. Peronists follow the figure of a leader rather than the ideology of a party. Similarly, clients follow charismatic brokers regardless of their political leanings. Still, contrary to what happens with charismatic national leaders, the personalistic ties that characterize clientelism

Anthropological perspectives on clientelism and politics   107

invariably provide clients with pragmatic (although always temporary) solutions to their problems. Clients can count on brokers to receive tangible benefits time after time.

A moral obligation to reciprocate permeates all types of exchanges discussed in this study. In spite of this, attention to local specificities sheds light on the different kinds of relationships that develop in particular contexts. As I have shown, networks of exchange in Italy, Russia, China, and Argentina have different requirements and goals. The types of actors involved also vary according to social and cultural evaluations that legitimate certain types of behaviours and condemn others. In China, for example, participation in *guanxi* is restricted to people who share strong ties based on friendship or kin. In Argentina, on the other hand, ties between brokers and clients can sometimes be quite loose, although belonging to inner or outer circles has implications in terms of the degree to which relationships are primarily emotional or instrumental. Unlike the Italian and Argentinian cases, *blat* and *guanxi* do not revolve around political goals. The purpose of the exchanges for those who participate in *blat* and *guanxi* is to obtain benefits through informal means in order to create better living conditions for themselves. This is also the case in Argentina, but mainly from the clients' point of view. Patrons and brokers have political goals in mind; thus, the clients' needs are never satisfied to the point where the patrons' or the brokers' help is no longer required.

Clientelism in football

The types of exchanges that characterize the ties between club officials and *barras* in Argentinian football differ from those observed in poor neighbourhoods. Following Auyero's description of interested action versus disinterested action, it is safe to say that the relationships between *barras* and officials are often based on interested action, although Moreira (2012) explains that these relationships are simultaneously defined by loyalty and emotional friendships. *Barras* receive free game tickets, plane tickets, buses, and food and beverage concessions, among other businesses, while club officials receive political support within and beyond the clubs in the form of votes and support at rallies, where the *barras* sometimes operate as henchmen who physically confront political rivals. In cases where club officials do not have political aspirations, entering agreements with the *barras* is a way of pacifying them. *Barras* often know where officials live, where their children go to school, where they park their cars, etc. Keeping them "satisfied" prevents officials from being threatened. Thus, the brand of clientelism observed in football often lacks the emotional component that is commonly found in other contexts. To borrow Wolf's term, clientelism in football is characterized by instrumental friendships, although in some cases, it might be more accurate to talk about instrumental *relationships*, as the "friendship" component is often missing.

In a decidedly defensive attempt to distance himself from any kind of association with the types of relationships that exist between different actors within football clubs, Hugo, the former leader of Ferreteros' *barra brava*, provided an

108 Anthropological perspectives on clientelism and politics

example of patronage by hinting at the fact that *barras* rely on the support of club officials to travel.

HUGO: I still want to make it clear to you that, I have been away for many years from… What happens is that, that, the core of, of, of this social circle is always the same. Heads change, interests change, violence changes, but the way people travel, um, how they go to the stadium… We used to travel by bus to other countries, now fans[11] travel by plane…

EP: And how is that financed?

HUGO: (*Long pause*) I wouldn't want to know.

EP: Ah, well, right…

HUGO: I suppose they do raffles, they give them jerseys, umm, they might have help from some sector… From politics, from labour unions.

Given his past as the leader of a *barra*, his answer could well mean that he *does* know how trips are financed, but would prefer to forget. In any case, his reference to politics indicates that *barras* are functional to the interests of political parties. This was further reinforced by Antonio, the former president of one of Argentina's most important clubs.[12] During our conversation, I made the grave mistake of mentioning an example that spoke poorly of the political party that Antonio sympathized with (as I later found out). My reason for mentioning this example had nothing to do with my personal political leanings and preferences. It was not meant as an attack on a particular party. Rather, I mentioned the first politician that came to my mind due to his widely publicized association with *barras*. When Antonio mentioned that other politicians and parties were also involved in agreements with *barras*, it did not matter that I sincerely and repeatedly agreed with him. Still, his comments were informative.

EP: In cases where it is known that there are strong ties between *barras* and officials, like the case of Quilmes,[13] for example, with Aníbal Fernández,[14] um, could it be that the officials don't want to have ties but are in a complicated position?

ANTONIO: I assure you they don't want to have ties.[15]

EP: So where does the pressure come from?

ANTONIO: You talk about Aníbal, let's see…

EP: Just to name a random example.

ANTONIO: But I don't know. It's your statement, not mine. Aníbal Fernández is a senator who is also the president of Quilmes as well as the president of the Argentinian Hockey Confederation. Now, if it turns out that he uses all of that to do politics, I can't say. What's strange is the emphasis on Aníbal Fernández, because Macri[16] also has people working with him; the Radicals[17] must have them too. In other words, it's not about one political party. So, when you emphasize, emphasize everyone, otherwise it's complicated… Unions, political parties, everyone. There

	isn't a single one of them that doesn't have ties with the guys from the *barras bravas*.
EP:	But is that because of the *barras'* pressure in the form of threats or...
Antonio:	Nooo, I don't know, I don't think so. Some of them (*the officials*) must even have friendly relations (*with the* barras)... Otherwise the *barras* would hit them during the week. They (*the* barras) go look for them at their workplaces and hit them.

Ironically, my mistake proved fruitful, as Antonio went out of his way to make clear that *all* political parties – as well as some unions – have ties with the *barras*. Interestingly enough, he did not categorically deny that the party he sympathizes with was involved with *barras*; instead, the emphasis was on the fact that all the other parties were involved *as well*. As MacLachlan (2006) explains, stating that everyone else is doing the same is an effective way of overriding guilt. More importantly, Antonio explained – rather ambiguously – that it is probable that many club officials and politicians maintain friendly relations with *barras*, meaning that they are not intimidated or threatened when it comes to making deals. This would point to ties that are at least partially based on emotional friendships, although I suspect that what he meant by friendly can be more accurately described as polite. If not intimidated or threatened, what interests could club officials and politicians have in establishing and maintaining friendly/polite relationships with *barras* who are known to resort to violence when their demands are not met? Considering that Antonio also mentioned that *barras* would not hesitate to go after those who do not comply with their demands, it is easy to imagine that many of the supposedly friendly ties are based on fear.

As a member of Los Troncos,[18] Miguel, the lawyer who represented a *barra*, believes that although some club officials negotiate with the *barras* out of fear and necessity, others actively seek to establish instrumental relationships with them in an attempt to solidify their position within the clubs through exchange networks that guarantee political support. In his view, the brand of clientelism observed in football is an extension of the clientelist practices observed elsewhere in Argentina.

EP:	You have the officials who believe that they are incapable of containing the problem of the *barras*, who think that they are incapable of fighting this problem, ummm, they say they need the state's involvement...
Miguel:	(*Interrupting*) You have two types of officials: The one who wants to fight against the *barras* (*long pause*), but is aware that the system does not accompany him. You have the one who is an associate of the *barra* and uses the *barra* as it happened at Newell's Old Boys,[19] for example. In many clubs, when the elections approach, you have to get the votes, and if you manage the *barra*, you get the votes.
EP:	Right.

MIGUEL:	I saw, for example, when Juan Pérez defeated Carlos García[20] to become the president of Los Troncos. Juan Pérez had the support of a union; the *barra* supported Carlos García.
EP:	And what do the *barras* get out of their involvement?
MIGUEL:	(*With a tone of obviousness*) Money.
EP:	In the form, for example, of…
MIGUEL:	It's like what happens with the political brokers. You take me to the election as a candidate; when I have the power I pay for your bus, I pay for your trip, I pay for your plane, I pay for your hotel, I give you 200 match tickets so that you can sell them…
EP:	How is clientelism a part of football and how does it transcend the world of football?
MIGUEL:	(*With a tone of obviousness*) It's the same thing.
EP:	Sure.
MIGUEL:	It's the same thing. *Barras bravas* are a part of politics.[21]
EP:	Sure, but there is the issue of a type of clientelism that is, in certain cases, somewhat forced. By forced, I mean that the *barras* sometimes threaten the officials, and the officials are in a situation where they say "well, we have to collaborate with something," and then there may be officials who willingly get involved with *barras*. It's not something that, let's say… Well, "I have no other choice, I do it because they threaten me" but rather, they do it because they have a personal interest.
MIGUEL:	Because they use the *barra*. In other words, there is a sector of a club's leadership that looks to the side and does not get involved, but gives something to the *barra* to avoid getting hurt, and then there are officials who say, "I'm going to gain control of the club through the *barra*." For example, at an assembly of representatives… I saw it at Los Troncos; they had stolen even the tap water. There were a lot of members in attendance with different cultural levels, to complain (*about an incident of theft inside the club*). The *barra* showed up, the assembly ended in two minutes, they approved everything. I… Hold on, I'm a member of Los Troncos, I love Los Troncos, I go to the assembly… Now, on top of everything I go so that they beat the shit out of me and a *barra* kills me? Nooo, I'm getting the fuck out of there, I'm going home dude.
EP:	Sure, of course.
MIGUEL:	I'm going home. That makes normal people step aside, because you have to talk to those characters, huh?

The power of negotiation that the *barras* exercise through intimidation and violence contrasts with the emotional and instrumental friendships described by Auyero (2000) and Wolf (2001). In football, it is the *barras* who often set the tone and determine the content of the exchanges, as will become apparent in the next chapter. Furthermore, as Miguel's example shows, the presence of *barras* during meetings and assemblies weakens the democratic process within clubs by preventing members from openly expressing their views for fear of retaliation.

When discussing how stadiums are used as venues for political propaganda, Hugo provided an example of the ways in which clientelist practices are manifested at football matches.

EP: You watch a game on TV and you see banners with political propaganda hanging from the terraces, and they don't always do that for free.

HUGO: Let me tell you, I haven't been around for many years, but everything has monetary value. Either monetary, or... "I'm going to do you a favour, so you have to do me one." "*Clarín* lies,"[22] a banner on both River's and Boca's terraces, with the same font, the same measurements...

EP: And where does that banner come from?

HUGO: It's not very difficult... (*pause*) with normal reasoning, to know where it comes from. I don't have to be the one to tell you where it comes from.

Hugo's comment points to the Front for Victory party supplying the banner to River's and Boca's *barras*, presumably in exchange for certain economic benefits. When it comes to doing politics, parties do not discriminate on the basis of a club's social and historical foundations. In this case, both Boca and River – Argentina's two biggest clubs by far and bitter rivals – were used as stages for political protest/propaganda. Similarly, where money and other benefits are involved, *barras* do not hesitate to form alliances with parties, independently of their own political inclinations.

Much like corruption, clientelism escapes easy definitions that present objective truths about the features and practices that characterize it. As the example of ancient Rome illustrates, clientelism's resilience and persistence as a form of problem-solving network points to the importance of face-to-face, dyadic relationships in the absence of formal state interventions. In Argentina, clientelist networks have been a ubiquitous part of political life since the early 19th century. The present-day brand of clientelism is often based on emotional ties through which clients feel a moral obligation to return the favours they receive from brokers. Emotional ties are an important component in networks of exchange, as evidenced by the role of *blat* in Russia, *guanxi* in China, and gift-giving in the Philippines. Still, it is important to remember that not all networks of exchange revolve around political goals. Thus, taking into account the political nature of the kinds of exchange that can be observed in Argentina, clientelism represents a type of problem-solving network that often combines emotional ties with interested action. The world of Argentinian football, however, deviates from the types of relationships that inform the interactions between brokers and clients in poor neighbourhoods. Further reinforcing the idea that clientelism must be understood in relation to local circumstances and specificities is the fact that football clubs serve as examples of contexts where instrumental ties are often the norm. Through these ties, *barras* receive economic benefits in exchange for political support within and beyond the clubs.

The topics examined in Chapters 3 and 4 lead to a consideration of the role of morality in Argentinian football and the ways in which it informs interactions between various actors, particularly in cases where these interactions contribute to the perpetuation of violence and corruption.

Notes

1 The name *Justicialista* is derived from the term "social justice" (*justicia social* in Spanish).
2 The so-called "desert" was, in fact, inhabited by Indigenous populations.
3 The Sáenz Peña Law is the law that introduced mandatory secret ballot elections.
4 Neighbourhood *caudillos*.
5 Plural form of *denarius*, a Roman unit of currency.
6 In the words of Beard, *tablinum* is "the name given to the relatively large room often found.... between atrium and peristyle – and used, we guess, by the master of the house" (2008:101).
7 A powerful local broker.
8 Secretary of Social Action.
9 UB stands for *Unidad Básica* (Basic Unit). UBs are neighbourhood committees ran by brokers. They provide basic goods (food, medicines, etc.) and services to the local community.
10 Literally "co-mother." The term here is used in place of "godmother."
11 Although he used the word *fans*, he was in fact talking about *barras*.
12 At the time of our interview, Antonio was planning on running for president once again.
13 Quilmes Atlético Club is a club that plays in the second division.
14 A well-known politician who held several positions, including Minister of Production, Minister of the Interior, Minister of Justice and Human Rights, General Secretary of the Presidency, and Chief of the Cabinet of Ministers. Former president of Quilmes Atlético Club.
15 This is debatable, as the case of Marcelo Mallo, discussed in the next chapter, shows.
16 At the time of the interview, Mauricio Macri was the Chief of Government of the Autonomous City of Buenos Aires.
17 "Radicals" refers to members of the *Unión Cívica Radical* (UCR) or Radical Civic Union, a centrist political party.
18 Los Troncos is the fictional name I have assigned to the club Miguel is a member of.
19 Club Atlético Newell's Old Boys is a first division club from the city of Rosario. Miguel's example refers to the relationship between Eduardo López, former president of Newell's, and Roberto "Pimpi" Camino, former leader of the club's *barra*, murdered in 2010.
20 Juan Pérez and Carlos García are pseudonyms.
21 Recall Duke and Crolley's (2001) description of Argentinian football as an extension of politics.
22 *Clarín* is one of Argentina's two most important national newspapers. It was critical of both the president of Argentina, Cristina Fernández de Kirchner, and her political party (Front for Victory). Front for Victory supporters often claimed that *Clarín* published lies about the president and the party; thus, the phrase "*Clarín* lies" became popular among the president's supporters. As Hugo mentioned, it was not uncommon at the time of the interview to see banners during football matches with the inscription "*Clarín* lies," pointing to one of the ways in which football is used for political purposes.

Chapter 5

Morality in Argentinian football

Moral relativism

I approached my analysis of people's behaviours from the perspective of moral relativism. As a result, I do not believe that ways of thinking about corruption and violence are based on objective and scientifically identifiable moral facts. Instead, I acknowledge the social, cultural, and psychological conditions that inform people's actions. Although it is possible to act according to a set of moral values that is knowable and makes sense in a particular context, the universality of morality remains epistemologically and ontologically unattainable. In other words, I claim that moral values do not exist as scientific facts independently of culture and society. In what he calls the fully developed argument of moral relativism, the philosopher Cook states:

> If we had acquired our moral views in the way we acquire scientific views, namely, by means of a rational fact-finding procedure, then we could criticize other cultures wherever their morality differs from ours.... But we do *not* acquire our moral views by discovering objective moral facts. (This becomes obvious when we realize that moral principles differ from culture to culture, for this state of affairs would not exist if there were a realm of objective moral facts *everyone* can discern – as everyone can discern that the sky is blue.) Moral principles are acquired, not by any *rational* process, but by the *causal* process of "enculturative conditioning," that is, they are impressed upon us in subtle ways by the culture in which we are raised.
>
> (1999:11; emphasis in original)

Eberhardt (2014), an anthropologist, offers a somewhat different view on morality. In her study, she combines a Durkheimian notion of morality whereby society acts as the ultimate source of moral authority with Piaget's interpretation of morality as a set of values that is developed through personal interactions and freely adopted by individuals as opposed to one that is imposed by society. As a developmental psychologist, Piaget's focus on his study of children's moral development was not concerned with what children did; rather, he was interested in how children

DOI: 10.4324/9781003458937-5

thought about what they did. In line with Durkheim and Cook, Piaget believed that, during the first stage of moral development, young children acquired moral values through exposure to particular social and cultural environments. During the second stage (which could be observed in older children), however, children's behaviours were characterized by an increasing tendency

> to accept as legitimate only those rules formed by the mutual consent of the parties involved. In this more advanced stage, children are much more likely to take into account the circumstances of the action and the intention of the actor when they are asked to make a moral judgment. These two stages constitute two very different perspectives on moral problems. Piaget found that the younger children he interviewed tended to reason according to the premises of the first stage, while those 10 and older tended to reason with the premises of the second stage.
>
> (Eberhardt 2014:304)

Piaget went on to explain that the transition from one stage to the other was mostly the result of the social relationships that children develop over time. Eberhardt proposes a hybrid understanding of morality that fuses the prominent role of culture and society as sources of moral values with the personal, microscopic, and situationally determined interactions between individuals.

For the purposes of a discussion of morality in the context of corruption, clientelism, and violence in Argentinian football, Piaget's second stage of moral development provides a useful lens through which to analyze the interactions between club officials, politicians, and *barras*. These interactions seem to be informed by a sort of internal moral code that is, at times, confined to specific environments, circumstances, and situations. While conversing with me (an outsider), Antonio, Hugo, and Miguel answered some of my questions in a tone that was at least partially defensive, indicating an awareness of the moral character/status of their actions.

Moral issues and dilemmas

In a conversation I had with Bergés, he described a typical game day experience at the gates of the *Bombonera*,[1] Boca Juniors' stadium. His account highlights the arbitrary nature of police searches and reveals the often amicable ties that the police maintain with the *barras* outside the stadiums. The neatly orchestrated cooperation between *barras* and the police at the turnstiles is particularly ironic considering that both groups tend to engage in physical confrontations with each other inside the stadiums. This fluid love/hate relationship is contextually adaptive, responding to different motivations at particular times. Thus, economic interests coupled with some degree of familiarity between police officers and *barras* based on frequent interactions might help to maintain friendly or, at the very least, respectful encounters, while the *barras'* displays of physical and

Morality in Argentinian football 115

verbal aggression before, during, and after a game are meant to convey a message of dominance as well as of physical and mental endurance and fortitude in the form of *aguante*. It is important to keep in mind that the general public's sense of injustice when it comes to the ways in which *barras* and paying fans are treated during police searches is heightened by blatant displays of what could easily be interpreted as collusion between *barras* and the police. Bergés eloquently expressed his frustration with the ways security operations are conducted by pointing to morally questionable practices that remain unpunished.

BERGÉS: I would arrive at the stadium, and... I would go with personnel from court, very few. For example, I remember that at that moment we had two secretaries who were young women, 30-something, I don't know. So, I would go (to the gates) and at a given moment the police officer who was there with his security operation – Boca was playing against... I don't know, it doesn't matter... Against Rafaela just to say something – would tell me: "ok, the fans are going to come in now," I don't know, and I would tell him as if I were a person who came from, from, from Algeria, so in other words I don't have the faintest idea what's going on, I would tell him "but listen to me officer," I tell him, "you are the one in charge of the operation, do what you want, I'm minding my own business, I'm observing what's happening," I tell him "but over there is the lineup that was formed by all those who brought their tickets in hand," cramped, hot, five people within one metre, all cra... "And these guys are just arriving and will enter the stadium walking, with their drums..." I don't know, "what, what do you think about it?" I ask him, "what's the deal? Why don't they line up like everyone else?" The officer looked at me as if I were crazy. But he looked at me like this (*eyes wide open*), he told me, "but doctor, this is not how it works," he said. "Well, *you* tell me that this is not how it works," I tell him, "officer, *you* tell me that this is not how it works," I said. I would tell him that delicately and with respect, right? "A person is supposed to enter the stadium with a ticket," I tell him, "where are these people's tickets? Do they all have their tickets?" "Well, some do, some don't," he tells me. So? I ask him, "can they go in with the flags?" "Well, some flags are allowed, others aren't," he says. "Are you going to control them? And the drums, do you check them, do you *not* check them? People who are drunk can enter anyway?," I ask him, "because those who are drunk in *that* lineup (*the one without 'privileges'*) are stopped and sent back home!" He says, "nooo, but this can't be done any other way." Ok, so I told him, "let's do the following: I have to take care of other things," I told him, "they are going to stay at the gate; the secretaries are going to stay," I tell him, "the secretaries are going to stay here." They were public officials! "The doctors will stay here." "Nooo, they can't stay here!" he says. "What do you mean they can't stay?," I tell him.

> They are going to stay here because I say so. They are going to stay here precisely to do this (*keep an eye on the security operation*), and besides, since you are a police officer, you have to protect them!

It is interesting to note that according to the police officer, things "can't be done any other way." To hear this statement from the officer in charge of the security operation – in other words, from a state representative tasked with ensuring the safety of the spectators – raises some questions regarding the possibility of implementing measures aimed at creating safe and secure environments for all spectators. Why is it that things cannot be done any other way? Do the police and the clubs not have the resources to properly monitor the stadiums' access points? Do they fear the consequences of not satisfying the demands of the *barras*?

Hugo offers an alternative interpretation on the way in which police searches are conducted.

HUGO: The search is the responsibility of the Federal Police.

EP: Right. And what I'm going to say is not something that *I* say, but complaints that one hears from the fans, right? They say that regular fans are searched from head to toe while other fans go in beforehand…

HUGO: (*With a tone of voice that indicates that the comments are not true*) They all go through the same search. What happens is that, let's see, I ask you this question: You are a police officer, your section (*of the stadium*) receives 4,000 people, how do you manage to search 500 people?

EP: Right, it seems complicated.

HUGO: With the first 30 people you are going to do a good job, but the rest? It's a deeper, more serious problem. The one who searches you earns 6,000, 7,000, 8,000 pesos. Why would I keep searching fans?

Hugo's explanation presents some contradictions. It is hard to believe his claim that all fans go through the same search when he immediately proceeds to invalidate it by saying that police officers are not motivated to do their job because they have to deal with too many fans and their salaries are too low. Ironically, the question he poses at the end of the interview excerpt lends some credibility to fans who complain about *barras* having benefits, including "express entry." Curiously enough, even if one were to agree with the claim that the officers' inefficiency is the result of their working conditions, it is the regular fans who are consistently searched. It seems like a striking coincidence that officers would almost exclusively get tired and frustrated when it is the *barras*' turn to get searched. What happens when *barras* arrive at the stadium *before* other fans? It does not seem plausible that officers would start their shifts in a state of exhaustion, letting the *barras* go through the turnstiles without searching them or asking to see their tickets, only to become energized later when it is time for all other fans to go through security. Bergés' conversation with the police officer in charge of the security operation at the Boca game he attended further belies Hugo's statements. The experiences of

Morality in Argentinian football 117

four research participants I interviewed, who would enter football stadiums for free, provide some justification for the fans' anger and frustration. In any case, Hugo proceeded to explain that all fans are treated poorly by the police.

HUGO: First you have to give the local and visiting fans good access to the stadiums, umm, I can guarantee you that the fans' entrance to the stadium, *any* stadium, is inhumane… It's inhumane. They look like animals, and are treated like animals.
EP: By whom?
HUGO: By the competent authorities.
EP: That would include officials? Police officers…?
HUGO: No… Police officers.

Although his comments indicate that *all* fans are treated like animals, it is only the *barras* (and accompanying "guests") who often get to enter the stadiums for free without being searched, without being asked for tickets, and without being asked to show identification.

The fans' frustration regarding security operations on match days has been expressed in newspaper articles on numerous occasions. One reader wrote,

THEY ASK ME TO SHOW IDENTIFICATION TO ENTER THE STADIUM AND THEN YOU SEE HOW GUYS LIKE DI ZEO[2] ENTER BOCA'S STADIUM AND I LAUGH MY ASS OFF. IT'S SHAMEFUL, ALWAYS BOTHERING THE GUY WHO PAYS HIS FEES AND GOES TO A MATCH, WHILE THE VIOLENT FANS WHO HAVE CRIMINAL RECORDS AND HANDLE ALL THE BUSINESSES ARE ALLOWED TO ENTER FREELY.

(Clarín 2016; my translation; all caps in original)

In an article titled "Everyone with the National Identification Card," published on the website of Argentina's most popular newspaper dedicated to sports, a reader commented: "Everyone with the National Identification Card; that is, fools like me who are members in good standing or bought a ticket. The darkies from the *barras* get in kicking turnstiles; the 'insecurity' committee fully involved" (Olé 2017; my translation). Another reader, commenting on the same article, added: "HA!! HA!! What a good joke, that comment about having to show identification to be able to enter the stadium. The *barras* get in and that's that. Who is going to ask them to identify themselves? Please…" (idem). Herrera (2018) further points to the preferential treatment that *barras* receive as a result of their privileged status within the clubs. Even though *barras* receive free tickets from club officials, these tickets are often scalped. Taking into account that ticket scalping is one of the *barras*' main businesses, and considering the *barras*' power of negotiation through intimidation, it is not surprising that they are granted access to the stadiums for free. This is one way to avoid confrontations with the police at the gates,

118   Morality in Argentinian football

and might partially explain why the head of the security operation who talked
with Bergés stated that things cannot be done any other way. Herrera explains
that, at San Lorenzo,

> the east goal stands are reserved for club members only, but the core
> fans – known as La Gloriosa Butteler[3] – had scalped the tickets they had
> received from the club, confident that they would enter the stadium anyway,
> given their connections with local authorities.
>
> (2018:470)

In this climate of impunity and complicity, *barras* are able to impose conditions
and gain almost unrestricted access to their clubs' stadiums. The freedom to roam
freely around the stadiums, a consequence of the clientelist ties they maintain
with club officials, affords the *barras* the opportunity to perpetuate acts of violence and aggression through displays of *aguante* and hypermasculinity, manifestations of passion as a form of war, offensive chants, and economic disputes
involving opposing factions of a *barra*.

Many club officials claim that they have no option but to tolerate the *barras*.
In other words, they are forced to negotiate and "collaborate" with them because
they are powerless to expel them from their clubs. Although this might certainly
be true in many cases, it would be misleading to categorize club officials as victims
and *barras* as opportunistic thugs. Officials often have an active interest in maintaining cordial relationships with the *barras*, as it is through these relationships
that they are able to pursue their political goals. It is ironic, then, that many
officials who publicly identify the existence of *barras* as a problem rely on *barras*
for political support at rallies and protests as well as for votes during municipal,
provincial, and/or national elections. As Leonardo, the police commissioner and
Head of Security at Club Barrial explains, there are many high-profile political
figures who have ties with *barras* and football clubs, a fact that highlights the
prominent place of football in Argentinian politics.

EP: Based on what you told me, there are many officials who make deals
           with the *barra* because if they don't, the *barras* won't leave them
           alone. There is *that* on the one hand.
LEONARDO: Yes.
EP: On the other hand, there are also some officials who have personal
           interests, right? For political reasons, right?
LEONARDO: Right! Correct, there's also that! And if you start conducting a study
           now, an analysis of all the clubs, you will see how many clubs have pol-
           iticians in their presidencies. They are renowned, umm, well-known
           people. The president of Lanús[4] is a candidate who is running for
           mayor now, mayor of Lanús. Moyano[5] is the president of Independi-
           ente, Meiszner[6] is the president of Quilmes, ehhh…
EP: Massa[7] in Tigre.[8]

LEONARDO:	Massa who was, until he became mayor (*of the city of Tigre*), president of Tigre.
EP:	Up to what point can a president have decision-making power… That's why I say that that will depend on each club, but for example I've been told by a former Atlanta official that at Atlanta there was this *barra* who would go to meetings of the board of directors with a gun; he would place the gun on the table and say, "ok, I would like this or that."
LEONARDO:	That's the kind of intimidation I was telling you about. People who come to a club in good faith, who want to do something, know that these guys will break their car.

Raúl Gámez, former president of Club Atlético Vélez Sarsfield,[9] and Javier Cantero, former president of Independiente, are examples of officials who tried to eradicate the *barras* from their clubs. They did not succeed. Cantero's case received considerable media attention due to his outspoken nature and open confrontations with the club's *barra brava*, led by Pablo "*Bebote*" ("Big Baby") Álvarez, one of Argentina's most infamous *barras*. Without external support from legal authorities, Cantero was ultimately cornered and forced to resign.

Gámez, who was president of Vélez on three occasions, was also the leader of Vélez's *barra brava*, known as La Pandilla ("The Gang"), in the 1980s. As was the case with Hugo at Ferreteros, having a prominent role in the *barra brava* gave "*Pistola*"[10] Gámez political leverage. Thus, it is not only officials who are able to pursue political careers as a result of their connections with *barras*. The reciprocal nature of these connections also allows *barras* to move up the social and political ladder. Ironically, however, Gámez has stated that club officials made many mistakes that allowed the *barras* to prosper. He said: "we were unable to stop them and the matter got out of hand" (Beer 2015; my translation). His comment is morally ambiguous, as it is likely that his role as leader of the club's *barra brava* allowed him to eventually become president. It is also likely that many of the voters who supported him during club elections were friends and acquaintances from La Pandilla. When it comes to justifying their dual roles as former leaders of *barras bravas* and club officials, Hugo and Gámez explain that, at the time when they were leaders of their respective *barras bravas*, acts of physical violence were confined to fist fights; there were no knives or firearms involved. Furthermore, there were no economic interests at play; confrontations took place between rivaling *barras* over displays of masculinity, strength, and endurance. In essence, the explanation is meant to minimize the impact of their actions by rendering them morally justifiable within their historical context. Having said that, Gámez mentioned that, during his presidencies, he had to reach agreements with the *barras*, as it was the only way to avoid conflicts within the club. In an interview published by the newspaper *La Nación*, he stated that he had admitted to Bergés, the judge who investigated him, that he gave the *barras* tickets and buses. Thus, although he recognized that officials had made mistakes by granting the *barras* some privileges, he nevertheless proceeded to negotiate with them in unequal terms that were beneficial for the *barras*, "pacifying" them while simultaneously allowing them to solidify their status within the club.

Perhaps more interesting is the fact that in a country where impunity is palpable and expected, people often feel free to reveal details about questionable practices in public without the fear of legal consequences. At times, the liberties that public figures take when disclosing morally questionable details borders on naïveté. When it comes to club officials, *barras*, and the police, their ties have become naturalized to the point where their exchange of "favours" is seen as a normal aspect of running a club and not as something that merits the attention of legal authorities, even in cases where these favours are responsible for acts of violence. Still, the fact that these ties are considered normal (in the sense that they are not well-kept secrets that the general public is unaware of) does not mean that they are widely accepted or celebrated; rather, they are tolerated.

From a moral perspective, Cantero and Gámez exemplify different ways of dealing with the impossibility of eradicating *barras* from their clubs. Although Cantero was unable to expel them, his resignation signaled that he was unwilling to contribute to their cause. Gámez, on the other hand, stated that the *barras* were a problem, but given his inability to distance himself from La Pandilla, he ended up becoming functional to the *barras'* demands, thus helping to perpetuate the very same practices that he publicly condemned. The argument in this case would be that if he did not negotiate with the *barras* to keep them satisfied and avoid conflicts, someone else would. Therefore, the fact that *another* president would likely find themselves in a position of having to reach questionable and, at times, illegal agreements with the *barras*, renders *his* own actions morally justifiable.

Gastón Gámez (Raúl Gámez's son) was also a member of La Pandilla. In his words, "my old man was an idol to many kids who are now with the fans"[11] (Perfil 2015; my translation). Although I do not have access to specific details regarding Gastón's circumstances, it would be interesting to know if the period in which he was a member of La Pandilla coincided with one or more of his father's presidencies.

Leonardo described the ambiguous relationships that officials maintain with *barras* by emphasizing the *barras'* dual role as enforcers who act on behalf of officials and as thugs who threaten officials when things do not go their way.

EP: Taking into account what you said, that some players are intimidated by the *barras* who are sent by the officials, what is the interest of the officials in cases like that?

LEONARDO: When there is a money conflict, and players want to go on strike, or don't want to play, or don't want to train,

EP: An official sends the *barras*.

LEONARDO: He sends them to threaten or intimidate them.

EP: And what do they (*the officials*) get?

LEONARDO:	Nothing, just that the *barras* are there to support them. And sometimes when the team is not doing well, they also go and intimidate them. The *barras* operate within the clubs. They have their tickets, and what happens? If you don't give them those tickets or don't give them those perks they have (*long pause*), you can't be a club official. Why? Because in our case, for example, we are a neighbourhood club, they (*the* barras) all live within ten blocks of the club. So they are guys who know where your grandchildren go to school, where you, your mom, your dad live, they scratch your cars, they provoke you. Why? Most of them are club members, do you understand? Most are members, now whether they pay the membership fees or not, we don't know.

Leonardo's comments beg the question: Why do some people decide to become club officials when the positions are not paid and they know in advance that they will have to deal with the *barras* and get into illegal businesses/agreements? From what perspective can officials justify their decision?

EP:	The officials must know who these people (*the* barras) are.
LEONARDO:	Of course. No no, not just the officials. The police know it; the Ministry of Security knows it; they all know them. The players know them, everyone. But nobody dares to fight them. That's why Mr. Mateo[12] took photos of himself and defied the authorities. Most of the cases related to the right of admission don't have a previous pending case; these cases are opened because they target certain characters... Very few of those cases have pending legal matters.

According to Hugo, Argentina's moral and economic decadence contributed to a social environment in which the culture of work has been lost. When asked about the place of *barras* within the clubs, he distanced himself from any kind of association with "contemporary" *barras*, although his answers indicate that he knew more than he was willing to share.

HUGO:	We are in a country where, I don't know how it happened, but decadence took hold, at almost every level.
EP:	Decadence in the moral sense?
HUGO:	Moral, economic... It used to be that those who did not work were frowned upon. Um, people like my father were raised with a culture of work.
EP:	Are there perhaps fans, fans of any kind, who take some advantage of clubs? Fans who could be said to be trying to make a living from the clubs nowadays?
HUGO:	It's what we have... It's what we have, but I don't know this, because I'm on the outside. Don't forget that I haven't been an official for almost ten years, and it's been ten years since... since I've been to the terraces.

122 Morality in Argentinian football

EP: And as an official did you see cases like that?

HUGO: I… um, at my level no… And because I understand the situation I was not interested in knowing. Um… There are times when the less you know, the better, but… no, it wasn't an issue that, that, that, that wouldn't let me sleep. I, I didn't, didn't have a… Because I'm a hard-working person, see? I would finish my workday and would go to the club that I love to dedicate my time to it, which caused many problems with my domestic partner and my job… When I ended my tenure, my shop was almost bankrupt because I had neglected it for four years.

Admitting that he "understood the situation" and as a result "was not interested in knowing" what went on inside the club was almost akin to saying that he knew well what went on.

When I asked Miguel about the reasons that encouraged police officers to become involved with *barras*, his answer was in line with Hugo's comments on Argentina's moral and economic decadence as well as with MacLachlan's (2006) description of a culture of impunity where "anything goes."

EP: Why the need for the police to get into these collusive relationships? Is it an economic matter? Is it partly because they have low salaries, or is it because, um… I'm also interested in how much of it is social, how much is cultural, and how much comes from somewhere else.

MIGUEL: If you ask me for a personal opinion, I think it is a cultural matter. That is, Argentina, and especially in the big cities, especially in Buenos Aires and its suburbs… and the same thing is happening in other big cities such as Córdoba, Rosario, and Mendoza… There is a cultural degradation. Certain values were lost. I believe the 70s were the last normal years; after that, people adopted an "anything goes" mentality, and… The state disappeared, the state is a bad payer, the state is a bad employer, the state is… corrupt, and that causes the police to go into business too.

EP: How do you get to the point where "anything goes"?

MIGUEL: The issue of football and the *barras bravas* is the issue of a society that has gradually been losing its moral values. During the crisis of 1929 (which came partly from Europe but particularly from the United States), Argentina had an economic problem, but public hospitals worked, the public education system worked, public security worked. Now, on the other hand, there is an economic problem *plus* a cultural problem. I'm going to give you an example: This is like a family, the father loses his job, he gets home and says, "I lost my job"; he has a good wife, he has two children who understand him. They (*the children*) start studying at night, they each look for a job, the man and his wife start doing odd jobs, and sooner or later that family will recover. Now, if the father loses his job and drinks every day, if the wife is a prostitute and the children are drug addicts, they have a ton of problems. *This* is Argentina. So, you have an economic problem, and that economic problem turned into a social problem.

Hinchadas Unidas Argentinas: The "stigmatization" of *barras*

Argentinian scholars and journalists (Alabarces 2005; Castillo 2011; Grabia 2009a; Moreira 2013; Moreira et al. 2023) have highlighted the opportunities for political and economic advancement provided by football clubs. In *Todo Pasa*, sports journalist Hernán Castillo describes the founding of a non-governmental organization called Hinchadas Unidas Argentinas (United Argentinian Fandoms or HUA). HUA congregated members from various *barras bravas*; its goal was to become the national team's official *barra*. The idea of an NGO that represents fans who have criminal records should be enough to raise concerns, but its existence becomes even more bizarre when taking into account that the mastermind behind this project was Marcelo Mallo, a *barra*/politician with strong ties to the Front for Victory, a centre-left political party. Mallo explained that the idea behind the NGO was to reinsert the leaders of the *barras bravas* into society (Castillo 2011). In a rather imprudent comment, however, he highlighted one of the ways in which football and politics are intertwined by unwittingly providing an example of clientelism during an interview with a news agency.

> I want to turn the *barras bravas* into a political group that provides Peronism[13] with votes and auditors. The fans of Chacarita come from 21 shantytowns; if they become social leaders and work in the neighbourhoods, tomorrow they will be tools that the government will have at its disposal. Here you have votes. Are we approaching internal elections and I need auditors? I ask the guys: how many will you bring me?
>
> (Castillo 2011:216; my translation)

In line with Mallo's statements, Duke and Crolley emphasize football's potential for clientelist practices beyond the clubs at the municipal, provincial, and national levels:

> It is the political role of the fans which has been distinctive in Argentine *fútbol*. The fans have been voters not only in elections for club officials, which.... have been themselves partly political, but also in local, regional and national elections. Therefore, ambitious politicians needed to cultivate a solid fan base of support. The more militant fans (*militantes*) participated in more than committed support for the team and the club; they also undertook political work on behalf of a politician who might be the club *presidente*, a candidate for club *presidente* or one of the club *dirigentes*. This direct relationship between politicians and fan groups was to reach its apotheosis.... in the form of the *barras bravas*.
>
> (2001:104)

Figure 5.1 An advertisement promoting the candidacy of Mariano Cúneo Libarona for president of Racing Club. Photo by author.

In a similar vein, Moreira highlights the political opportunities available to successful club officials beyond football:

> Having a successful tenure in an elite club has an impact on the construction of the positive image of club officials who wish to try their luck in other spaces of power. Club officials who are successful in the world of football can transform their fame and prestige into useful resources to participate in alternative spaces. It is common for club officials with successful careers to be summoned as (municipal, provincial, or national) State officials, or as candidates for political parties.
>
> (2013:67; my translation)

When I mentioned HUA's plan to reinsert *barras* into society to Hugo, he pointed out that it is not possible to reintegrate them because they were never social misfits.

EP: Within those groups (*barras*), some have criminal records, not all, but some do. Hambo's[14] perspective is to reintegrate them into society.

Hugo: If you reintegrate them it's because they are outside (*of society*), and I don't think they are outside! Do you understand what I'm saying? The *barra*'s profile, from what I see on TV, umm, the interviews they have... They are no longer the "darkies"[15] who drank a demijohn of red wine... They are businessmen. Don't think that they are only uneducated, poor people, there's a bit of everything. I believe that the leaders are no vagabonds, no illiterates, eh? There may be some, but society has progressed.

Although I would not go as far as saying that most *barras* are formally trained businessmen, I do agree with Hugo's comment regarding the fact that *barras* are not outside of society. The media often refer to *barras* as social misfits, but in practice, *barras* are perfectly adapted to a social, cultural, and political environment that rewards their role within football clubs.

Débora Hambo supported the creation of HUA as a way to combat the stigma associated with being a *barra*. HUA was promoted as the official supporters group of Argentina's national football team. This meant that *barras* who joined the NGO would get the benefit to follow the national team everywhere, all expenses paid. According to Hambo,

> generally, *barras bravas* are made up of people who have a marginal life, and do not have much chance or hope of getting out of that marginality; so, this plan allowed them not to be marginal for a little while.
>
> (Vázquez & Cayón 2014:206; my translation)

Here, Hambo rejects the *barras'* "stigma" by romanticizing their socioeconomic situation. It would be easy (simplistic, to be more precise) to accuse someone who raises concerns about an NGO dedicated to sponsoring *barras* of being reactionary. The problem with Hambo's argument is that it does not seem to take into account that the marginality of the *barras* (in cases where they *do* come from marginalized populations) is *one* kind of marginality. It would certainly be misguided to stigmatize vulnerable populations on the basis of their poverty, but at the same time, it would be inaccurate to assume that *barras* are representative of a universal form of marginality. Some of the *barras'* distinctive features include the use of violence, intimidation, and extortion. In fact, their identities revolve around displays of physical and mental fortitude that are often expressed through acts of physical violence. It is not uncommon for some of them to carry firearms. Taking this into account, it does not seem unreasonable to question the wisdom of sponsoring their trips in support of Argentina's national team.

Hambo was asked: Why would fans who always found a way of life in violence and confrontation suddenly stop being violent? She said: "Because violence does not pay, it is pointless to be violent" (Vázquez & Cayón 2014:207; my translation). There are two problems with her answer. On the one hand, as many of my interviewees have explained, violence in football *does* pay, *literally*. On the other hand, the academic literature on *barras* shows that being violent is far from pointless for the actors involved as confrontations act as rituals that reinforce feelings of belonging and notions of identity, expressed through (sometimes symbolic) displays of *aguante* and masculinity (see, for example, Aragón 2007).

126 Morality in Argentinian football

Beyond Hambo's characterization of HUA as an NGO that strived to reintegrate *barras* into society (it is unclear how sending *barras* to international matches would have accomplished this), Mallo's plans for them, which included turning them into brokers with the intention of recruiting party followers, pointed to relationships that revolved around interested action (Auyero 1999). The NGO was dissolved in 2014 by its members.

Moral inconsistencies

Some of the conversations I had with my interviewees revealed inconsistencies between what was said and what was done. Keeping in mind Piaget's interpretation of morality as a partially fluid set of values that change and adapt to different contexts, interactions, and circumstances at a microscopic level, it is interesting to note how interviewees responded to morally sensitive issues that they had experienced firsthand.

Antonio openly admitted that he had had ties with the *barras* during his presidency at Sporting Potrero.[16] Much like Gámez, he said that he would like to eradicate *barras* from his club, but lamented the fact that he had "no choice" but to collaborate with them (two possible choices would be to not become an official or to resign).

EP: Many club officials say that they don't have the tools or the ability to eradicate violence and that they need help from the state, while the state says that the matter is mainly the responsibility of the clubs...

ANTONIO: It's very... Let's say that everyone is right. The club official is right and the state is right. When they ask me how problems are solved, we say the state solves them, but we are all the state. We can't look sideways when we have to look straight ahead. I don't think that there are any officials in Argentina who want to have ties with the *barras*; I doubt it. But in all honesty the *barras* exist; the officials who say that they don't know them lie, because we all know those guys because we spent years at the club and these guys grew up doing this[17] within the club under different leaders, so those who say that they don't know them, lie. I know them, we are part of that, that, that history. In one way or another, um, you collaborate, let's say, with buses, with silly things that should not exist, but it is also no less true that the *barras* have ties with the police. This is a well-known fact. Put differently, today the *barras bravas* fight over businesses. They don't fight over a team's flag like they used to; now it's all about money.

Antonio mentions "silly things" (buses provided by the club to the *barras* to help them reach their destination at no cost seem to fall under this category) in what sounds like an attempt to minimize the moral responsibility of club officials in perpetuating practices that encourage and validate the actions of the *barras*. The defensive tone employed by Antonio becomes even more evident when he mentions the ties that the police have with the *barras*. If the *police* negotiate or "collaborate" with *barras* – not that they *have* to – how can club officials be reasonably expected to remain oblivious to the *barras'* demands? This is yet another example of the ways in which people's feelings of guilt over morally questionable practices are minimized or erased. As long as others are doing the same, no individual in particular should be accused of engaging in these practices.

On the one hand, Antonio mentions that no club official wants to have ties with the *barras*; on the other hand, anyone who wants to become a club official in Argentina knows that they will have to have ties with *barras* if they hope to have a successful or, at the very least, moderately peaceful tenure. From a moral perspective, the dilemma is whether it is preferable and more desirable to become an official knowing beforehand that concessions will have to be made to the *barras*, or to not become an official at all. It is important to note that since clubs in Argentina are non-profit civil associations, managerial positions are *ad honorem*, meaning that there is no financial incentive to consider when assessing the pros and cons of joining a club. Some, however, might take into account the political potential of clubs in their decision to "put up" with the *barras*.[18] Needless to say, there are well-intentioned officials who seek to sever all ties with the *barras* in what they see as a noble – albeit romantic, I would argue – cause to eradicate violence from the stadiums. Their efforts, however, are generally short-lived. More often than not, they are either forced to negotiate ("collaborate," if one were to borrow Antonio's term) with the *barras*, or to resign from their positions, as was the case with Javier Cantero.

Miguel, who had previously talked to me about Argentina's cultural degradation and loss of moral values, described in detail a legal case in which he represented Mateo.[19] Although he did in fact defend Mateo, he initially downplayed this seemingly uncomfortable detail in a series of contradictory sentences.

MIGUEL: I have a particular case... I, umm, defended... I did not *defend* him, it just happened to me by coincidence, Mateo appeared here. Mateo had a problem regarding his right of admission at Los Troncos. He came to see me through a lawyer friend of mine, he shows up here, ummm, and I give him legal protection. To me... It's a little similar to what you do... You see, he caught my attention because I wanted to meet the character.[20] Apart from that, since I know Los Troncos, it hurts, I know the officials at Los Troncos, so I say, "let's see how all of this works." I'm going to tell you what Los Troncos' problem is today. Anyway, I provide him with legal protection, I prepared a good case... I was very lucky, because in the Province of Buenos Aires the case is drawn before any judge. In other words, you may get a family judge, a labour judge, a criminal judge; I got a criminal judge, which is important because in front of a character like Mateo, a criminal judge has more balls, more presence to stand his ground. He is more used to these things. A family judge or a labour judge hears about a *barrabrava* and they get defensive. Mateo is a character, a character, intelligent, not cultured but intelligent. Um, if you look at him, he's worth nothing. 60 kilos, skinny... Never mess with him. He's respectful, and loves Los Troncos very much. He speaks of Los Troncos as if Los Troncos were his. For example, he could not enter the stadium, he entered anyway, I think, but he put together what is called "the circus," the flags, the party... He said to me "Doctor, did you like the party that I put together the other day?" Well, normally the kind of case I presented dies; it's dismissed from the start. There is an oral hearing that is done within the procedure of the Province of Buenos Aires where Mateo has to come. In that hearing you present your case and the other party replies. Mateo had to come. I assure you that he showed up well-dressed; if you would see him in any fancy restaurant in Buenos Aires you would think he's an executive. Shaved, combed, wearing a fashionable outfit, impeccable, not tacky, his shoes... He was a yuppie. The judge was speechless, he wanted to meet him separately.[21] The judge turned out to be the son of a federal judge who was my partner. Well, what's the reality? Mateo's legal protection against the right of admission should have been granted, because the right of admission was poorly applied. The judge rejected it, but in the last point of his speech, point 3, he complains about Los Troncos for all the bad things that Los Troncos does, and now I tell you why. Because this guy (*Mateo*) has been hung for two years, and since they don't know what to do about him, they do nothing, and apply the wrongly applied right of admission. What happens is that that judge, I understand him, he's a 40-year-old boy, he didn't dare to approve the legal protection, do you know why? I know the father, because I assure you that I was *this* close to winning the case... Because the father told him, "if you sign in favour of the protection, and the next day something happens at Los Troncos' stadium, your career is over." Because you then get the request for impeachment, so you have to take care of yourself.

EP: In what sense, as you say, was the right of admission misapplied?

MIGUEL: Because the facts on which it is based are false. It is based on an alleged deprivation of liberty that Los Troncos' president himself says did not occur.

EP: In other words, that would mean not letting a person like Mateo, for example, enter the stadium.

MIGUEL: Right.

EP: How did they (*the club officials at Los Troncos*) manage to misapply the right of admission?

MIGUEL: Well, because it's used for political purposes. It's not legal; you use the rule to settle your internal problems. So, since you (*talking about Los Troncos' president*) came to fight against the corruption of the previous board of directors, you do politics by screwing Mateo. You don't care about whether he is guilty or not guilty. No, you sign anything. Ultimately, you are as corrupt as the one who left. But you use what you can to do politics. Before the media, you appear as the one fighting against violence... That's why the reality of D'Onofrio[22] seems to me much more honest, because D'Onofrio knows that he has The Drunkards of the Terrace[23] (*inside the club*)... Los Troncos' president was a fool, a pusillanimous man; nobody knew him and when he began to appear in newspapers he thought he was Gardel.[24]

Mateo's case is an interesting one from a moral perspective. Apart from what Miguel told me, I have no knowledge of the circumstances under which the right of admission was applied to deny Mateo access to Los Troncos' stadium. It could be that Miguel was right in saying that the club had no legal justification for applying it *in this particular case*. Having said that, Mateo had legal precedents, including prison sentences, and a long history of involvement in criminal cases.[25] Miguel's moral justification for defending him (he made it sound as if he had no choice but to defend him because Mateo "appeared in his office by coincidence") is based on the particular details of the case, rather than on his history of criminal activities. Still, at one point during our conversation in which we were talking about impunity, Miguel implicitly acknowledged Mateo's problematic criminal history by saying, "not only does impunity exist, it's growing more and more! Imagine the extent to which it's growing, considering that Mateo wants to become president of Los Troncos." This is an interesting comment, as it indicates that Miguel considers the possibility of Mateo becoming president of Los Troncos an example of impunity. This, in turn, means that he is aware of Mateo's criminal background (which makes sense considering that he is a criminal lawyer who represented him). In spite of this, he was very vocal in his defence of Mateo during the legal case regarding his right of admission at Los Troncos. Coming from someone who claimed to be extremely familiar with the issues afflicting Argentinian football, his comment is thought-provoking. On the one hand, it is important to look at the specificities of the case, but on the other, it makes sense to take Mateo's criminal record into account in relation to his intentions at Los Troncos.

To be clear, the main point here is not about Mateo's right of admission. Rather, this example highlights the moral inconsistencies in Miguel's assessment of Mateo's situation and status. As a member of the legal system, the admiration he expressed for Mateo as well as his insistence that Mateo be allowed to enter Los Troncos' stadium in spite of the fact that he considers his desire to run for club president an example of impunity is problematic. This is particularly relevant since, as I will discuss in the concluding chapter, some interviewees consider the legal system to be slow and ineffective, describing it as a revolving door that allows people who commit criminal acts – including *barras* – to resume their activities without fear of long-term legal consequences. Indeed, one might reasonably wonder if *barras* benefit from lawyers such as Miguel, who represent them to make sure that they continue to enjoy guaranteed access to the stadiums, from where they can establish relationships with officials which allow them to participate in acts of violence and aggression motivated by passion, *aguante*, a sense of belonging, and economic interests.

The rival is the enemy: Passion and morality

There is a tendency among the most fervent football fans in Argentina to equate "rival" with "enemy." Media sources, on the other hand, insist on romanticizing sports as activities that have an innate ability to promote the values of friendship, tolerance, cooperation, and teamwork. An example of this can be seen in feel-good promotional materials for global events such as the summer and winter Olympics, and the FIFA World Cup. Nadia Fernández, a provincial legislator in the province of Córdoba, stated that

> football exists to promote the values of honesty, courage, brotherhood, tolerance and peace in a society. Football integrates and welcomes people; it does not exclude, persecute or discriminate against anyone. Therefore, we must all work together to make it a peaceful celebration of life again.
>
> (2014; my translation)

In direct opposition to Fernández's assessment, Burstyn states that "the problem – if the myriad difficulties of modern sport can be connected in one phrase – is that sport…divides people in ways that are often destructive and antisocial. Sport divides people against themselves" (1999:27). While different analyses of the social role of sport present valid arguments regarding the positive and negative aspects of participation in sports (whether as an athlete or as a fan/spectator), I argue that a more balanced view of the possible effects of sports on people's attitudes and behaviours is necessary. The examples mentioned above conceptualize football as an entity that possesses certain values independently of the actors that bring football to life. My argument, from a morally relativist perspective, is that team sports do not *inherently* promote noble values, nor do they inevitably cause violent confrontations. Rather, the varying ways in which team sports express particular values and sentiments are determined by the actors involved. Still, given the confrontational nature of contact team sports such as football, it is hard to imagine that they are better equipped to promote peaceful interactions between rival athletes and spectators than they are to encourage animosities. The objective, after all, is to *defeat* the rivals. In order to achieve this, teams must strive to be *better* than their opponents. Moreover, teams represent a neighbourhood's, city's, province's, or country's honour. In this regard, team sports thrive in the "Othering" of rivals. It is in contrast to the rivals that teams' identities are forged. In other words, differences matter. *We* are what *they* are not. In this context, there is a thin line between rival and enemy. In his analysis of the early history of football in Argentina, Frydenberg states:

> Rivalry quickly turned into enmity. Participation in tournaments and leagues implied being part of a shared space, where everyone competed against everyone. This interest in positioning oneself within the totality of the competitive world was carried out through the defence of small, group, and neighbourhood spaces. Football practice was thus becoming a vehicle for the recognition of one's own spaces and that of others, the latter being perceived as threatening. In short, being a member of the football environment meant participating in that symbolic universe governed by rivalry-enmity.
>
> (2011:79; my translation)

Sergio, founder of the NGO Hecho Club Social, emphasizes the importance of the "Other" in football:

> Football's folklore is fine with me, what seems stupid to me is the irrationality that there cannot be one person wearing a Boca jersey, and another one wearing a River jersey, and a San Lorenzo fan, and an Independiente fan, watching a game together, or walking down the street together, as it should be, and I say, we can make fun of each other and that's great, but afterwards, coexistence is... Football, without the "Other" does not exist.

The example of a Boca fan who went out for a run wearing Boca's jersey in the vicinity of River's stadium resonates with Sergio's comment. The fan was beaten by a River fan (Perfil 2019). After the incident, a police officer asked the Boca fan to take off his jersey to avoid further problems.

The conceptualization of the rival as the enemy is not confined to fans. In the city of Rosario, one of Newell's Old Boys' Academy players gave a motivational speech inside the club's tunnel before coming out onto the field, where the Academy team was about to play a game against the Academy team of city rivals Rosario Central. Since this was not a game between both clubs' first teams, there were no fans in attendance. This means that there were no fans to impress. During his speech, the player said,

> Today is the game, the game of our lives and the game we all want to play. It's Central, dude! You have to step on Central's head! You have to leave them lying on the floor, we cannot fall! You have to kill Central! It's the rival we all hate! A fan of Central walks down the street, they[26] come across a fan of Newell's and they want to kill each other! We have to kill them! Let's stop messing around, let's kick their asses!
>
> (La Capital 2017; my translation)

Taking into account the role of a variety of actors in the creation of sports-based friendly and hostile environments, I argue that sports are neither a unifying force nor a divisive one. They are what participants make of them, and what they make of them will vary significantly according to their life histories and local contexts.

132 Morality in Argentinian football

Put differently, there are no inherent qualities in sport that make it a force for positive or negative social change; rather, sports have the potential for both, and the direction they take is indivisible from their sociocultural contexts. In Argentina, fans of professional football often encourage and promote an image of the rival as the enemy. This creates hostile and, at times, violent environments at football matches. Furthermore, football's propensity to encourage animosity on the field spills over to the fans, who in some instances feel compelled to make clear that their team is the best in the neighbourhood, city, province, country, continent, world, or at the very least, that the fan base they belong to is the best/most passionate/most supportive.

In this chapter, I have examined the ways in which a variety of actors within the world of football make sense of the moral contradictions, inconsistencies, and dilemmas that emerge from their role and participation in certain practices. From a morally relativist perspective, their choices and actions shed light on the social and cultural mechanisms that contribute to the perpetuation of a system of organized chaos through which corruption, impunity, and violence thrive.

Taking this into account, what exactly would change have to look like in the context of Argentinian football for it to be feasible and effective? Given the difficulties in finding a local solution, there have been attempts at importing measures that have been applied in European countries such as England and the Netherlands. Within these European contexts, these measures have been relatively successful in reducing football-related acts of violence.

Notes

1 *Bombonera*, the nickname given to Boca's stadium, means bonbon box. The official name of the stadium is Alberto J. Armando, in honour of one of the club's former presidents.
2 Rafael Di Zeo is one of the leaders of Boca's *barra brava*.
3 La Gloriosa Butteler is the name of San Lorenzo's *barra brava*.
4 Club Atlético Lanús is a first division club from the city of Lanús, in southern Greater Buenos Aires.
5 Apart from being the president of Independiente (one of Argentina's big five clubs), Hugo Moyano is one of the Argentinian Football Association's three vice presidents. He was also the leader of the Truckers Union and secretary general of the General Confederation of Labour. In 2008, he founded Club Atlético Social y Deportivo Camioneros (Truckers Social and Sporting Athletic Club), a club that currently plays in the country's third division. His son, Pablo Moyano, is the club's president.
6 José Luis Meiszner, a lawyer by training, was president of Quilmes Atlético Club, on and off, for approximately 20 years. Aníbal Fernández, mentioned in the previous chapter, succeeded Meiszner as president of Quilmes from 2011 to 2016. Quilmes' stadium was called Estadio Centenario José Luis Meiszner ("José Luis Meiszner Centennial Stadium") from its inauguration in 1995, under Meiszner's presidency, until 2016, when it was renamed Estadio Centenario Ciudad de Quilmes ("City of Quilmes Centennial Stadium"). The stadium was renamed due to the negative association of

its former name with acts of corruption attributed mainly to Meiszner and Fernández. In the words of Jairo Gomelsky, who is currently one of Quilmes' vice presidents, "what we want to do is change the club's image, wash its face. We didn't want the club to be linked to the mafia or illegal acts. Changing the name of the stadium was an important part of that process" (Tamagni 2016; my translation).

7 Apart from being president of Club Atlético Tigre and mayor of the city of Tigre, Sergio Massa was also Argentina's Chief of the Cabinet of Ministers.

8 Club Atlético Tigre was founded in the city of Tigre but is currently located in the nearby city of Victoria, in the province of Buenos Aires.

9 Vélez is a first division club from the western neighbourhood of Liniers, in Buenos Aires.

10 Among members of La Pandilla, Gámez was known as *Pistola* ("Pistol").

11 In this context, "the fans" is a euphemism for "the *barra brava.*"

12 Mateo is a *barra* who was represented by Miguel in a legal case.

13 Peronism is arguably Argentina's most influential political movement. The name is derived from its founder, General Juan Domingo Perón.

14 Débora Hambo was the NGO's lawyer. She also represents Pablo "*Bebote*" Álvarez, one of Argentina's most famous *barras*.

15 The Spanish word used by Hugo when talking about "darkies" (*morochitos*) refers to people of tanned/dark skin who are usually perceived as having the manners and level of education of people belonging to the lower classes.

16 Sporting Potrero is a fictional name.

17 By "doing this," presumably he means being and behaving like *barras*.

18 To name one example, Mauricio Macri, a businessman, took advantage of his public image as president of Boca Juniors from 1995 to 2008 to become Chief of Government of the Autonomous City of Buenos Aires for two consecutive terms, from 2007 to 2015. He then became Argentina's president from 2015 to 2019.

19 Mateo is the pseudonym I use to refer to one of Argentina's most infamous *barras*. Even though he is a public figure who has appeared in numerous newspapers, I use a pseudonym in my writing to protect Miguel's identity.

20 Even though I would be interested in knowing more about Mateo's life, there is a difference between being curious about the character and representing him in court.

21 According to Hugo, some *barras* are celebrities in the eyes of the fans. His comment seems to fit Miguel's example, as Mateo made quite an impression on Miguel and the judge.

22 Rodolfo D'Onofrio was River Plate's president at the time of my interview with Miguel.

23 The Drunkards of the Terrace (known in Spanish as *Los Borrachos del Tablón*) is the name of River Plate's *barra brava*.

24 Carlos Gardel was a famous tango singer and songwriter. In Argentina, to say that someone thinks they are Gardel is akin to saying that they think too highly of themselves.

25 Incidentally, he was one of the many founders of the NGO United Argentinian Fandoms.

26 The Spanish word he used is gender neutral.

Chapter 6

Conclusion

Foreign solutions

Any attempt at copying measures and policies from one context and implementing them in another must carefully consider the social, cultural, historical, and political conditions under which they were developed. Although it may be possible to share and even transfer some strategies between contexts, these strategies would most likely need to be modified to account for each context's specificities. In some cases, however, the contextual differences may be too big to consider this option. When it comes to violence in football, to uncritically apply measures developed in one country in other countries betrays a lack of familiarity with the local conditions that perpetuate violence.

In *Sport Matters*, Dunning (1999) is openly critical of microscopic studies, advocating instead a grand theory approach. One of the main problems with this approach is its ambiguity. In his search for "cross-national" explanations, as he calls them, he overlooks the social, cultural, and political specificities that characterize different contexts. In a chapter titled *Soccer Hooliganism as a World Social Problem*, he states that

> in order to develop a cross-nationally adequate theory of soccer hooliganism what would ideally be required would be a systematic, in-depth cross-national study carried out by an international team of sociologists in terms of a standardized set of concepts and methods and directed towards testing an agreed-on theory or set of theoretical propositions.
>
> (1999:153–154)

Given my ethnographic and qualitative inclinations, it should come as no surprise that I do not consider standardization or the testing of an agreed-on theory the best approach to a global study of football-related violence. These approaches are too rigid and limit the scope of interpretive analyses that emerge from a careful consideration of local factors. It would be a mistake to assume that the strategies developed to tackle football hooliganism in England could be readily adopted by Argentinian authorities in an effort to decrease the levels of football-related

DOI: 10.4324/9781003458937-6

violence. Thus, when it comes to football violence in England and Argentina, to name two examples, the similarities that emerge from a comparative perspective do not make up for the different causes, motivations, and tensions that require contextualization. As Dyck explains, "anthropologists remain skeptical about the wisdom of wielding universal and categorical definitions of human arrangements as if these comprise unquestionable means for investigating and understanding social and cultural phenomena" (2012:10). In his comparative chapter on football in Europe and Latin America, Giulianotti further stresses this point by refuting the Leicester School's universalizing approach to the global study of violence in football, which revolves around an English understanding of the phenomenon: "Researchers from Scotland, Italy and Argentina have highlighted the separate social histories of football in these nations. Concomitantly, the violence of these fans cannot be simply pinned on the lower working classes and their peculiarly 'rough' socialization" (1999:46). In a similar vein, other scholars have emphasized the need to carefully consider and analyze the specificities that characterize different contexts (Archetti 2003, 2008; Armstrong 1998; Armstrong & Hognestad 2003). Studies conducted by Aragón (2007), Alabarces (2004, 2005), Armstrong (1998), Duke and Crolley (2001), Giulianotti (1995, 1999), Testa and Armstrong (2010), Gil (2006, 2007), Spaaij (2007), Watson (2022), Magazine (2007), Garriga Zucal (2010), and Moreira (2013), among others, serve as examples of how football studies in varying geographical, historical, and sociocultural contexts have produced different conclusions regarding the causes of football-related violence. Far from dismissing the relevance of shared features and commonalities, the point here is that similarities between two or more contexts do not necessarily suggest universal explanations and solutions. Watson, for example, explains that the similarities that exist between Argentina and Colombia when it comes to some of the features that characterize football and politics cannot properly account for the varying ways in which football is used and experienced by social actors for particular goals in these different sociocultural contexts. As he put it, "Argentinian football.... has often served as a model or 'father' for Colombian football, something to be learned from and ideally surpassed; the Colombian situation, however, differs in various ways" (Watson 2022:35). As I have previously discussed, ethnographic methodologies are well positioned to examine the potential for social and cultural change at the local or microscopic level without losing sight of larger processes. Put differently, ethnography's contribution to the study of social and cultural phenomena lies in its ability to create personal relationships with the people who are directly affected by particular social issues. It is by interacting with the actors that ethnographers are able to assess social issues in relation to people's feelings, thoughts, and desires. Rigid scientific approaches tend to be ill-suited to account for social and cultural phenomena, as people's actions and motivations are often unpredictable, non-generalizable, and non-replicable.

The inefficacy of approaches that seek to standardize concepts and methods in an attempt to develop universal solutions becomes apparent when looking at the Argentinian case. In 2009, the Subsef (Subsecretaría de Seguridad en

Espectáculos Futbolísticos or Undersecretariat of Security at Football Events) hired Otto Adang, a Dutch specialist in public order who had previously worked as a counsellor for UEFA (Union of European Football Associations) during the 2000, 2004, and 2008 editions of the European Cup, to address the issue of violence in Argentinian football. In a sports newspaper, he explained:

> The European solution is impracticable in Argentina. There, the hooligans were concentrated in marginal groups with no relation to the system. Here, the *barras* are linked to businesses to a surprising extent. They own player transfers, they manage the merchandising on the streets, they are in charge of parking lots, they sell drugs and have astounding ties to political power. That is why the problem in Argentina is much more serious than elsewhere in the world, because here you have to change the whole system. Until that happens, it is naïve to think of reeducating the *barras* or to generate a complete turnaround based on the education system.
>
> (in Grabia 2009b; my translation)

Adang's assessment is in line with Bergés'. During our conversation, he mentioned the impossibility – and ridiculousness – of importing ready-made solutions from other countries.

BERGÉS: One sees that Chelsea's[1] owner has nothing to do with England's everyday politics. On the other hand, here, Moyano[2] might declare a strike tomorrow, and he is the president of Independiente! A national strike! Of course politics is related to football! Angelici[3] is a person who, they say he is like the boss of the entire area of La Boca, Barracas,[4] and others at the political level. Well, he is the president of Boca! In Argentina the solution cannot be foreign, it has to be an indigenous solution. Foreign solutions have come here, eh? I remember about eight years ago, the secretary of security and his team went to the Netherlands. It was done with good intentions, because I know him. They went to the Netherlands and the guys brought with them, not the solution; rather, they saw how the issue (*of violence in football*) was handled there.

EP: They brought Otto Adang, who is a Dutch specialist.

BERGÉS: Well, but, but it is clear that this person, umm, they brought the Dutch solution but the Dutch solution is as if we were in the middle of Mars! That is, because of our way of being. Is it clear?

Bergés' comments point to the inadequacy of standardized measures that conceptualize human populations as mere biological organisms, downplaying the social and cultural features that define and guide them. Although a grand theory approach might dismiss or minimize the relevance of the idiosyncratic features of a given society, I argue that it is indispensable to take into account the particularities that give meaning to people's actions and interactions. This does not mean that commonalities between different societies at a macroscopic level should be brushed aside. There are indeed some similarities between English hooligans and *barras*. Still, when it comes to football-related violence in Argentina inside the stadiums and beyond, it is only by considering the experiences, feelings, motivations, and incentives of the actors involved in relation to their social and cultural environment that adequate solutions may be proposed.

Leonardo, in his capacity as Head of Security at Club Barrial and police commissioner, offers insight regarding the possibility of implementing foreign measures in Argentinian stadiums from a law enforcement perspective.

LEONARDO: As a result of these problems that they (*the English*) had for many years, they decided to fight them, and they succeeded. How did they fight them? By having prosecutors in the stadium, so that the team that committed excesses was tried right there in the stadium and those responsible for the excesses went to jail, their passports were withheld every time a team from England played abroad so they could not leave. They slowly "surrounded" them.

Interestingly enough, interviewees often highlight punitive measures. As Plaza Schaefer and Cabrera (2021) explain, punitive measures have been the focus of policies and interventions aimed at improving security at football stadiums for the past 35 years or so. In Leonardo's case, this is perhaps not surprising given his professional background, but considering the ties that exist in Argentina between politicians, club officials, *barras*, and the police, it might be useful to consider long-term alternatives to punitive measures that are often relied on as Band-Aid solutions. The temporary and superficial effects of supposedly exemplary punitive measures become apparent when taking into account the fact that acts of violence related to football (including those that have little to do with the sport and everything to do with money and politics) have increased during the past few decades. What types of non-punitive reforms could be carried out by the state to prevent or reduce violence and corruption? Leonardo's comments suggest that it might be impossible to expel the *barras* from the clubs given the interests of club officials and politicians.

LEONARDO: (*An English guest who specialized in football violence*) was asked about what he thought about the situation here in Argentina, based on what he knew, because he said he had some knowledge. And he said "look, here in Argentina they will never be able to eradicate the *barras*." Then they asked him "but why?" "Because they are linked to politics." So, it's very difficult to combat the *barras*. Because the one who is going to play the drum on Sunday during a match is a *barra*. Those who intimidate the players within the clubs are sent by the club officials. When there's an election at a club, when the posters are going to be put up, the *barras* are the ones who get involved.

138 Conclusion

Keeping in mind the local conditions that preclude the application of foreign solutions, I turn my attention to a consideration of the possibility of producing change in Argentinian football from within.

On change: Social and cultural impediments

Consulted about the prospect of reducing the levels of violence that have affected Argentinian football for years, some interviewees expressed optimism. Regarding the type of violence that revolves around passion, the appropriation of flags and displays of masculinity and *aguante*, Antonio said:

ANTONIO: That's over. It's all in the past. Now, Boca fans fight Boca fans, River fans against River fans, Racing fans against Racing fans.[5]

EP: Right, but then… I mean, if club officials know about this, do you think that something can be done about it?

ANTONIO: Obviously! You can always do something.

EP: Like what, for example?

ANTONIO: Like what? First, you have to educate people. Argentina is now going to introduce a very good measure which is the digitalization of stadium access,[6] meaning that if you are not registered in the system, you will not be able to enter the stadium. If you committed a felony related to football and you haven't paid for it, you will not be able to enter. They are going to expel a lot of people from the stadiums, people who cause trouble. The thing is, issues have to be resolved in the moment, when they happen, otherwise people forget. You have to judge them immediately with state representatives who have to be in all the stadiums.

As mentioned in the previous section, Leonardo expressed a similar view when discussing the presence of prosecutors at English stadiums. He insisted on the need to have prosecutors available inside Argentinian stadiums in order to expedite the arrest of violent fans.

LEONARDO: The solution, I think, is that all stadiums should have two, three prosecutors, in a place with their own desks. They send the guy (*who was involved in a violent incident*), he is arrested, done. There is a CCTV system for that, which never… I always argue over a ball that goes missing in the stands, I never get… They never catch anyone who takes a ball?

The problem with this approach is that arresting fans who commit acts of violence inside the stadiums is a short-term solution at best. On top of this, it should be noted that many acts of violence take place outside the stadiums. It is not uncommon for rival *barras* to ambush each other. Intra-*barra* conflicts are also sometimes "resolved" outside the stadiums. The case of Gonzalo Acro, a River *barra* who was murdered in 2007 outside a gym by *barras* belonging to a different faction of the same *barra brava*, serves as an example of the complexity of cases of violence related to football in Argentina. Acro's case made national headlines when the authorities in charge of the investigation determined that he had been shot in the leg from a motorcycle at close range, before being shot twice in the head by *barras* sent by the Schlenker brothers, leaders of one of the factions of River's *barra brava*. Acro was a member of the rival faction commanded by Adrián Rousseau. The murder took place in the Buenos Aires neighbourhood of Villa Urquiza, approximately five kilometres from River's stadium. As Plaza Schaefer and Cabrera explain,

> many of the confrontations or violent incidents that used to take place in the quintessential public space of the football spectacle, that is, the stadiums on match days, have now moved to "private" environments that have little to do with sports fields. It is common to see that several of the latest football-related deaths – mainly associated with clashes between *barras* – occur in neighbourhood squares, night bars, concerts or dances, and club facilities, among others.
>
> (2021:91; my translation)

Although arresting fans inside the stadiums might discourage violent behaviour in some cases, it would do little to significantly alter a system that incentivizes violent fans by offering them the opportunity to establish mutually beneficial relationships with the police, club officials, and politicians (recall HUA, the NGO created by Marcelo Mallo, discussed in the previous chapter). Regarding the technologies used at football stadiums to monitor the spectators' behaviour, Leonardo unwittingly pointed out once again the inefficacy of CCTV systems. Antonio had a similar experience at Sporting Potrero.

ANTONIO: Argentinian clubs have invested a lot of money in everything related to security cameras, *a lot* of money, but… They were installed, but evidently the results are negative because, umm, the police never arrested anyone.

EP: And why is it that they don't arrest anyone?

ANTONIO: Oh, I don't know! You should ask the police. We would need to ask Berni[7] for a hearing.

His comments are in line with Leonardo's experiences. In short, the Head of Security at Club Barrial, the former president of Sporting Potrero, and a former club official at Atlanta have told me that the police have never caught anyone as a result of using CCTV systems. Bearing in mind the case involving referee Sergio Pezzotta, CCTV systems, rather than detecting acts of violence,

140   Conclusion

seem to exacerbate suspicions of corruption and connivance between club officials, *barras*, and the police.

APREVIDE (Agencia de Prevención de Violencia en el Deporte or Agency for the Prevention of Violence in Sport) is a provincial government agency that was established to tackle the issue of violence in sports in general, although it is most often mentioned in relation to security operations conducted during professional football matches. Considering that fatal cases of violence in football have increased over the past few years, I wanted to find out more about the role of APREVIDE in terms of measures aimed at reducing violence in football stadiums. Since Leonardo had participated in meetings held by the agency, I asked him about its function.

EP: You, being the Head of Security at Club Barrial… Can you tell me what exactly is the function of agencies such as APREVIDE?

LEONARDO: Well, I don't know. Why do they exist? I don't know. I go to the meetings because I represent the club but I look around and think "why am I here?"

EP: So you have meetings with people from APREVIDE?

LEONARDO: Sure, with the secretary of… Three or four people, plus the police commissioners who are part of the security operations during matches.

EP: What do these people say at the meetings? I mean, what do they plan?

LEONARDO: We fight over the number of police officers, because if the police come they always ask you to hire 200 officers instead of 100. The club has to pay for that; it's very expensive. The police operation is *very expensive*.

EP: If you asked a person who works in one of these agencies, what would they say to you, what is their function? What do they do?

LEONARDO: Nothing, APREVIDE never prevented anything, and sometimes they cause it (*i.e. the violence*).

EP: How do they instigate violence?

LEONARDO: Well, the search, easy. If you don't get along with them, they will search you. They make you wait for three hours, they search the fans badly, they push them, the officers come and make them stand in line… They provoke a reaction. As long as they (*the security operations conducted by APREVIDE*) don't send anyone to prison, nothing is being done.

Regarding the possibility of implementing measures aimed at reducing violence, Antonio remained optimistic. This is hardly surprising, taking into account that he was, at the time of our interview, the former president of a big club who was planning on running for president once again. Boldly claiming that there is little that can be done to change the situation would not be the smartest campaign strategy. This is not to say that he was being dishonest about his hopes for the future, but it does mean that I took his answer with a grain of salt.

ANTONIO: Change is possible, for sure. But not doing what the English did, forcing all spectators to seat inside the stadium. I don't believe in that; that measure expels people from lower-income backgrounds. Instead of being a sporting spectacle that is tied to our culture, it mutates into an economic spectacle where only the ones who can afford it actually attend the games, while those who can't, have to watch them on TV, and I am against that, *totally* against that.

Although turning matches into economic spectacles available only to a small section of the population might not be desirable, emphasizing football's ties to local culture is somewhat problematic, as the features that characterize the Argentinian context are precisely what gave rise to the types and levels of violence observed in football today. In other words, an excessive emphasis on preserving the local cultural practices and traditions might hinder the development of long-term solutions. On the one hand, it is understandable that the notion of a large-scale change in people's mentality, including cultural customs and practices, might generate a fear of losing a sense of local/national identity that is firmly rooted in particular ways of thinking about the world and experiencing it. On the other hand, insisting on preserving harmful practices and ideas that perpetuate the conditions that allow violence to thrive is counterproductive. Taking into account the increasing number of cases of violence that plague Argentinian stadiums (even after the ban on visiting fans), looking for solutions within the current social, cultural, and political context is unsustainable. The current conditions may make football matches accessible to almost everyone (according to Antonio), but they also expose spectators to acts of physical violence, verbal aggression, and discrimination.

Antonio mentioned to me that he had spoken with security agencies but gave no details regarding the specific measures that the clubs coordinate with the agencies. As mentioned in a previous interview excerpt, Leonardo believes that security agencies such as APREVIDE are, simply put, useless. Being a police commissioner as well as Head of Security at Club Barrial, and having participated in meetings held by APREVIDE, he is arguably better qualified to comment on the role of security agencies than club presidents.

During our conversation, Antonio insisted on the feasibility of projects that seek to transform stadiums into safe spaces.

ANTONIO: Some might say that this problem (*violence in football*) will never disappear in Argentina, that it is here to stay. I don't think so. I think that we can do something about it, we have to make an effort, we have to work on a project, and expel the *barras* from... (*pause*)

EP: And what would a project entail? I mean, what... I don't know if you have an idea, even if it's something... (*pause*)

ANTONIO: I have an idea, a project. I am working with my own security committee and we are going to present the project to society, but I can't

142 Conclusion

describe it to you in five minutes because that would mean that I'm being partial and if I'm partial the project will have no merit. But we do have a group that is conducting studies with security professionals as well as people who can understand and interpret the sense of being a fan. This (*violence*) is a problem and we are going to present our project. We are working; we are putting a lot of hours and professionalism.

Antonio maintained an ambiguous discourse throughout the interview, playing the role of a politician who claims to have answers and solutions without ever actually feeling the need or the urge to elaborate on them. Considering that he has political aspirations within a club and that political offices are partial by nature, I fail to see the problem with his project reflecting his political bias. In other words, why would a project aimed at reducing the number of cases of violence inside and around the stadiums need to remain impartial or apolitical? Can such a project remain morally and politically detached? How would presenting his ideas to a larger audience during a one-hour televised announcement instead of explaining them to me "in five minutes" render them more impartial? The heightened level of secrecy surrounding his project made me suspect that it was in its very early stages, but without more details, I can only speculate. Still, in spite of his optimism, he was somewhat ambiguous regarding the possibility of finding a solution.

ANTONIO: The day we open up, the day we tell the truth – which we are all familiar with – the problem will be solved. It is not difficult to solve it. It is not easy either, otherwise it would probably have been solved already. We are going to collaborate in order to have a security project.

It is difficult to decipher what he meant by "telling the truth," but he was presumably referring to the fact that people are well aware of the presence of *barras* inside the clubs. It should be noted that during his tenure as president of Sporting Potrero, the club's *barra brava* was as active as it had ever been. He had complained to me about the president of the rival club having *barras* hanging around and inside the club with impunity, overlooking the fact that the situation at Sporting Potrero during his presidency was no different.

Antonio seemed to be unaware of the existence of NGOs dedicated to tackling the issue of violence and corruption in football (the NGOs are not widely known by the general public), but consulted about their role, he said that he was open to having conversations as long as they remained apolitical.

EP: I can think of at least two or three NGOs that stand against violence in football. Do you think that a collaboration between clubs and NGOs would be useful, or is there a sort of split…?

ANTONIO: Every person who might have an innovating project to overcome this problem is welcome. We would have to see what the NGOs think about it. It goes like this: If the issue is not politicized, it has a solution.

> If it becomes politicized, it does not have a solution. Do you know why?
> Because people's interests start to take over.

I find it curious that he refers to political interests as inherently negative. This revolves around the implicit understanding that politics in Argentina is based exclusively on personal interests, a notion that is reinforced by MacLachlan's (2006) blunt but accurate description of the workings of Argentinian politics, mentioned earlier. Antonio seems to have little faith in the idea that political interests can revolve around the collective well-being of a population. Within the Argentinian context, his scepticism is unsurprising, especially considering that cases of corruption facilitate an image of politics that equates political interests with personal interests.

When discussing the NGOs' ability to produce change with Javier, a journalist and politician, he highlighted the importance of having a clear political project before thinking about possible solutions. In this regard, his approach was diametrically opposed to Antonio's.

EP: Do you think that grassroots movements can emerge from the clubs? Because I'm thinking about the NGOs that tried to do something but were not formed specifically within the clubs...

JAVIER: What happens with the NGOs is that if they don't consider having a vocation for power, to be able to combat the football clubs' corrupt environments, they will never be able to control them.

EP: Right. It seems that five years ago, when I talked to Mónica, they (*the NGO Let's Save Football, better known as SAF*) were very enthusiastic about the NGOs. Then, little by little, things fell apart; they fell apart because they saw that they had no support. Liliana[8] is tired; she will be president of SAF until the end of the month, but will then step down...

JAVIER: She is tired! What happens with that NGO... The thing is if you don't have a political project that aims to change the situation you end up being an NGO that only files complaints, which is not bad, but it is very hard to maintain that because the complaints that you file never produce change because there is no will to change. This is an issue that transcends the political environment. It has to do with the political, social, and cultural aspects of our people.

Javier points to systemic impunity by referring to the inefficacy of filing complaints or lawsuits, as they are often archived and ignored. On top of this, people who witness acts of violence may not always be willing to cooperate with the authorities for fear of being targeted by the perpetrators. In 2008, Mónica explained to me that while she was working at Atlanta, a *barra* entered the club with a hammer and broke a TV, a computer, a cash register, and windows. Even though she reported the incident to the police, the two Atlanta employees who

144 Conclusion

had witnessed it made excuses to avoid having to identify the *barra* because they were afraid of the consequences. Given the impunity with which *barras* handle themselves, there is little incentive to take action against them, particularly when doing so might put a person at risk.

In line with other interviewees, Javier believes that the issues that afflict Argentinian football are rooted on the social and cultural features that inform people's interests, behaviours, and interactions. From this perspective, legal measures aimed at reducing violence are often rendered inefficient by a culture of impunity that allows the actors involved in cases of violence to circumvent the legal system through connivance.

In his capacity as a lawyer and former federal judge, Bergés believes that the legal system is well equipped to drastically reduce cases of violence in spite of the political, social, and cultural hurdles that hinder the development of viable, long-term solutions. Having said that, his observations refer more to the legal system's *potential* to reduce violence than to measures that have been proven to work in the Argentinian context in the past.

BERGÉS: We have here this issue of this special relationship with politics that is very noticeable in small clubs... In the big clubs, the violent fan seeks to benefit from the club. He wants tickets, he wants to manage the club's restaurant, the parking lots, he wants free trips when the club is doing well, umm well, all of that. He wants that. And the club in many cases ends up giving it to him. When the club is small – the so-called neighbourhood clubs – the violent fan has a lot of influence within the neighbourhood. It is something, it is something more political, more... The broker, the, the, the, there is a whole relationship tied to City Hall many times. It is different. River is huge, so that is why I get angry with D'Onofrio[9] when he says "I can't handle the *barra*." No! *Ituzaingó*[10] cannot handle it, but you can handle it if you have money to pay for private security. In other words, if you don't want the *barra* to enter the stadium, it will not enter! When Macri was president of Boca, it was one of the bloodiest times of Boca's *barra brava*. Because they allowed them! And there was also a tourism agency, to arrange the trips, everything was well scheduled. There was always something that was given to them. So, the problem we have is that; we have the problem of politics. Still, I think that many things can be done by the state! In other words, I think that in terms of structural violence within football, it seems to me that with some changes... I would say that in the time it takes to play two championships, I think that violence can be lowered from 100% to 50%. It is a lot!

EP: Interesting! (*Incredulous laugh*) Like what kind of changes for example?

BERGÉS: No no, the thing is, what happens is that I experienced that being, being, being a magistrate, being a judge. I mean, uh, in Argentina we have a concept... This is a personal idea, maybe I'm wrong, but it's a matter that has to do with my life experience... I believe the following, we – because we also see it in other parts of the world – we in Argentina have a way of seeing life whereby it is much more pleasant for us to have some pressure from an authority than not to have it. When I say pressure, it is not in the form of intimidation, but the pressure that ensures that the law is going to be applied.

Considering that football-related violence has increased over the past decades in spite of legal measures such as a ban on visiting fans, it is hard to imagine that it could be reduced by as much as 50% within a period from one to two years. In any case, whenever I asked interviewees about possible measures, changes, and solutions, the answers tended to be either abstract or ambiguous. While Antonio mentioned a plan that he could not – or *would* not – reveal (one that, by his own admission, was still being developed), Bergés was unclear about the ways in which violence can be lowered. He referred to Argentinians as *children of rigour*. This phrase is a local expression that suggests that people will only behave properly and do the right thing when forced to by some sort of authority. While there might be some truth to this, to say that it is "pleasant" for people to be legally forced to behave in certain ways is an exaggeration. Still, he seems to suggest that, in the absence of a strong legal authority, personal interests invariably trump collective ones.

Being curious about the specific measures that he had in mind, I insisted on the subject in an attempt to get an answer that would clarify his position.

EP: Are there any concrete solutions that can be implemented, perhaps from a legal framework? Can you produce a change in mentality from that legal framework, or is it something that...

BERGÉS: No. I think not. I think not because from my opinion, from my perspective, the laws in Argentina are perfectly adequate. We have a system of powers that is divided into three, the legislative power, the judicial power, and the executive power. I believe that the problem lies in the executive branch and in the judicial branch, in that order, but both are very close together. The legislative branch, I would be encouraged to say that it is the one that has done the most. What I am sure of is that just because we have ten new laws, it does not mean that things will change. Of that I am sure.

Indeed, creating new laws would accomplish little. As Bergés pointed out, an excessively permissive legal system generates impunity. This is not to suggest that an authoritarian regime would be a good alternative. His argument revolves around the idea that adequate laws already exist, they just need to be *applied*. This is a simple enough idea. In practice, however, political corruption and personal relationships make it seem, at times, like an almost impossible task.

146 Conclusion

Leonardo has little confidence in the legal system. To some extent, his views coincide with Bergés'. Regardless of whether he thinks the laws are adequate or not, his point is that the laws that exist on paper are often ignored or misapplied.

EP: What can be done from a legal point of view, for example? If everyone at the club knows who these people are... That is, what measures are implemented by club officials to try to... I don't know if to prevent, but...

LEONARDO: If you don't have the support of the authorities, you can't do anything. 80% (*of barras*) are criminals... 80% are criminals! They sell drugs, they steal. If you don't have support... Because there is also collusion with the police. So, if you don't have the support of the justice system, which here in Argentina is totally devalued, what are you going to do? If you knew that you report one of these guys and he goes to jail, ok... But no, he will enter through one door and exit through the other.

It is particularly relevant and enlightening to hear from a police commissioner that the *barras* are in collusion with the police. Given the widespread levels of corruption, it would be impossible for Leonardo to monitor the behaviour of every police officer or security guard under his supervision. This is especially true considering that police officers spend many hours working on the streets, where they are free to establish relationships with *barras*. Thus, police officers might agree to liberate a zone,[11] allowing one *barra brava* to ambush another without fear of police intervention, in exchange for a percentage of the earnings of one of the businesses managed by the *barra brava*. In this scenario, it seems almost utopian to think of effective measures aimed at reducing violence and corruption in football. Taking as an example the love-hate relationships that characterize the interactions between *barras* and the police, who are both enemies and business partners depending on the occasion, it becomes apparent that the factors that contribute to and encourage acts of violence and corruption severely limit the possibility of producing change from a law enforcement perspective.

According to Miguel, only those who have firsthand experience with the workings of Argentinian football are qualified to offer solutions and solve the problem of violence and corruption. Making use of a delicately nuanced lexicon, he explained that "armchair observers" risk misunderstanding football's context by focusing on stories presented by the media.

MIGUEL: I start from the basis that, if you don't know the problem, you can't comment on it based on what the newspapers say. I can talk to you because I'm a criminal lawyer, in the criminal justice system, I defended a *barrabrava*, I go to the stadium, I went to the stadium as a boy; that is, I know the whole environment. I can be wrong, eh? Now, from the point of view of... (*in a mocking tone*) "oh what a horror! What a shame!

What a mess! How unsustainable!" I send a letter to La Nación[12] and they publish it, no no no. Get down to where the shit is, put your hand in the shit, because you know what this is like? This is like poop. Even the Pope shits, right? This is how it is, and it has a smell, so it exists. You have to get to know it, dude. Who can solve football's problems? The guy who knows about them.

Although it is true that relying solely on newspaper accounts of cases of violence and corruption in football would be misguided, I find his analysis deeply troubling from a moral standpoint. He explained that only those who know about football's problems can solve them. He also mentioned that he is very familiar with "the whole environment," both in his capacity as a criminal lawyer and as a football fan. This means, presumably, that he would be able to suggest solutions. Putting aside the fact that no long-term solutions have been suggested, his discourse is contradictory. Not only did he casually mention that he defended one of Argentina's most infamous *barras* because he was "curious" about the character, he also called Bergés an idiot for having tapped a famous senator's phone during an investigation. Regarding this incident, he explained that the other senators sided with the person who was being investigated, which ultimately led to Bergés losing his position. According to Miguel, "you have to be a moron to think about tapping a senator's phone; that's what he got for playing detective." Even though I am not familiar with the circumstances surrounding the case, Miguel's harsh words were not based on its specific details; rather, it was the thought of investigating a person in a position of power such as a senator that he considered dumb. Regardless of the wisdom (or lack thereof) of Bergés' decision, Miguel implicitly suggests that politicians in positions of power are better left alone. This perspective, however, poses a problem. If politicians feel that they are untouchable, there is little to discourage them from becoming involved in corrupt arrangements. Thus, if Miguel believes that the issue of violence and corruption in football can be solved, I would be interested to know how this could be achieved in a context where corrupt politicians have immunity, as only "idiots" would be unwise enough to investigate them.

A new paradigm

I remain highly sceptical about the possibility of producing change under the current social, cultural, and political conditions. Except for the temporary fixes suggested by Antonio and Leonardo, who believe that having prosecutors at football stadiums would discourage acts of violence, most interviewees were vague regarding specific measures, ideas, or proposals that could serve as long-term solutions to the issue of violence and corruption. Within the Argentinian context, legal reforms would do little to modify the social and cultural characteristics that perpetuate the types of football fans, politicians, and security forces that contribute to a violent and corrupt football environment. The laws might be perfectly

148 Conclusion

adequate, as Bergés put it, but unless there is a change in mentality, cases of violence and corruption will continue to be subjected to a parade of laws that keep failing, not because there are inherent flaws in them, but because no law is infallible. To some extent – depending on the context – laws are only as effective as the people acting on them. Given the willingness of people in positions of authority (including politicians, club officials, and police officers) to circumvent the law, and considering the ease with which they are able to do so, it is clear that laws are, in this particular scenario, often little more than words on a piece of paper. As Plautus put it in his comedy "Trinummus":

> Why, "custom's" gained control over our very laws and has 'em under its thumb more than children have their parents. The poor old laws are even hung on walls and nailed there, where our cursed "custom" should far more fittingly be spiked.... The sanctity of law guards nothing from it: laws are slaves of "custom," yes, and "custom" makes short work of sweeping everything away, sacred and civic.
>
> (1952:203)

As I mentioned, foreign solutions, developed in countries with social and cultural realities that differ considerably from Argentina's, would be ill-suited to tackle the challenges that have impeded the development of viable solutions. Thus, the fact that the solutions will have to be local is unfortunate, because it means that they will somehow have to emerge, against all odds, from a context where a culture of *aguante* is glorified, football rivalries create enmities, political interests are at play, and corruption and impunity are rampant.

The insistence on the need to develop local solutions has one unfortunate side effect: it emphasizes the value of local understandings and interpretations and downplays the relevance of analyses done by outsiders who are conceivably unfamiliar with the country's social reality. Antonio, for example, was highly sceptical about the possibility of foreigners being able to make sense of Argentinian culture and society. He asked me:

ANTONIO: Where are you going to present your findings?
EP: In Canada.
ANTONIO: (*With a derogatory tone and a deadpan, humourless expression*) In Canada they don't understand anything about who we are.
EP: (*Laughter*) That's precisely why I'm here, so that you can tell me about the situation to try to understand!
ANTONIO: And if you want to explain it to them, when you finish explaining it, they don't understand you. Umm, because, let's see... This cannot be understood. It cannot be understood, but oh well...

The problem with this reliance on the insider's perspective is that a "fully native" approach might be limited by cultural factors in its capacity to formulate ways of thinking about and experiencing football that exceed local understandings. Put differently, most locally proposed solutions are bound by the particular cultural characteristics and idiosyncrasies that define the Argentinian context. As I previously discussed, to look for solutions that seek to reduce violence inside and around football stadiums while simultaneously preserving the "colourful" traditions that often instigate acts of violence is both unsustainable and incompatible. To clarify, being open to analyses and observations made by foreigners in relation to the specificities that characterize the Argentinian context is not the same as suggesting that ready-made foreign solutions should be imported and transplanted. Still, although familiarity with the local context is important and necessary, outsiders might be better positioned to adopt a critical distance that enables them to identify patterns and behaviours that may be too ingrained for locals to notice.

What is required, then, is a sweeping cultural transformation. As long as the laws, customs, traditions, and policies currently in place continue to operate under the influence of a cultural environment that celebrates manifestations of violence and rewards those who are "wise" enough to do things "under the table," violence and corruption will thrive unchallenged. In his book *Corruption, an Argentinian culture*, Pomer similarly points to the difficulties in producing cultural change:

> In Argentina, certain conditions are maintained because the behaviours that engender, reproduce and assure them a robust and deplorably healthy life never disappeared from social life. They were never swept away by social changes that brought with them a radically different culture that was transformative.
>
> (2004:47; my translation)

Alabarces identifies cultural change as a prerequisite for tackling violence in football:

> The key lies in a broad cultural change: the replacement of a culture of *aguante* by a festive culture that recovers the old festive value of football, the predominance of the comic over the tragic ... This can only be achieved in the very long term, in no less than ten years, but those are the times of profound transformations ... And for that, well-planned and systematic media and educational campaigns are needed to convince civil society to join them.
>
> (2004:115; my translation)

When it comes to the timeframe needed for a cultural transformation to occur, I am decidedly less optimistic than Alabarces. I would be pleasantly surprised if I were to witness the kind of change needed to reconfigure Argentinian football and society within my lifetime. In the time since Alabarces' book was published, cases of football-related violence continued to rise, with more than 120 fatal victims according to SAF ("Lista de víctimas," n.d.). This period includes the ban on visiting fans. Needless to say, levels of violence should not be measured exclusively by the number of fatal victims, but at the very least, they serve as an indication that things are not going well.

Taking into account the political and economic conditions that create social resentment in certain sectors of the population, I am also sceptical about the extent to which media and educational campaigns would be able to successfully promote an image of football that is detached from expressions of violence.

Plaza Schaefer and Cabrera (2021) believe that the current focus on punitive measures should shift to preventive approaches that incorporate the voices of different actors, including those who are embedded in practices that revolve around the symbolic and affective dimensions of violence. In line with Alabarces (2004) and Plaza Schaefer and Cabrera, Branz et al. (2020) propose educational campaigns with the goal of raising awareness of the ways in which people legitimize the logic of *aguante* and its associated violence and aggression. As an example, they suggest working on a campaign that demonstrates "to what extent all actors make football a space where violent practices are accepted" (Branz et al. 2020:91; my translation). Although their proposed campaigns target not only fans but also club officials, players, and coaches, they make no mention of political and economic interests. Still, the ties – both emotional and instrumental – that exist between political leaders, neighbourhood brokers, club officials, union leaders, the police, businesspeople, and *barras* are explicitly acknowledged in their article. Keeping this in mind, well-planned educational campaigns aimed at reducing violence in football seem destined to fail in the absence of larger social, cultural, and economic transformations that address a collective mentality that fuels a thriving culture of impunity. In spite of their efforts within and beyond academia to raise awareness of the issues that contribute to violence in football, Branz et al. claim that

> we are worse than we were twenty years ago, when we began this journey, because, regardless of the small satisfactions of our work, such as the support of our colleagues and our students, not only have we not convinced anyone, but we have continued to record deaths, injuries, damages, and other incidents. We have not saved a single life.
>
> (2020:93; my translation)

With regard to corruption in football, former "referee of bribery" Humberto Rosales asks: "Has the time come to begin a serious and responsible investigation into the acts of corruption in Argentinian football?" (2013:15; my translation). He then offers an answer that points to the difficulties in producing long-term changes within the Argentinian context:

> I believe, almost without fear of being mistaken, that this investigation will never take place. If carried out, it would compromise, as in my days as a referee, the 'good name' of many leaders and officials with too much power.
>
> (idem)

Conclusion   151

I could end my analysis of politics, corruption, and violence in Argentinian football on a moderately positive note by talking about hope. When all else fails, it is easy to hang on to hope. In his book, whose title translates to *The Atrocious Charm of Being Argentinian*, Aguinis (2001) discusses the behavioural traits and peculiarities – many of them less than flattering – that inform the notion of "Argentinianness." In the concluding chapter, however, he paints a positive picture of the country's future, making reference to past accomplishments and present virtues. I argue that, when it comes to short- or medium-term cultural and behavioural changes, it would be condescending to talk about hope. Furthermore, it would be irresponsible to sugar-coat a social, cultural, political, and economic reality that is in desperate need of a cultural transformation. The current way of doing politics, combined with an "everyone for themselves" mentality (MacLachlan 2006), a deeply rooted culture of impunity where politicians, the police, club officials, and *barras* enter into agreements without fear of legal consequences, and cases of violence and verbal aggression at football matches (and beyond) that are tied to group identity performances, political interests, economic interests, and displays of *aguante*, makes it difficult to imagine a scenario where significant, transformative change could occur without a cultural transformation.

Outside observers such as Adang (Grabia 2009b), Gaffney (2009), MacLachlan (2006), and Darwin (1913), have recognized the difficulties in producing change under conditions that perpetuate violence and corruption. In a sense, Argentina represents a sort of inversion of Radcliffe-Brown's (1952) structural functionalism. By this, I mean that, contrary to Radcliffe-Brown's understanding of structural functionalism as a system that tends to promote harmony and stability, Argentinian institutions perpetuate a system of organized chaos. This organized chaos (consider the case of HUA) rewards those who take advantage of the opportunities provided by rampant levels of impunity. That Darwin's observations, made over 100 years ago, remain accurate to this day, indicates that it will be difficult to break the self-sustaining cycle of corruption, particularly when there is no political will to disrupt it.

My intention here has not been to polemicize, but rather to raise awareness of the fact that most of the proposed solutions will continue to fail unless they are accompanied by a push for cultural change. In short, what is needed is a new paradigm, a new way of evaluating social relations and engaging with others.

Throughout this book, I have examined the mechanisms through which corruption, impunity, clientelism, and violence contribute to the perpetuation of a system of organized chaos in Argentinian football and society. Far from existing in a vacuum, the world of Argentinian football, which has been the focus of my study, exemplifies the social, cultural, and political obstacles that impede the country's socioeconomic development.

Notes

1 Chelsea Football Club is an English Premier League club from London.
2 Bergés mentioned Hugo Moyano as an example because he has organized countless strikes and political rallies throughout the years.
3 At the time of the interview, Daniel Angelici was the president of Boca.

152 Conclusion

4 The Buenos Aires neighbourhoods of La Boca and Barracas share a border.

5 This makes reference to the fact that physical confrontations between members of the same *barra* over economic interests are increasingly common. Murzi and Segura Trejo (2018), on the other hand, explain that cases of violence involving fans, the police, players, and club officials are still quite common in spite of being underreported in comparison with cases involving *barras*.

6 He is referring to a system that was to be called AFA Plus. This system was going to replace paper tickets with biometric technologies in an attempt to eliminate scalping and falsified tickets. It was also meant to prevent *barras* with criminal records from entering the stadium. The system never came to fruition.

7 At the time of the interview, Sergio Berni was Argentina's Secretary of Security.

8 At the time of my interview with Javier, Liliana Suárez was the president of SAF. She also founded FAVIFA (Familiares de Víctimas del Fútbol Argentino or Relatives of Victims of Argentinian Football) after her son was killed on July 11, 1995, by *barras* of Club Atlético Tigre and Club Deportivo Morón in Uruguay, where Argentina's national team was playing the Copa América, a South American continental tournament. Both Tigre and Morón are Argentinian clubs.

9 Rodolfo D'Onofrio was River's president at the time of the interview.

10 Club Atlético Ituzaingó is a club that plays in the fourth division. Bergés' point is that small clubs such as Ituzaingó are unable to confront the *barras* because they lack the financial resources.

11 In Argentina, a liberated zone is an area that *should* be under police protection but has been left unprotected to allow an individual or a group to commit criminal acts, including acts of violence, with impunity. There have been many cases of theft and violence suspected to have been facilitated by liberated zones around football stadiums.

12 *La Nación* is a national newspaper.

Appendix A

A note on methods

During the course of my research, I relied on ethnographic methods of data collection such as participant observation, observant participation, semi-structured interviews, and fieldnotes. These qualitative methods are well suited to determine the causes and motivations of groups and individuals by focusing on aspects of social life such as local customs, beliefs, and culture that are (perhaps unwittingly) overlooked by quantitative and statistical methods. Furthermore, the participatory and long-term nature of fieldwork allowed me to establish a degree of trust and openness with some research participants that would have been hard to attain through non-ethnographic approaches. A view of society from below or, put differently, an approach where the individuals' experiences, opinions, and beliefs are taken into consideration makes it difficult to stick to a neatly predefined theory when conducting fieldwork. Having said that, this does not mean that the lack of a "readily applicable" theory results in abstract analyses where nothing can be interpreted and determined with certainty. Grounded theory emerges from the data and is based on empirical observations.

In addition to the interviews and observations I conducted, attending a River game granted me the opportunity to observe and document the process of getting into the stadium as well as the crowd's behaviour.

Appendix B

On subjectivities and the validity of research findings

It could well be argued that, far from being detached observers with no political agendas, ethnographers are in a position to exercise agency in support of particular social goals. In fact, many anthropologists (Bourgois 1991; Green 1995; Scheper-Hughes 1995) argue that ethnographers *should* take a political stance that actively strives for social and cultural change. As Khasnabish explains,

> Green constructs a discipline which takes as its first ethical priority the obligation to give voice to the experiences of the powerless, the oppressed, the victimized, and to serve as a vehicle for realizing social change, not simply one which articulates social critique. For Green, there can be no meaningful anthropology of human suffering if its practitioners do not choose to actively 'cast their lot' on the side of the powerless in opposition to the powerful.
>
> (2004:65)

While it is undeniable that ethnographers have particular views and opinions regarding the issues they study, some of the advocates of an "anthropology of liberation" are critical of scholars who focus their attention on the production of fieldwork-based knowledge within the "safety" of academia. The lack of active and persistent involvement on the part of ethnographers in the struggles of those affected by the issues being studied is equated with a lack of concern for their personal and social well-being. Scheper-Hughes believes that

> anthropologists who do not take explicit moral and political positions with regard to situations characterized by conflict are not only guilty of not working to achieve human emancipation but are in fact guilty of perpetuating the very violence to which they bear witness.
>
> (Khasnabish 2004:67)

The logic behind her argument is dubious, but the point here is not that the practice of an engaged, activist anthropology should be discouraged in favour of analytical perspectives that remain detached from the field. It is indeed important for ethnographers to think critically about their roles as agents of social and cultural change in fieldwork situations. A socially committed approach to fieldwork research that seeks to prioritize the voices and concerns of the participants might be well positioned to produce change on their terms. For the purposes of my research, however, it is the extreme versions of the activist approach, such as that of the anthropology of liberation, that I found problematic. Considering this, I have not approached my research from an "either *with* them (i.e. the participants) or *against* them" perspective. Rather, a more nuanced approach, such as the one proposed by Khasnabish (2004), is better able to account for the social, cultural, and moral complexities of the contexts and situations ethnographers encounter on the field while remaining committed to social justice.

In the Afterword to *Cultural Intimacy*, Herzfeld (2005) discusses the role of ethics in politically sensitive anthropological field studies. He rejects the "hands off" approach by arguing in favour of the anthropologist's political involvement in the communities/societies where they conduct fieldwork:

> the.... negative consequence of avoiding political engagement with the nation-states we study is that it allows our desire not to embarrass a geopolitically weaker country to overwhelm our concern for the disadvantaged within. What is more, if we take seriously our hosts' wishes to be treated as moral equals, as indeed we should, such avoidance of criticism is not only condescending but inconsistent as well. We should be equally free to argue with the abuse of power at whatever level we encounter it. In the places where we do our work, moreover, there are often intellectually vivacious individuals who are able and willing to make the official, majority case to us. With such people it is surely insulting to refuse engagement. We expect them to speak openly to us about their views; why should we hide our own?
>
> (2005:213)

An intellectual concern for objectivity – a term often deified in the social sciences to the point where its eternal elusiveness becomes the source of unnecessary anxiety – should not preclude anthropologists from voicing their views on particular matters, provided that these views are not based purely on preconceptions and prejudices. In this regard, Haraway states:

> Throughout the field of meanings constituting science, one of the commonalities concerns the status of any object of knowledge and of related claims about the faithfulness of our accounts to a 'real world,' no matter how mediated for us and no matter how complex and contradictory these worlds may be.
>
> (1988:591)

In his argument for a militant middle ground between positivism and hyperrelativism in the social sciences, Herzfeld criticizes the audit-culture approach to ethics for its rigidity, explaining that it "cannot accommodate the sometimes agonizing choices that anthropologists must make among conflicting interests within the community under study" (idem). His social poetics approach to ethnographic research emphasizes the need to respond to the challenges posed by ethical prescriptions that limit the scope and depth of analytical and interpretive studies of culture and society. As Herzfeld aptly put it, "the role of the social critic is never easy, and an anthropologist who refuses that role has walked away from the world and entered the safe antisepsis of theory, structure, and pure reason" (2005:224). Khasnabish distances himself from the extreme views endorsed by Scheper-Hughes and instead proposes an approach that is more in line with Herzfeld's middle ground between positivism and hyperrelativism:

> In pursuing the work of an ethically committed anthropology, rather than committing ourselves to agendas and frameworks which cloak ethical and intellectual dilemmas in the language of liberation and emancipation, we must instead reaffirm our commitment to the people with whom we work, to the challenge of conveying as effectively and widely as we can the richness, the complexity, and sometimes even the harshness and the horror of human experience. Anthropologists can be witnesses, we can lend our voices and our access to those with whom we work in an ethical and responsible manner. What we should not do is allow ourselves to be seduced by a rhetoric of "liberation" and self-righteousness, which, while claiming the ethical and moral high ground, serves instead to obscure the very complexity of the worlds, we, and the individuals and communities with whom we work, inhabit.
>
> (2004:85)

Needless to say, social and cultural practices and performances can be analyzed and interpreted in many different ways by different researchers, as has become apparent in my analysis of the fans' performances at football matches in Argentina. Still, an effort to account for one's own biases should not amount to repressing one's views on the issues at hand. Whose interests are served (in the name of an illusory objectivity) by satisfying ethical prescriptions that are often detached from the social settings and cultural contexts where ethnographers conduct fieldwork?

While the strengths of ethnographic methodologies are many, the postmodern critique of ethnography described (but not endorsed) by Brewer poses a challenge to anthropology's role as a discipline concerned with the understanding of systems of knowledge, human interactions, and different accounts of social reality:

> All accounts are constructions and the whole issue of which account more accurately represents social reality is meaningless.... This is called the crisis of representation. Inasmuch as ethnographic descriptions are partial, selective, even autobiographical in that they are tied to the particular ethnographer and the contingencies under which the data were collected, the traditional criteria for evaluating ethnography become problematic.
>
> (2000:24–25)

Although the hyperrelativism that characterizes postmodernism exaggerates the impossibility of knowing anything about social reality with any degree of certainty, the issue of reliability is a valid concern. It is indeed true that ethnographic accounts are bounded in space and time, and that an ethnographer working in a particular place at a particular time will interact with groups of people and witness a variety of events that another ethnographer working on the same topic might not have access to. As a result, different accounts of the same social issue in a given place might reach very different conclusions. Different actors undoubtedly make different interpretations of the world around them. For an ethnographer, this means that the fieldwork data, far from being objective in any way that would satisfy a positivist, is itself informed by the beliefs, ideologies, and evaluations of the research participants, even before it reaches the stage where the ethnographer analyzes and interprets the data according to their own personal background. In the words of Hofstede,

> the values of the researcher determine to a large extent the way he or she observes, describes, classifies, understands, and predicts reality. There is no way out of this dilemma but to (1) expose oneself and one's work to the work of others with different value systems and (2) try to be as explicit as possible about one's own value system.
>
> (2001:15)

Validity is a concern to the extent that it is difficult (at times, impossible) for ethnographers to check the truth or accuracy of the stories conveyed by the research participants. Even in cases where participants are well intentioned, their accounts might be unwittingly influenced by their feelings and opinions. Needless to say, the burden of validity should not fall exclusively on informants. Considering that ethnographers tend to work alone, it would be easy for someone conducting fieldwork to manipulate, alter, and cherry pick pieces of data in ways that fit his or her intentions or "agenda." Studies on hooliganism conducted by the School of Leicester have in fact been accused of making their (predominantly non-ethnographic) data fit their hypothesis. According to Archetti and Romero, the School of Leicester's analytical approach "is marked by a reliance on the normative historical model and by a kind of 'social distance' which permits easy generalizations" (1994:42). When it comes to the difficulties in presenting qualitative data and findings, Beuving and de Vries acknowledge the criticism that dismisses ethnographic studies based on grounded theory as purely subjective enterprises:

> The findings collected in a naturalistic inquiry are usually presented to the reader as a narrative; as a story about society. This raises the question of whether your story may be different from my story; in other words, naturalistic inquirers are frequently accused of subjectivism that bears more resemblance to fiction than to (social) science.... The term 'subjectivism' must be read as synonymous to violating the principles of validity and reliability.
>
> (2015:42)

158   Appendix B

With this criticism in mind, Beuving and de Vries (2015) enumerate tools that help avoid accusations of subjectivism. Among these, they highlight the role of grounded theory as a procedure that revolves around constant comparison, the use of different data collection methods that allows researchers to triangulate their findings by exposing them to a variety of methods, and a reflexive attitude through which researchers confront their assumptions and inclinations with their field observations.

To be sure, my methodological concern lies not with reliability but with validity. According to Honigmann, "there is practically a zero probability of ever testing the reliability of a comprehensive ethnographic report, so one ought to stop talking about replication as a technique of verification" (1976:246). In a similar vein, Mitchell explains that in ethnographic research,

> it is perfectly justifiable for the analyst to operate with a simplified account of the context within which the case is located provided that the impact of the features of that context on the events being considered in the analysis are incorporated rigorously into the analysis.
>
> (1983:205)

Another perceived limitation of ethnographic methodologies revolves around the issue of generalizability. The impossibility of making general claims about the way a society, community, or group of people works is a common criticism, often endorsed by positivists who tend to favour strictly scientific approaches to the study of human social and cultural interactions.[1] Nicholas acknowledges this criticism in relation to the ethnographic study of social movements:

> The problem of understanding movements is rooted in an empirical ethnographic problem. Anthropologists collect their data and test their theories through "fieldwork" and through comparisons with the results of other fieldwork. The techniques of fieldwork are adapted to microsocial settings, yet increasingly it is clear that the tribes, peasant villages, and nowadays cities or urban neighborhoods studied by anthropologists are only "part-societies with part-cultures".... Moreover, we do not know if the units of our research are "representative" of anything larger than themselves and, if so, what that something is.
>
> (1973:64)

Unsurprisingly, researchers who put a strong emphasis on generalizability also rely on comparative analyses to assess the validity of their findings. While comparative approaches are in fact very useful in the analysis of the causes and effects of particular social and cultural issues, the focus of ethnographic research need not be on generalizability and universal explanations; rather, it is more productive to concentrate on social, historical, and cultural specificities. This begs the question: Does every case need to be replicable for it to be indisputably relevant? Too much emphasis on generalizability risks obscuring and perhaps even rendering invisible many of the socially, historically, and culturally specific factors that shape people's lives.

For the purposes of this book, the argument is not that there are no commonalities between different social and cultural contexts when it comes to analyses of violence in football. Rather, my point is that many of the differences are significant enough to warrant special attention to local specificities. Thus, in the case of football-related violence and corruption, while it is important to acknowledge that similarities can often be identified, it would be naïve to assume that universal solutions can be applied uncritically and independently of a context's historical, social, cultural, and political circumstances.

Note

1 Approaches to the study of football violence such as those of the School of Leicester, for example, rely on generalizations that tend to homogenize sociocultural contexts by seeking universal solutions to issues that are born of local specificities.

References

Agar, Michael (2007) "Emic/etic." In G. Ritzer (Ed.), *The Blackwell Encyclopedia of Sociology* (pp. 1371–1374). Malden, MA: Blackwell Publishing.

Aguinis, Marcos (2001) *El atroz encanto de ser argentinos*. Buenos Aires: Planeta.

Alabarces, Pablo (2004) *Crónicas del aguante: Fútbol, violencia y política*. Buenos Aires: Capital Intelectual.

Alabarces, Pablo (Ed.) (2005) *Hinchadas*. Buenos Aires: Prometeo Libros.

Alabarces, Pablo & Garriga Zucal, José (2008) "El 'aguante': una identidad corporal y popular." *Intersecciones en Antropología* 9:275–289.

Alabarces, Pablo, Garriga Zucal, José, & Moreira, María Verónica (2008) "El 'aguante' y las hinchadas argentinas: una relación violenta." *Horizontes Antropológicos* 14(30): 113–136.

Alconada Mon, Hugo (2018) *La raíz de todos los males: Cómo el poder montó un sistema para la corrupción y la impunidad en la Argentina*. Buenos Aires: Planeta.

Amit, Vered (Ed.) (2000) *Constructing the Field: Ethnographic Fieldwork in the Contemporary World*. London; New York: Routledge.

Anderson, Benedict (1991) *Imagined Communities: Reflections on the Origin and Spread of Nationalism*. London; New York: Verso.

Anderson, Craig A. & Bushman, Brad J. (2002) "Human aggression." *Annual Review of Psychology* 53:27–51.

Aragón, Silvio (2007) *Los trapos se ganan en combate: Una mirada etnográfica sobre las representaciones y prácticas violentas de la "barra brava" de San Lorenzo de Almagro*. Buenos Aires: Antropofagia.

Archetti, Eduardo (2003) "Playing football and dancing tango: Embodying Argentina in movement, style and identity." In N. Dyck & E. Archetti (Eds.), *Sport, Dance and Embodied Identities* (pp. 217–229). Oxford; New York: Berg.

Archetti, Eduardo (2008) "El potrero y el pibe. Territorio y pertenencia en el imaginario del fútbol argentino." *Horizontes Antropológicos* 14(30):259–282.

Archetti, Eduardo & Romero, Amílcar (1994) "Death and violence in Argentinian football." In R. Giulianotti, N. Bonney & M. Hepworth (Eds.), *Football, Violence and Social Identity* (pp. 37–72). London; New York: Routledge.

Armstrong, Gary (1998) *Football Hooligans: Knowing the Score*. Oxford; New York: Berg.

Armstrong, Gary & Harris, Rosemary (1991) "Football hooligans: Theory and evidence." *The Sociological Review* 39(3):427–458.

Armstrong, Gary & Hognestad, Hans (2003) "'We're not from Norway': Football and civic pride in Bergen, Norway." *Identities* 10(4):451–475.

References   161

Atkinson, Michael & Young, Kevin (2008) *Deviance and Social Control in Sport*. Champaign, IL: Human Kinetics.

Auyero, Javier (1999) "'From the client's point(s) of view': How poor people perceive and evaluate political clientelism." *Theory and Society* 28(2):297–334.

Auyero, Javier (2000) "The logic of clientelism in Argentina: An ethnographic account." *Latin American Research Review* 35(3):55–81.

Auyero, Javier (2001) *Poor People's Politics: Peronist Survival Networks and the Legacy of Evita*. Durham, NC; London: Duke University Press.

Auyero, Javier (2007) *Routine Politics and Violence in Argentina: The Gray Zone of State Power*. Cambridge: Cambridge University Press.

BBC Mundo (2017) "La trágica historia de Emanuel Balbo, el hincha que murió al ser lanzado desde la tribuna al vacío en un partido de fútbol en Argentina." April 17.

Beard, Mary (2008) *Pompeii: The Life of a Roman Town*. London: Profile Books.

Beer, Carlos (2015) "Raúl Gámez: 'Sí, pacto con los barras.'" *La Nación*, January 24.

Beuving, Joost & de Vries, Geert (2015) *Doing Qualitative Research: The Craft of Naturalistic Inquiry*. Amsterdam: Amsterdam University Press.

Bourgois, Philippe (1991) "Confronting the ethics of ethnography: Lessons from fieldwork in Central America." In F. Harrison (Ed.), *Decolonising Anthropology: Moving Further Toward an Anthropology for Liberation* (pp. 111–127). Washington, DC: American Anthropological Association.

Branz, Juan Bautista et al. (2020) "Violencias en el fútbol argentino: claves para pensar su deconstrucción." *Debates en Sociología* 51:77–95.

Brewer, John D. (2000) *Ethnography*. Buckingham; Philadelphia: Open University Press.

Briquet, Jean-Louis (n.d.) "Clientelism." *Encyclopaedia Britannica Online*.

Bull, Martin J. & Newell, James L. (1997) "New avenues in the study of political corruption." *Crime, Law & Social Change* 27:169–183.

Bull, Martin J. & Newell, James L. (Eds.) (2003) *Corruption in Contemporary Politics*. Hampshire; New York: Palgrave Macmillan.

Bundio, Javier Sebastián (2018) "La construcción del otro en el fútbol: Identidad y alteridad en los cantos de las hinchadas argentinas." *Cuadernos de Antropología Social* 47:195–212.

Burstyn, Varda (1999) *The Rites of Men: Manhood, Politics, and the Culture of Sport*. Toronto; Buffalo; London: University of Toronto Press.

Buzzella, Hernán (2007) "De chico acomodado a barrabrava fiel." *Clarín*, August 9.

Callaway, Helen (1992) "Ethnography and experience: Gender implications in fieldwork and texts." In J. Okely & H. Callaway (Eds.), *Anthropology & Autobiography* (pp. 29–48). London; New York: Routledge.

Cámara Argentina de Comercio (2015) *Panorama demográfico de la Provincia de Buenos Aires*. Buenos Aires.

Castillo, Hernán (2011) *Todo pasa: Fútbol, negocios y política de Videla a los Kirchner*. Buenos Aires: Aguilar.

Cavallo, Domingo (1997) *El peso de la verdad: Un impulso a la transparencia en la Argentina de los 90*. Buenos Aires: Planeta.

Centenera, Mar & Rivas Molina, Federico (2018) "Las causas judiciales contra Cristina Kirchner." *El País*, August 19.

Clarín (2016) "Amenazas en la General Paz recrudecen la interna de la barra de River." September 18.

Clarín (2023) "Murió el hincha de Lanús baleado en la cabeza en medio de un cruce entre barrabravas." July 31.

162 References

Co, Edna Estifania A. (2007) "Challenges to the Philippine culture of corruption." In S. Bracking (Ed.), *Corruption and Development: The Anti-Corruption Campaigns* (pp. 121–137). Basingstoke; New York: Palgrave Macmillan.

Cook, John W. (1999) *Morality and Cultural Differences.* New York: Oxford University Press.

Creswell, John W. (2009) *Research Design: Qualitative, Quantitative, and Mixed Methods Approaches* (Third Edition). London; Thousand Oaks, CA: Sage Publications.

Darwin, Charles (1913) *A Naturalist's Voyage Round the World: The Voyage of the Beagle.* London: John Murray.

De la Torre, Carlos (1992) "The ambiguous meanings of Latin American populisms." *Social Research* 59(2):385–414.

Douglas, Delia D. (2005) "Venus, Serena, and the women's tennis association: When and where 'race' enters." *Sociology of Sport Journal* 22:255–281.

Dubowitz, Mark & Dershowitz, Toby (2019) "Argentina's new leadership carries old baggage of corruption and conspiracy allegations." *NBC News THINK*, December 23.

Duke, Vic & Crolley, Liz (2001) "*Fútbol*, politicians and the people: Populism and politics in Argentina." *International Journal of the History of Sport* 18(3):93–116.

Dunning, Eric (1999) *Sport Matters: Sociological Studies of Sport, Violence and Civilization.* London; New York: Routledge.

Dyck, Noel (2012) *Fields of Play: An Ethnography of Children's Sports.* Toronto: University of Toronto Press.

Dyer, Elizabeth A. (2006) "Argentina." In H. J. Birx (Ed.), *Encyclopedia of Anthropology* (Vol. 1, pp. 272–274). Thousand Oaks, CA; London; New Delhi: Sage Publications.

Eberhardt, Nancy (2014) "Piaget and Durkheim: Competing paradigms in the anthropology of morality." *Anthropological Theory* 14(3):301–316.

Eggers Brass, Teresa (2006) *Historia Argentina: una mirada crítica (1806–2006).* Ituzaingó: Editorial Maipue.

Eisenstadt, Shmuel Noah & Lemarchand, René. (Eds.) (1981) *Political Clientelism, Patronage and Development.* Beverly Hills: Sage Publications.

Eisenstadt, Shmuel Noah & Roniger, Luis (Eds.) (1984) *Patrons, Clients, and Friends: Interpersonal Relations and the Structure of Trust in Society.* Cambridge: Cambridge University Press.

El Cronista (2023) "'Incapaz, ausente y poco transparente': cómo percibe la sociedad argentina al Estado." March 22.

Eriksen, Thomas Hylland (2004) *What Is Anthropology?* London: Pluto Press.

Estévez, Alejandro M. (2016) "Encuesta de percepción de los jóvenes argentinos sobre la corrupción y el comportamiento ciudadano." Universidad de Buenos Aires, Facultad de Ciencias Económicas.

Fernández, Nadia (2014) "Ellos o nosotros." *La Voz*, November 17.

Ferradás, Carmen Alicia (2001) "Argentina." In M. Ember & C. R. Ember (Eds.), *Countries and Their Cultures* (Vol. 1, pp. 77–92). New York; Detroit; San Francisco; London; Boston; Woodbridge, CT: Macmillan Reference USA.

Fox, Jonathan (1994) "The difficult transition from clientelism to citizenship: Lessons from Mexico." *World Politics* 46(2):151–184.

Frosdick, Steve & Marsh, Peter (2005) *Football Hooliganism.* London; New York: Routledge.

Frydenberg, Julio (2011) *Historia social del fútbol: Del amateurismo a la profesionalización.* Buenos Aires: Siglo Veintiuno Editores.

Gaffney, Christopher (2009) "Stadiums and society in twenty-first century Buenos Aires." *Soccer & Society* 10(2):160–182.

References 163

Galasso, Norberto (2006) "La década infame." *Cuadernos para la Otra Historia* 20:2–18. Buenos Aires: Centro Cultural Enrique S. Discépolo.

Gallo, Ezequiel (1986) "Argentina: Society and politics, 1880–1916." In L. Bethell (Ed.), *The Cambridge History of Latin America Volume V: C. 1870 to 1930* (pp. 359–391). Cambridge: Cambridge University Press.

Gallotta, Nahuel (2016) "'El Pony', el adolescente que cambió el fútbol por el delito." *Clarín*, October 6.

Galvani, Mariana & Palma, Javier (2005) "La hinchada de uniforme." In P. Alabarces (Ed.), *Hinchadas* (pp. 161–182). Buenos Aires: Prometeo Libros.

Garguin, Enrique (2007) "'Los Argentinos Descendemos de los Barcos': The racial articulation of middle class identity in Argentina (1920–1960)." *Latin American and Caribbean Ethnic Studies* 2(2):161–184.

Garriga Zucal, José (2010) *Nosotros nos peleamos: Violencia e identidad de una hinchada de fútbol.* Buenos Aires: Prometeo Libros.

Gil, Gastón Julián (2006) "'Te sigo a todas partes'. Pasión y *aguante* en una *hinchada* de fútbol de un club del interior." *Intersecciones en Antropología* 7:333–348.

Gil, Gastón Julián (2007) *Hinchas en tránsito: Violencia, memoria e identidad en una hinchada de un club del interior.* Mar del Plata: EUDEM.

Giordano, Verónica (2000) "La corrupción política en Argentina, 1886–1890: Una mirada desde The Times de Londres." *Sociohistórica* 7:251–268.

Girling, John (1997) *Corruption, Capitalism and Democracy.* London; New York: Routledge.

Giulianotti, Richard (1995) "Participant observation and research into football hooliganism: Reflections on the problems of entrée and everyday risks." *Sociology of Sport Journal* 12:1–20.

Giulianotti, Richard (1999) *Football: A Sociology of the Global Game.* Cambridge: Polity Press.

Glaeser, E., Di Tella, R. & Llach, L. (2018) "Introduction to Argentine exceptionalism." *Latin American Economic Review* 27(1):1–22.

Gledhill, John (2000) *Power and Its Disguises: Anthropological Perspectives on Politics.* London; Sterling: Pluto Press.

Golden, Miriam A. (2003) "Electoral connections: The effects of the personal vote on political patronage, bureaucracy and legislation in postwar Italy." *British Journal of Political Science* 33:189–212.

Goldstein, Donna (2003) *Laughter Out of Place: Race, Class, Violence, and Sexuality in a Rio Shantytown.* Berkeley; Los Angeles; London: University of California Press.

Goldstein, Donna (2012) "How corruption kills: Pharmaceutical crime, mediated representations, and middle class anxiety in Neoliberal Argentina." *City & Society* 24(2):218–239.

Grabia, Gustavo (2009a) *La Doce: La verdadera historia de la barra brava de Boca.* Buenos Aires: Editorial Sudamericana.

Grabia, Gustavo (2009b) "El problema más grave de barras está en la Argentina." *Olé*, March 4.

Green, Linda (1995) "Living in a state of fear." In C. Nordstrom & A. C. G. M. Robben (Eds.), *Fieldwork Under Fire: Contemporary Studies of Violence and Survival* (pp. 105–128). Berkeley: University of California Press.

Grondona, Mariano (1993) *La corrupción.* Buenos Aires: Planeta.

Guano, Emanuela (2003) "A color for the modern nation: The discourse on class, race, and education in the *Porteño* middle class." *The Journal of Latin American Anthropology* 8(1):148–171.

164 References

Guilbert, Sébastien (2006) "Violence in sports and among sportsmen: A single or two-track issue?" *Aggressive Behavior* 32:231–240.

Gupta, Akhil (2005) "Narrating the state of corruption." In D. Haller & C. Shore (Eds.), *Corruption: Anthropological Perspectives* (pp.173–193). London; Ann Arbor, MI: Pluto Press.

Haigh, Roger M. (1964) "The creation and control of a caudillo." *Hispanic American Historical Review* 44(4):481–490.

Haller, Dieter & Shore, Cris (Eds.) (2005) *Corruption: Anthropological Perspectives.* London; Ann Arbor: Pluto.

Hallin, Daniel C. & Papathanassopoulos, Stylianos (2002) "Political clientelism and the media: Southern Europe and Latin America in comparative perspective." *Media, Culture & Society* 24:175–195.

Haraway, Donna (1988) "Situated knowledges: The science question in feminism and the privilege of partial perspective." *Feminist Studies* 14(3):575–599.

Hasicic, Germán (2016) *Fútbol e identidad. Prácticas y rituales en el estadio del Club Atlético River Plate.* (Unpublished thesis). Universidad Nacional de La Plata, La Plata, Argentina.

Heeks, Richard (2007) "Why anti-corruption initiatives fail: Technology transfer and contextual collision." In S. Bracking (Ed.), *Corruption and Development: The Anti-Corruption Campaigns* (pp. 258–272). Basingstoke; New York: Palgrave Macmillan.

Herbert, Ian (2018) "Was 1978 the DODGIEST World Cup ever? Match-fixing claims, allegations of corruption and a fascist dictator… The incredible story of how Argentina swept to victory 40 years ago." *The Daily Mail*, June 1.

Herrera, Eduardo (2018) "Masculinity, violence, and deindividuation in Argentine soccer chants: The sonic potentials of participatory sounding-in-synchrony." *Ethnomusicology* 62(3):470–499.

Hersey, Will (2018) "Remembering Argentina 1978: The Dirtiest World Cup of all time." *Esquire*, June 14.

Herzfeld, Michael (2005) *Cultural Intimacy: Social Poetics in the Nation-State.* New York: Routledge.

Hofstede, Geert (2001) *Culture's Consequences: Comparing Values, Behaviors, Institutions, and Organizations Across Nations.* Thousand Oaks, CA; London; New Delhi: Sage Publications.

Honigmann, John (1976) "The personal approach in cultural anthropological research." *Current Anthropology* 17(2):243–261.

Hopkin, Jonathan (1997) "Political parties, political corruption, and the economic theory of democracy." *Crime, Law & Social Change* 27:255–274.

Hopkin, Jonathan (2006) "Conceptualizing political clientelism: Political exchange and democratic theory." *APSA Annual Meeting: Panel 46-18 'Concept Analysis: Unpacking Clientelism, Governance and Neoliberalism.'* Philadelphia. 1–19.

INDEC (2012) *Censo Nacional de Población, Hogares y Viviendas 2010.* Buenos Aires.

infobae (2017) "El día que Cristina Elisabet Kirchner defendió a los barrabravas." April 17.

infobae (2022) "Una encuesta muestra que la clase media asocia la corrupción y los privilegios con la dirigencia política." March 26.

James, Wendy (2008) "Well-being: In whose opinion, and who pays?" In A. Corsín Jiménez (Ed.), *Culture and Well-Being: Anthropological approaches to Freedom and Political Ethics* (pp. 69–79). London; Ann Arbor: Pluto Press.

Keep, Joel (2014) "Argentine drug probe zeroes in on Presidential Palace." *Miami Herald*, September 5.

References 165

Kennedy, David (2013) "A contextual analysis of Europe's Ultra Football supporters movement." *Soccer & Society* 14(2):132–153.

Kettering, Sharon (1988) "The historical development of political clientelism." *The Journal of Interdisciplinary History* 18(3):419–447.

Khasnabish, Alex (2004) "'Zones of conflict': Exploring the ethics of anthropology in dangerous spaces." *Nexus* 17(1):63–87.

Kottak, Conrad Phillip (2009) *Mirror for Humanity: A Concise Introduction to Cultural Anthropology.* New York: McGraw-Hill.

La Capital (2017) "El video de la violenta y preocupante arenga de Newell's en la previa del clásico de reserva." May 15.

La Nación (2011) "Por el camino de las presiones." June 30.

La Nación (2017) "El hincha de Belgrano arrojado de una tribuna, en estado crítico: 'Tiene pocos signos de vitalidad cerebral.'" April 16.

La Nueva Mañana (2017) "Está grave el hincha arrojado desde la tribuna durante el clásico." April 16.

La Nueva Mañana (2019) "Cayó porque fue golpeado violentamente en su intento desesperado por huir." March 28.

Lanata, Jorge (2014) *10K, la década robada: Datos y hechos en los años de la grieta.* Buenos Aires: Planeta.

Lancaster, Thomas D. & Montinola, Gabriella R. (1997) "Toward a methodology for the comparative study of political corruption." *Crime, Law & Social Change* 27:185–206.

Larraquy, Marcelo (2017) *Argentina. Un siglo de violencia política.* Buenos Aires: Sudamericana.

Lemarchand, Rene & Legg, Keith (1972) "Political clientelism and development: A preliminary analysis." *Comparative Politics* 4(2):149–178.

Levitsky, Steven (2005) *La transformación del Justicialismo: Del partido sindical al partido clientelista 1983–1999.* Buenos Aires: Siglo XXI.

Lista de víctimas (n.d.) Retrieved from salvemosalfutbol.org/

Llach, Juan J. & Lagos, Martín (2014) *El país de las desmesuras: Raíces del retraso de la Argentina.* Buenos Aires: El Ateneo.

Lobato, Mirta Zaida (2000) "Estado, gobierno y política en el régimen conservador." In M. Z. Lobato (Ed.), *Nueva Historia Argentina Tomo 5: El progreso, la modernización y sus límites (1880–1916)* (pp. 179–208). Buenos Aires: Editorial Sudamericana.

Lopes, Fernando (2007) "Partisanship and political clientelism in Portugal (1983–1993)." *South European Society and Politics* 2(3):27–51.

Lynch, John (1992) *Caudillos in Spanish America 1800–1850.* Oxford: Clarendon Press.

Lyth, Jason (2007) *Playing in the City: Football Fandom and Street Protests in Buenos Aires.* (Unpublished master's thesis). Simon Fraser University, Burnaby, Canada.

MacLachlan, Colin M. (2006) *Argentina: What Went Wrong.* Westport, CT; London: Praeger.

MacLeod, Murdo J. (1984) "Aspects of the internal economy of colonial Spanish America: Labour; taxation; distribution and exchange." In L. Bethell (Ed.), *The Cambridge History of Latin America Volume II: Colonial Latin America* (pp. 219–264). Cambridge: Cambridge University Press.

Macor, Darío (2001) "Partidos, coaliciones y sistemas de poder." In A. Cattaruzza (Ed.), *Nueva Historia Argentina Tomo 7: Crisis económica, avance del Estado e incertidumbre política (1930–1943)* (pp. 49–95). Buenos Aires: Editorial Sudamericana.

Magazine, Roger (2004) "'You can buy a player's legs, but not his heart': A critique of clientelism and modernity among soccer fans in Mexico City." *The Journal of Latin American Anthropology* 9(1):8–33.

Magazine, Roger (2007) *Golden and Blue Like My Heart: Masculinity, Youth, and Power Among Soccer Fans in Mexico City*. Tucson: The University of Arizona Press.

Mason, Jennifer (2002) *Qualitative Researching* (Second Edition). London: Sage Publications.

Medina, Walter C. (2020) "Las causas judiciales que preocupan a Mauricio Macri." *nueva-tribuna.es*, January 31.

Meneley, Anne & Young, Donna J. (Eds.) (2005) *Auto-ethnographies: The Anthropology of Academic Practices*. Peterborough, ON: Broadview Press.

Mény, Yves & Rhodes, Martin (1997) "Illicit governance: Corruption, scandal and fraud." In M. Rhodes, P. Heywood & V. Wright (Eds.), *Developments in West European Politics* (pp. 95–113). London: Macmillan.

Miller, David (2014) *Introduction to Collective Behavior and Collective Action*. Long Grove, IL: Waveland Press.

Mills, C. Wright (1959) *The Sociological Imagination*. Oxford: Oxford University Press.

Mitchell, J. Clyde (1983) "Case and situation analysis." *Sociological Review* 31(2):187–211.

Moreira, Verónica (2012) "Juego electoral y relaciones políticas en el fútbol argentino." *História: Questões & Debates* 57:127–149.

Moreira, Verónica (2013) "Fútbol, violencia y política: redes de relaciones en Argentina." *Revista Colombiana de Sociología* 36(1):65–76.

Moreira, Verónica et al. (2023) "A Duel of 'Hinchadas': Chile and Argentina, a comparative study." In B. Buarque de Hollanda & T. Busset (Eds.), *Football Fandom in Europe and Latin America: Culture, Politics, and Violence in the 21st Century* (pp. 215–236). Cham; Switzerland: Palgrave Macmillan.

Moutoukias, Zacarías (2000) "Gobierno y sociedad en el Tucumán y el Río de la Plata, 1550–1800." In E. Tandeter (Ed.), *Nueva Historia Argentina Tomo 2: La sociedad colonial* (pp. 355–412). Buenos Aires: Editorial Sudamericana.

Mundlak, Yair, Cavallo, Domingo & Domenech, Roberto (1989) "Agriculture and economic growth in Argentina, 1913–1984." *International Food Policy Research Institute* Research Report 76.

Murzi, Diego & Segura M. Trejo, Fernando (2018) "Hacia un mapa de la 'violencia en el fútbol': Actores, dinámicas, respuestas públicas y desafíos en el caso de Argentina." *Revista de Gestión Pública* 7(1):43–75.

Navrátilová, Hana (2014) *"Good Times in Buenos Aires": Being an "Expat" in the City of Foreigners*. (Unpublished master's thesis). Stockholms universitet, Stockholm, Sweden.

Nicholas, Ralph (1973) "Social and political movements." *Annual Review of Anthropology* 2:63–84.

O'Donnell, Guillermo (1993) "On the state, democratization and some conceptual problems: A Latin American view with glances at some postcommunist countries." *World Development* 21(8):1355–1369.

Olé (2011) "Para Pezzotta que no lo mira por TV." July 8.

Olé (2017) "Todos con DNI." March 22.

Olweus, Dan (1993) *Bullying at School: What We Know and What We Can Do*. Malden, MA; Oxford; Carlton: Blackwell Publishing.

O'Neill, Megan (2005) *Policing Football: Social Interaction and Negotiated Disorder*. Hampshire; New York: Palgrave Macmillan.

Ortner, Sherry B. (2006) *Anthropology and Social Theory: Culture, Power, and the Acting Subject*. Durham, NC; London: Duke University Press.

Pardo, Daniel (2018) "Clásico River-Boca por la Libertadores: ¿qué tan cierto es que Boca Juniors es el equipo del pueblo y River Plate el de la élite?" *BBC Mundo*, November 23.

References   167

Pardo, Italo (Ed.) (2004) *Between Morality and the Law: Corruption, Anthropology and Comparative Society*. London; New York: Routledge.

Parrish, Charles T. & Nauright, John (2013) "Fútbol cantitos: Negotiating masculinity in Argentina." *Soccer & Society* 14(1):1–19.

Perfil (2015) "Los Gámez, dinastía de barra bravas." September 21.

Perfil (2019) "Salió a correr con la remera de Boca y le pegaron." February 12.

Perfil (2022a) "Violencia en el fútbol: cinco casos recientes que muestran un incremento." September 13.

Perfil (2022b) "La Justicia 'se deja influir': el 66% desconfía de su independencia en causas de corrupción." September 26.

Pigna, Felipe (2004) *Los mitos de la historia argentina: Del "descubrimiento" de América a la "independencia."* Buenos Aires: Grupo Editorial Norma.

Pigna, Felipe (2006) *Los mitos de la historia argentina: De la ley Sáenz Peña a los albores del peronismo*. Buenos Aires: Planeta.

Plautus, Titus Maccius & Nixon, Paul (1952) *Plautus in Five Volumes: V*. London: William Heinemann Ltd.; Cambridge, MA: Harvard University Press.

Plaza Schaefer, Valeria & Cabrera, Nicolás (2021) "Violencias, seguridad y dilemas metodológicos: Una mirada sociológica de la experiencia en el Club Atlético Belgrano de Córdoba, Argentina." *Runa* 42(1):83–102.

Pomer, León (2004) *La corrupción, una cultura argentina*. Buenos Aires: Leviatán.

Press TV (2007) "Argentina has most corrupt judiciary." June 11.

Que Pasa Salta (2018) "'No viajen a Bolivia, es terrible', la advertencia de una salteña que vivió un calvario." March 6.

Radcliffe-Brown, Alfred R. (1952) *Structure and Function in Primitive Society: Essays and Addresses*. Glencoe, IL: The Free Press.

Rebossio, Alejandro (2015) "Buenos Aires, la ciudad con más campos de fútbol del mundo." *El País*, August 17.

Respighi, Emanuel (2006) "Las historias oficiales son como una creación fantástica." *Página/12*, November 18.

Rocchi, Fernando (2000) "El péndulo de la riqueza: la economía argentina en el período 1880–1916." In M. Z. Lobato (Ed.), *Nueva Historia Argentina Tomo 5: El progreso, la modernización y sus límites (1880–1916)* (pp. 15–70). Buenos Aires: Editorial Sudamericana.

Rock, David (1975) *Politics in Argentina 1890–1930: The Rise and Fall of Radicalism*. New York: Cambridge University Press.

Rock, David (1985) *Argentina 1516–1982*. Berkeley: University of California Press.

Romero, José Luis (2004) *Breve historia de la Argentina* (Fifth Edition). Buenos Aires: Fondo de Cultura Económica.

Romero, Luis Alberto (2006) *A History of Argentina in the Twentieth Century*. Buenos Aires: Fondo de Cultura Económica.

Romero, Luis Alberto (2012) *Breve historia contemporánea de la Argentina: 1916–2010* (Third Edition). Buenos Aires: Fondo de Cultura Económica.

Rosales, Humberto (2013) *Los árbitros del soborno*. Córdoba: Raíz de Dos.

Roudakova, Natalia (2008) "Media-political clientelism: Lessons from anthropology." *Media, Culture & Society* 30(1):41–59.

Saba, Roberto P. & Manzetti, Luigi (1997) "Privatization in Argentina: The implications for corruption." *Crime, Law & Social Change* 25:353–369.

Safford, Frank (1985) "Politics, ideology and society in post-Independence Spanish America." In L. Bethell (Ed.), *The Cambridge History of Latin America Volume III: From Independence to c. 1870* (pp. 347–422). Cambridge: Cambridge University Press.

Sarmiento, Domingo Faustino (2003) *Facundo: Civilization and Barbarism.* Berkeley; Los Angeles; London: University of California Press. (Original work published 1845).

Scalia, Vincenzo (2009) "Just a few rogues? Football *Ultras*, clubs and politics in contemporary Italy." *International Review for the Sociology of Sport* 44(1):41–53.

Scheper-Hughes, Nancy (1995) "The primacy of the ethical: Towards a militant anthropology." *Current Anthropology* 36:409–440.

Sissener, Tone K. (2001) "Anthropological perspectives on corruption." Working Paper available at: http://bora.cmi.no/dspace/bitstream/10202/209/1/WP2001-05.PDF

Soca, Ricardo (2010) *La fascinante historia de las palabras.* Rey Naranjo Editores.

Soria, Horacio (2020) "'Beyond worst nightmares:' Argentina's child poverty rate soars amid pandemic." *Reuters*, July 5.

Spaaij, Ramón (2007) "Football hooliganism in the Netherlands: Patterns of continuity and change." *Soccer & Society* 8(2/3):316–334.

Statistics Times (2020) "List of Countries by GDP (nominal) per capita." January 21.

Stokes, Susan C. (2005) "Perverse accountability: A formal model of machine politics with evidence from Argentina." *American Political Science Review* 99(3):315–325.

Szwarcberg, Mariela (2013) "The microfoundations of political clientelism: Lessons from the Argentine case." *Latin American Research Review* 48(2):32–54.

Tamagni, Rodrigo (2016) "Por qué el estadio de Quilmes dejará de llamarse José Luis Meiszner." infobae, August 26.

Télam (2017) "Un hincha de River se cayó de la tribuna y está en grave estado." June 18.

Testa, Alberto & Armstrong, Gary (2010) *Football, Fascism and Fandom: The UltraS of Italian Football.* London: A & C Black.

The Telegraph (2013) "Former Argentine leader Menem to serve 7 years for arms smuggling." June 14.

Tsoukala, Anastassia (2009) *Football Hooliganism in Europe: Security and Civil Liberties in the Balance.* Basingstoke: Palgrave Macmillan.

Tuastad, Dag (1997) "The political role of football for palestinians in Jordan." In G. Armstrong & R. Giulianotti (Eds.), *Entering the Field: New Perspectives on World Football* (pp. 105–121). Oxford; New York: Berg.

Uliana, Santiago & Godio, Matías (2013) "Separar, dividir y mortificar. Los dispositivos culturales de seguridad en los estadios del fútbol argentino." In J. Garriga Zucal (Ed.), *Violencia en el fútbol: Investigaciones sociales y fracasos políticos* (pp. 297–319). Buenos Aires: Ediciones Godot.

Vázquez, Bernardo & Cayón, David (2014) *Fútbol para todos: La política de los goles.* Buenos Aires: Sudamericana.

Veiga, Gustavo (2004) "La cara siniestra del fútbol." *Página/12*, June 27.

Waldman, Peter (1986) *El peronismo: 1943–1955.* Buenos Aires: Hyspamerica.

Watson, Peter J. (2022) *Football and Nation Building in Colombia (2010–2018): The Only Thing That Unites Us.* Liverpool: Liverpool University Press.

Wolf, Eric (2001) *Pathways of Power: Building an Anthropology of the Modern World.* Berkeley; Los Angeles; London: University of California Press.

Wolf, Eric R. & Hansen, Edward C. (1967) "Caudillo politics: A structural analysis." *Comparative Studies in Society and History* 9(2):168–179.

Yarroch, Gustavo (2006) "La 12 se alquila para el tour Pura Adrenalina." *Clarín*, October 6.

Yglesias, Matthew (2012) "The four types of economies and the global imbalances." *Slate*, April 17.

Zatat, Narjas (2017) "Man dies after Argentina football crowd pushed him off stand mistaking him for rival fan." *The Independent*, April 18.

Index

Note: *Italic* page numbers refer to figures and page numbers followed by "n" denote endnotes.

Acro, Gonzalo 67n39, 139
activist anthropology 154–155
Adang, Otto 136, 151
AFA *see* Argentinian Football Association (AFA)
Agar, Michael 9
agency 10, 140, 144
aggression/aggressive 26–27, 47; behaviour 44; cartoonish displays of 51; definitions of 15; and fun 26, 33, 34; human 27; and humour 33; verbal 26, 28
aggressiveness 26
Agosti, Orlando Ramón 96
aguante 15, 125, 130; culture of 64; expression of 63; form of 115; legitimate carrier of 63
Aguinis, Marcos: *Atrocious Charm of Being Argentinian* 151
Alabarces, Pablo 5, 53–55, 62, 80–81, 135, 150
Alconada Mon, Hugo 57, 60, 64, 82–83, 111, 116–117, 121, 125
ambiguity 27–28, 75–76, 134
Amit, Vered 20
amoral familist behavior 83
Anderson, Craig A. 28
anthropologist/adventurer 13
anthropology: emic approaches to 9–10; of liberation 154–155; political 2
anti-corruption: models 72; programmes 73
APREVIDE 140–141

Aragón, Silvio 13, 135
Archetti, Eduardo 1, 5, 157
Argentina 135; context 9; culture 1, 9, 83, 127; football, clientelist relationships in 2; moral and economic decadence 121; political corruption and impunity in 2–4; prosperity 30; social and political history 80
Argentinian demographics 31, 32
Argentinian Football Association (AFA) 3, 25, 84, 89–90
Aristotle 74
Armstrong, Gary 135
associated violence 81, 150
Atkinson, Michael 27
Atrocious Charm of Being Argentinian (Aguinis) 151
autobiographical reflexivity 14
autoethnography 14, 38, 39
Autonomous City of Buenos Aires 11, 23, 31, 57
Auyero, Javier 74, 93, 98–99, 101–105, 107, 110

bad government 100
Band-Aid solutions 137
ban on visiting fans 35, 41, 47, 49, 145, 149
barbarism, in football 15, 28–34
barras 13, 21–22, 26, 34, 45, 53–54, 60, 66n30, 68n51, 79, 83, 85, 91n7, 107–108, 114–115, 129, 137, 143–144, 146,

150–151, 152n5; actions and discourses of 44; clientelism 4, 18n7, 55, 89, 104, 107–111, 118, 123; contemporary 121; demands 120; financial agreement with 86; illegal businesses/agreements 121; intimidation 4, 55–57, 86, 110, 117, 125; movements and interactions 88; participation 89–90; physical confrontations with 57; for political support 56; power of negotiation 117; presence of 35–36, 142; relationships with 109, 146; rival 138–139; role of 57; stigmatization of 123–126; violent behaviour 18n7

barras bravas 3, 5, 13, 15, 17n6, 53–62, 64–65, 65n1, 67n38, 83–84, 107–108, 110, 123, 139, 146; Alabarces' description of 57; in football and politics 78; role of 55, 78, 119

Basic Units 71, 95–96

Beard, Mary 97, 98, 112n6

behavioural/behaviours 77, 107; changes 151; corrupt 73; of fans and protesters 42; intolerant 34

Belgrano 22, 49–51, 66n11, 87, 91n17

"benevolent" corruption 74

Bergés, Mariano 67n44, 118, 136, 147

Beuving, Joost 7–8, 158

"big five" football clubs 11

blat 102–103, 107

Boca 20, 22, 32, 33, 35, 59, 60, 65n1, 66n11, 111, 116, 144

Boca Experience 19, 21

Boca fans 32–33, 36, 66n12, 66n17, 131, 138

Bolivian/Bolivia: fans 33; immigrants 33

Bombonera 52, 114, 132n1

Branz, Juan Bautista 64, 150

bribery 75, 78, 89, 103–104, 150

brown zones 70

Buenos Aires 1–2, 11, 22, 25–26, 31, 77, 84, 127–128, 132; football matches in 23–24; map of 23; neighbourhood of 32

Bull, Martin J. 69, 72

Bundio, Javier Sebastián 40

Burstyn, Varda 32, 130

Bushman, Brad J. 28

Cabrera, Branz 150

Cabrera, Nicolás 5, 137, 139, 150

Cantero, Javier 84–85, 119, 144

Castillo, Hernán 123

cathartic rituals 67n33

caudillismo 93

caudillos 93–95

Cavallo, Domingo 79

CCTV 87, 88, 91n18, 139

Celman, Miguel Ángel Juárez 78

census data 31, 65n5

Chacarita Juniors 81

chanting/chants 32–36, 38–39, 42; and dancing 37; proliferation of 36

Chelsea Football Club 151n1

children, moral development 113–114

civic culture 101

civic values 82

civilization 15, 28–32; and barbarism 28–32

clientelism/clientelist 2, 4, 12, 14, 78, 99, 106–107, 123; analysis of 71; anthropological analysis of 92; Argentinian brand of 104; brand of 109, 111; comparative perspectives 16, 101, 105; definition of 16; differences and similarities 105; dual role 74–75; ethnographic and qualitative studies on 98; in football 4, 71, 99, 107–111; functions 93; in Greater Buenos Aires 71; historical background 16; issue of 100; networks 70; and politics (*see* politics); practices of 97, 103; problem-solving network 93, 96, 106, 111; prominent role of 97; reciprocity 71; relationships 98; social and cultural specificities 93, 98, 103; social welfare 73, 74; study of 101

clients' voting behaviour 71

Club Almagro 43

Club Atlético Belgrano 49

Club Atlético Defensores de Belgrano 62

Club Atlético Talleres 49

Club Atlético Vélez Sarsfield 119

Club Barrial 59, 118, 139, 141

Club Leandro N. Alem 49

Club Luján 49

Club Nacional de Fútbol 54
clubs 60, 82, 137; economic advancement 123; elections 119; financial situation of 85; management 56; officials 61–62, 84–85, 99, 108, 118, 126–127; political 94, 123; security 83–84
Co, Edna Estifania A. 103
cognitive: anthropology 9–10; dissonance 39–49
collective action, opportunities for 99–100
Colombia 135
compadritos, intimidation of 94
complicity 85, 118
concealment 80
conflicts of interests 80–81
Conquest of the Desert 93–94
Conservative Party 95
constraint-based theory 10
contextual differences 103, 134
contextualization 71, 135
Cook, John W. 113–114
Córdoba's Football League 91n10
Coronel, Joaquín 48–49
corrupt behaviour 73–75, 90, 103, 106
corruption 4, 11–12, 16, 78–79, 142, 151; acts of 76; in Argentina 69–91, 106; Argentinian Football Association 84; article on 106; cases of 147; causes of 69; and clientelism 4, 12, 82, 100; conceptualizations of 69, 72; contextual understandings of 71; cycle of 4, 89; definitions of 15–16, 69–76, 106; extensive history of 90; in football 84–90; global and local understandings 69; indictments of 80; infatuation 84; issue of 100, 106; laws and control 83; local specificities 103, 159; media coverage of 14; and morality 76, 114; perpetuation of 111; qualitative research on 14; study on 101–102; survey data 73, 84, 90; and violence 77–84
Creswell, John W. 7
Crolley, Liz 3, 123, 135
cultural/culture 148; analytical and interpretive studies of 156; change 10, 17, 135, 149, 151, 154; contexts 15–16, 101–102, 158; environment 137;

impediments 138–147; of impunity 82, 86; transformation 10, 17, 149, 151
Cultural Intimacy (Herzfeld) 155

Darwin, Charles 77, 83, 151
Daskal, Rodrigo 33
Década infame 95
de facto government 79, 81
degree of familiarity 114–115
degrees of corruptness 76
dictatorship 78, 79, 81, 96; political discourses of 80
discrimination 32; against immigrants 32
Douglas, Delia D. 31
Duke, Vic 3, 123, 135
Dunning, Eric: *Sport Matters* 134
dyadic relationships 74, 111
Dyck, Noel 135

Eberhardt, Nancy 113
economic: interests in football 2, 4–5, 17, 54, 60; power 106
educational campaigns 17, 149–150
electoral fraud 78, 94–95
Emanuel Balbo case 15, 49–50, 64
emic and etic perspectives 5
emic approach 8–9, 15, 37–39, 55
emotional: attachments 7; friendships 97, 99, 103, 107, 109
English hooligans 65n4, 137
entertainers/entertainment 6, 54–55
environments 103, 131–132
Estadio Antonio Vespucio Liberti 25
ethnographers/ethnographic/ethnography 8–9, 12, 135; approach 99; critique of 156; definition of 7; descriptions 9–10; inclinations 134; methodologies 8, 156, 158; research, opportunity for 21
etic approach 9, 46
European Cup 136
European immigration 78, 94
"everyone for themselves" mentality 5
exchange networks 105, 107, 109
extractive immigrants 31

Fabbri, Alejandro 33
familiarity 8, 114–115, 134, 149

fans 3, 25, 32–33, 41, 53–55; anger and frustration 117; behaviour at football stadiums 37–39; Boca 32–33, 36, 66n12, 66n17, 131, 138; Bolivian 33; clashes and interactions between 35; organized 3, 26, 65n4; River 19–20, 32–33, 35–36, 66n12, 131; violent 138
fatal cases of violence 140
FAVIFA 152n8
Fernández, Nadia 108, 130
fieldwork 8, 11–13, 72, 103, 154–157; analysis of football fandom 37; in Buenos Aires 30; experiences 20; research 155
1978 FIFA World Cup 78, 79, 81
flags, appropriation of 138
football: Argentinian identity 30; business 3, 59; carnival 46, 51; description of 1; environment 147–148; fandoms 44; fans 32–33, 41; formal structures of 3; gender and violence in 35; hooliganism in England 134–135; law enforcement 137, 146; matches 111; and politics 3–4, 135; practice 131; psychology 5, 6; public policy 6, 7; public prominence 11; religion 1; as a right and a basic necessity 6; social and political role of 6, 20; social status of 14; stadiums 15, 37, 41, 51, 147; violence 17, 145, 159n1; see also clubs; fans
football clubs 2–3, 17n1, 33; "big five" 11; violence and corruption within 16
fraudulent administration 80; see also corruption
friendship: emotional 97, 99, 107, 109; instrumental 99, 103; types of 99
Front for Victory 111, 112n22, 123
Frydenberg, Julio 130
Fútbol Para Todos ("Football for All") 6–7; programme 7; psychological benefits of 6–7

Gaffney, Christopher 1, 13, 81–82, 85, 151
Gallardo, Marcelo 65n2
Gallo, Ezequiel 94
Galvani, Mariana 47
Garguin, Enrique 29
Garriga Zucal, José 53–55, 135

generalizability 158
gift-giving in the Philippines 103
Gil, Gastón Julián 45–46, 57, 61, 135
Girling, John 73–76
Giulianotti, Richard 135
Glaeser, E. 80
Godio, Matías 48
Golden, Miriam A. 100–102
Goldstein, Donna 70
Gómez, Oscar 49–50, 64
grand theory 8, 134
Grondona, Julio Humberto 84
Grondona, Mariano 75; La corrupción 76
grounded theory 7–8, 16, 75, 153, 157–158
group identity 4, 54, 62, 151
Grupos de Tarea 81, 91n5
Guano, Emanuela 30
guanxi 104, 107
Guilbert, Sébastien 28
Gupta, Akhil 84

Haigh, Roger M. 93
Hambo, Débora 125–126
"hands off" approach 155
Haraway, Donna 155
Hecho Club Social 5–6, 18n9, 38
Heeks, Richard 71–72
Herbert, Ian 79
"heroic" demonstrations 61
Herrera, Eduardo 39–40, 118
Herzfeld, Michael 155–156; Cultural Intimacy 155
Hess, Rudy 43
hincha 54, 55
Hinchadas Unidas Argentinas 16–17, 123–126, 151
HMS Beagle 77
Hofstede, Geert 157
Honigmann, John 158
Hopkin, Jonathan 70
hostile environments 15, 45
human aggression 27
hybrid anthropologist 9, 12, 20
hyperrelativism 155–157

identification checks 23
ideology 6, 30, 44, 106
illicit association 80

imagined community 30
immigrants 31, 42; discrimination against 32; of Indigenous backgrounds 34
impunity 61–62, 118; culture of 73; cycle of 4, 89; exorbitant levels of 4; extensive history of 90; in football 21, 85, 86, 89, 120, 129, 144; levels of 83
Indigenous populations as the Other 30
Indigenous races 31
inductive 7
instrumental friendships 99–100, 103, 110
instrumental relationships 107, 109
interested action 111, 126; *vs.* disinterested action 107
interpretive 7, 45, 72, 75, 134
interpretivism 7–8
intimidation 44, 55–56, 86, 94, 99, 110, 117, 145
intra-*barra* conflicts 35, 138–139
intra-barra confrontations 57, 65
intragroup violence 48
investigative journalism 14

James, Wendy 98–99

Khasnabish, Alex 154–156
Kirchner, Cristina Fernández de 60, 80
Kirchner, Fernández de 60–61, 80–81
Kirchner, Néstor 68n50, 80
Kissinger, Henry 79
Kottak, Conrad Phillip 8–9
Kuznets, Simon 80

La corrupción (Grondona) 76
Lacoste, Carlos Alberto 79
Lancaster, Thomas D. 102
law enforcement 137
legal consequences 120
legal system 145–146
Legg, Keith 93
Leicester School 135, 157, 159n1
Lemarchand, Rene 93
Lezama Park 66n26
Libarona, Mariano Cúneo *124*
Libertad 15, 19, 22, 25, 28, 38–39
liberated zone 85, 91n9, 152n11
list of victims of violence in Argentinian football 47

local specificities 9, 103, 107, 159
López, Manuel Alejandro 48–49
Los Troncos' stadium 128–129
loyalty 107
Lyth, Jason 37–40, 46

Machiavelli, Niccolò 82
MacLachlan, Colin M. 16, 82–83, 100, 109, 122, 143, 151
Macri, Mauricio 108
Magazine, Roger 135
Mallo, Marcelo 123, 139
Mario Alberto Kempes stadium 49
masculinity 58, 118–119, 125, 138
Massera, Emilio Eduardo 96
match fixing 79, 89–90
Mateo 127–129, 133n12, 133n19
media 4–5, 10–11, 22, 119, 125, 129, 146, 150; coverage 14
Mendoza, Pedro de 90n1
Menem, Carlos Saúl 79, 81, 96
Mény, Yves 72
Mills, C. Wright 8
Mitchell, J. Clyde 158
Mix Up Exchange 21–22, 24, 32–34
Molina, Matías Ezequiel Oliva 50
money laundering 80, 85
Montinola, Gabriella R. 102
Monumental stadium 25–26, 46
moral: absolutism 74; advancement 76; development 113–114; inconsistencies 16, 126–130; issues and dilemmas 114–123; relativism 113–114; values 113
morality: and corruption 76; discussion of 114; Durkheimian notion of 113; Hinchadas Unidas Argentinas 123–126; homogeneous conceptualization of 76; inconsistencies 126–130; interpretation of 126; issues and dilemmas 114–123; passion and 130–131; relativism 113–114; relevance of 73; universality of 113
Moreira, Verónica 107, 124, 135
Mundlak, Yair 78
Murzi, Diego 57
myth of origin 28

National Identity Card 21–22, 24–25
National Survey on Media and Justice 73

Index

naturalistic inquiry 157
Nauright, John 62
Navrátilová, Hana 30–31
Newell, James L. 69, 72
new paradigm 147–152
newspaper comments 43
Nicholas, Ralph 158
Nizzardo, Mónica 55
non-ethnographic approaches 153
non-punitive reforms 137
normative strengths 73–74
Núñez 22, 23

objectivity, intellectual concern for 155
Ocampo, Moreno 76
O'Donnell, Guillermo 70
Olweus, Dan 27
Omar Actis 79
O'Neill, Megan 12
oppressive economic policies 77
organized chaos 4, 10, 83, 132, 151
organized fans 3, 26, 47–48, 55, 57, 65n4, 82, 99–100
organized groups of fans 55, 99
Ortner, Sherry B. 10
"othering" in football 130

Palma, Javier 47
Pardo, Italo 14
Parrish, Charles T. 62
participant observation 12
participants, access to 11–14
participatory sounding-in-synchrony 38, 40, 43
passion 1–3, 17, 19, 47, 58, 60–62, 64, 118, 130–131
patronage politics 2, 3, 16, 97, 99, 100, 104, 106
patron-client relationships 16, 92–93
Peronism 106, 123, 133n13
Peronist Basic Units 96
Peronist Justicialista Party 93
Peronist Party 95–96
Peronist political strategies 106
Perón, Juan Domingo 95
perpetuation of practices 10
personal: contacts 11, 13, 102; wellbeing 154

Pezzotta, Sergio 87–88, 139–140
physical: aggression 114–115; barriers 48; violence 5, 15, 35, 42, 45, 47
Piaget, Jean 113, 114, 126
Pigna, Felipe 77
Plautus, Titus Maccius 83, 148
Plaza Schaefer, Valeria 5, 137, 139, 150
play 37, 39; cognitive dissonance 39–49; public performances during football matches 41, 42
police 57, 87; corruption 84, 87, 146; preferential treatment by 21–22; reputation 46; searches 116
political/politics/politicians 11, 14, 57, 118, 151; in ancient Rome 96–98; in anthropological studies 98–107; anthropology 2; aspirations 142; bias 142; brief background 93–96; clubs 94; contexts 5; control 94; corruption 73–75, 82, 145; culture 100–101; definitions 92–93; economy approach 70–71; in football 107–111, 135; ideology 44; image of 143; interests 2, 17, 54, 60, 143; leanings 108; media coverage of 14; power 106; prominent cases of 14; propaganda 111; rallies 57; violence 78
Pomer, León 26–27, 82
populism: definitions 106
positivism 155–156
poverty 7, 29–30, 32, 73, 93, 101, 106, 125
power: abuse of 155; corruption 74; perversion of 74; positions of 94, 147
practice theory 10
preconceptions 155
preferred term 53–54
prejudices 155
preventive approaches 150
principal-agent argument 101
privatization of violence 80–81
problem-solving networks 105–106
Process of National Reorganization 81
psychological well-being 5–6
public: funds 76, 78, 98; money 6–7, 70; resources 70, 74, 92, 103; scrutiny 42, 50
punitive measures 17, 137, 150
punteros 96

qualitative inclinations 134
qualitative methods 105, 153
quantitative methods 8, 153

race/racial/racism 32, 42–43
racial ideology 30
Radcliffe-Brown, Alfred R. 4, 10, 151
Radical Party 94–95
Raúl Gámez 67n40, 119–120
referees 40, 61, 87–90, 150
relationships: developing and maintaining 104; between politicians 3–4; types of 11–12, 105
reliability 157, 158
religion 1, 42–43, 77
research findings, subjectivities and validity of 154–159
Revolución Libertadora (Liberating Revolution) 96
Rhodes, Martin 72
rival *barras* 138–139
rivals as enemies 5, 34, 49, 130–132
River 1, 22, 33, 35, 46, 65n2, 65n11, 87
River Experience 19–21
River fans 19–20, 22, 25, 28, 32–33, 35–36, 38–39, 66n12, 111, 131
Rock, David 28, 30, 95
role play 39–49, 51–52, 64
Romero, Amílcar 1, 5, 157
Rosales, Humberto 89–92
Roudakova, Natalia 92, 101–102

Salvemos al Fútbol 47, 55, 87
Sarmiento, Domingo Faustino 29–31
Schaefer, Plaza 150
Scheper-Hughes, Nancy 154, 156
security agencies 141
security checks 23, 25, 64
Segura M. Trejo, Fernando 57
sense of security 47
Sissener, Tone K. 75, 102–103, 106
slums 31, 43, 65n8
Soca, Ricardo 54
social: change 135, 154; class 44; consciousness 32; contexts 15–16, 158; and cultural environments 103; and economic hardships 92; environment

137; impediments 138–147; leaders 17; movements, ethnographic study of 158; poetics 156; reality 156–157; scientists 17; transformation 10; welfare programme 73; wellbeing 154
society 148; analytical and interpretive studies of 156; idiosyncratic features of 136–137
sociocultural contexts 5, 132, 135
socioeconomic development 4, 60, 151
socioeconomic status 48, 71
solutions 5, 17, 134–138, 148, 149
South American Cup 19, 22, 25, 36, 65
Spaaij, Ramón 135
spectators 26, 41, 51–52
sponsoring 125
Sporting Potrero 126, 139, 142
Sport Matters (Dunning) 134
stadiums 23, 44–45, 47, 49, 60–61, 81, 116, 138, 140–141, 153; access points 116; for free 117; guaranteed access to 129–130; identity check 25; screening process 22; security 23, 25, 47, 59, 64, 144; spatial configuration of 47–48; *see also* violence
statues, of football stars 2
structural functionalism 4, 10, 151
structure 10, 93
subjectivism 157–158
superclásico 1, 17n1
supporters 15, 19–20, 39–40, 45, 47–48, 52–53
survey-based approaches 8, 73
symbolic power 86
systemic corruption 73–75, 82

tango music 1
Testa, Alberto 135
ticket scalping 19, 32, 117
tickets/ticketing system 21–22, 25
Tittarelli, Maximiliano 50
tolerance thresholds 37
Torre, Carlos De la 106
tourism 11–12, 59, 144
Transparency International report 2007 82
trapitos 59, 67n43

176 Index

Uliana, Santiago 48
Unidades Básicas 71, 93, 95
urban: agglomeration 11; settings 12

validity 20, 54, 154–159
verbal aggression 4–5, 15, 26, 28, 39, 42, 114–115
Vergara, Martín Darío 50
Videla, Jorge Rafael 96–87
violence 2, 11, 14, 67n32, 134, 142, 150–151; acts of 4–5, 47, 65, 152n11; and aggression at football stadiums 26–27; *aguante* 62–65; in Argentinian football 136; *barras bravas* 55–62; cases of 48, 147; chants 32–36; civilization and barbarism 28–32; cognitive dissonance and role play 39–49; conceptualization of 48; definitions of 15, 27–28; dimensions of 150; Emanuel Balbo 49–51; fan behaviour at football stadiums 37–39; fans 53–55; in football 2, 4, 5, 11, 12, 14, 16, 19–68, 72, 81, 125, 134, 137, 140, 145, 149, 150, 159; global study of 135; illegitimate use of 80; instigate acts of 149; levels of 141, 149–150; manifestations of 4; media coverage of 14; *Monumental* 25–26; obtaining tickets 21–22; outside stadium 22–25; perpetuation of 111; preventing acts of 89; prominent cases of 14; River Experience 19–20; spectators 51–52; supporters 52–53; type of 138, 141; use of 57
violent behaviour 4, 18, 26, 45, 50, 139
Vries, Geert de 7–8, 158

Watson, Peter J. 135
welfare system 7
well-being 5–6, 98
Wolf, Eric 99–100, 103, 110

Young, Kevin 27